MOTHERS ALONE

MOTHERS ALONE

Strategies for a Time of Change

SHEILA B. KAMERMAN
ALFRED J. KAHN
The Columbia University School of Social Work

 Auburn House Publishing Company
Dover, Massachusetts

Library of Congress Cataloging in Publication Data

Kamerman, Sheila B.
  Mothers alone.

  1. Single parents—Services for—United States.
2. Single-parent family—United States.   3. Family
policy—United States.   4. Child welfare—United
States. I. Kahn, Alfred J., 1919–   .   II.   Title.
HQ759.915.K36   1988   362.8'2   88–6195
ISBN 0-86569-183-5

Printed in the United States of America

PREFACE

Major change is occurring in the composition of single-mother families, the importance of the group, and public perception of what these mothers and children need by way of assistance. We write in the midst of what could be a policy watershed with regard to "welfare" and public financial aid for single mothers and their children. Whether or not the enacted reform will be adequate, it could signal dramatic policy changes.

Our objective is to contribute to knowledge, understanding, and awareness of the available public policy choices over the next several years. Our intended audience, therefore, consists of concerned citizens, policymakers, public officials, and scholars in the field.

In addressing such groups, we face a dilemma. Some want to know the story, the "argument": Documentation and footnotes get in the way. Others challenge paragraph by paragraph: Where are the data from? How can one learn more? Our attempt is to satisfy both constituencies. The appropriate chapters have many footnotes; the reader who wants easy access to the analysis is free to ignore them.

We here acknowledge the support of the Rockefeller Foundation which funded the research and, then, waited patiently as we adapted the analysis to a rapidly moving target. Dr. Phoebe Cottingham was the supportive program officer. A small supplement from the Stamer Foundation made it possible to update our European analysis. A subsequent and special project financed by the German Marshall Fund of the United States, as a by-product, significantly enriched Chapter 3.

With this, our 13th jointly written policy study (there also are two co-edited works), we acknowledge the good fortune of a research collaboration whose agenda remains vital. We are fascinated by the problems of social policy facing advanced industrial societies and believe that research, writing, and debate remain essential to wise politics.

March 1988 THE AUTHORS

CONTENTS

INTRODUCTION

The topic is of no small importance. As we write,

- More than one-quarter of all families with children in the United States are single-parent families. Of these, about 90 percent are headed by women.
- About 60 percent of children born in this decade are likely to live in lone-mother families, at some time, whether briefly or for longer periods.
- Some 40 percent of those who now are or soon will be the country's young women can expect to become single mothers before their youngest child reaches an 18th birthday.
- About 25 percent of working women with children are single parents.

Nor is life in the mother-alone family merely an oddity to be counted and observed: Those who become single parents must anticipate possibly serious problems for themselves and their children. Involved in departures from traditional life-styles and community patterns, they face challenges in managing daily living routines. Some—on the other hand—find in their status relief from or improvements over the alternatives already experienced. Most important, and for a very significant proportion, there is the possibility of poverty or near-poverty, whether briefly or for a lifetime.

At the same time, for the society, there are significant economic costs as well as threats to traditional family forms and ways of doing things. From some vantage points, the very foundations of the moral order seem to be at hazard.

The problem for social policy in responding to the single mother and her family is, first, to clarify just how the phenomenon can be understood and, then, to determine what a desirable societal stance and response might be. We have observed that the diagnoses are often far too simplistic. As a consequence, the remedies adopted are inevitably inadequate, albeit superficially or momentarily attractive.

Study of efforts in the United States at the present time and over the years and examination of the range of policies adopted in other advanced industrial societies as well lead us to the view that the main choices currently facing humane and just societies that seek a sympathetic response to the circumstances or plights of mother-alone families may be described as follows:

1. *An anti-poverty strategy.* Help single parents by establishing a national uniform policy of financial assistance for all poor families. Providing a guaranteed minimum income for all the poor could improve the economic situation of most single-mother families very substantially and permit them to remain at home while rearing their children.

2. *A categorical, single-mother strategy.* Helping single-parent families by providing a special cash benefit for all single mothers that would permit them to remain at home until their children attend school a full day and are of an age when they can go to and from school alone. This is a way of meeting their single-parent problem without commitment to the more costly and controversial first option.

3. *A family policy strategy with a special focus on young children.* Providing modest cash benefits to all families with children and supplementing these further for families with very young children, so that their mothers (or—in theory—fathers) may remain at home. Such a policy would have the advantage of not singling out single-parent families, yet could help them significantly while pursuing broader objectives. The focus is on all families with children—not just the poor; the help for single-mother families is a by-product.

4. *A family policy strategy of integrating work and family life.* Help single-parent families by enabling these parents to live as do most other parents, working at a job and carrying out parenting and home responsibilities. Thus, policies would be designed to facilitate participation in the labor force and provide both the economic benefits and the social supports which are essential if parents of young children are to work. The fact of successful work is the critical variable in coping, and such a policy would satisfy a core societal value.

These four currently observable policy regimes may be considered as options to be debated as the United States enacts measures and develops resources. They proceed from the selective (for the poor), to the categorical (single-parent families), to the more general and universalistic among policy responses. This volume reports on an effort to choose among the options presented, to seek a constructive, informed societal attitude, a stance, a policy with regard to mother-only families, and to identify the programs that could implement such a perspective.*

Inevitably, the first question to be addressed is: What are the criteria by which a policy—or policies—could be shaped today? What are to be the "decision rules," to employ the vocabulary of the professional policy analyst? What, in short, would make a policy or a program desirable or undesirable? On what basis may one recommend a policy to the American people?

Americans are not and do not choose to become a monolithic country. Our many and varied religious, racial, ethnic, and cultural traditions, constantly renewed by immigration, have yielded a diverse society. In our struggle to sustain essential national coherence and purpose, we continue, as well, to support and even to value such diversity.

Families and family structures show constant change, shaped by large-scale economic, educational, and cultural evolution. Hence, the picture is one of considerable divorce, separation, unmarried cohabitation, out-of-wedlock childbearing, and much else. Despite militant allegiance by some to the patterns of the past, most Americans would not act punitively to control such family change unless the costs of inaction were so overwhelming in their consequences as to become unacceptable. There are concerns, however, that could inspire other than repression or punishment or at the least, generate debate. For one thing, individuals in their deliberate and conscious actions on behalf of their own preferences or interests have no right to impose high economic costs upon others. Public assistance ("welfare") costs, for example, are paid for out of the taxes of the working poor and the hardly affluent lower-middle class, not just by the rich. A society has a right to consider such costs and ways of controlling them—or of targeting benefits— again, within the bounds of its preferences and core values.

Even more central is the matter of the well-being of children. A humanitarian society gives high priority to protecting and nurturing its children. A forward-looking society invests in child rearing and the welfare of children because of their contributions to its future. "What does it do to or for children?" should be a constant question in policymaking. A community's inability to answer the

---

*Of course, there also are single-parent families headed by fathers alone, but they are a very small minority and most do not face serious economic problems. Moreover, measures designed to alleviate the noneconomic problems of mother-only families would improve the quality of life for lone fathers as well.

question with confidence about many matters can become a source of program or policy uncertainty and hedging.

There is the related question of the well-being of mothers, of women. Policy should consider the quality of life that can be supported or encouraged for people who have somehow encountered life's obstacles, misfortunes, and discrimination, or who—whatever their derivations—have developed visions of more tolerable or even richer possibilities and alternatives. What can be done—with consideration always of children's stakes in the outcomes as well as the potential economic and social costs to the larger society?

The fundamental American tradition cannot be ignored; liberty, opportunity, and individualism are part of the baseline. Decency and fairness are deeply rooted in the country's social ethic.

The challenge for the analyst is to translate all of these into their implications with regard to specific measures proposed or tried. Obviously, to the extent that reported and analyzed experience and controlled research can help us determine objectively and systematically just where proposals lead, such data must be featured above myth, fad, or allegation.

These, then, are the parameters, the sources of criteria with which the discussion begins. This is a liberal, pluralistic society, and it wishes to so continue. This is a responsive and compassionate society but also a responsible one, and we do care about imposing on our fellow beings costs that they believe unfair to take on. We would be, above all, a humane and caring society, whose policies cannot ignore the well-being of children and disadvantaged mothers.

How, then, does this help us to consider mothers alone and their young children? How does this help us in choosing among alternative policy options? In the chapters that follow, we elaborate the criteria and explore the specifics.

Chapter 1 surveys, overall, what we actually know about single mothers and their children. It asks: What is the phenomenon? How is it perceived? What is its importance? A brief review of the facts leads one to reject any option that would ignore the very considerable diversity among single mothers. Certainly, a policy for the poor (or a "welfare reform" strategy) would not alone be adequate by itself (Option 1). Nor would a single-mother strategy (Option 2)—which assumes likeness within the group—cope with the range of circumstances and needs. However, it also becomes clear that the question of income must be central to policy and that welfare reform cannot be ignored—even though other issues remain as well. Here one refers to social supports, time, and child care.

Chapter 2 offers some historical perspectives. In effect, it reviews the U.S. history of Options 1 and 2, and focuses on single-mother families per se and our abortive, inadequate, and categorical efforts at implementing anti-poverty strategies. The record suggests that the society finds it difficult to enact and implement a constructive policy for all, or for all poor mother-alone families because of a variety of concerns and conflicts. Current developments have in any case turned welfare reform toward work programs and child support collection—all aimed at bringing people into the mainstream, rather than at-home support for poor single mothers until the children grow up. That option is no longer an acceptable response.

At this point, in Chapter 3, we look at the four options in some detail as they are now being experienced in several other industrial societies. Here, too, as in the first two chapters, one sees the limitation of the first two options—an anti-poverty focus alone or a categorical program for single mothers and their children. On the other hand, one is challenged to consider the other two possibilities: (1) general societal support for those who are rearing very young children, and (2) stronger encouragement and help for labor force participation by almost all mothers of young children.

The exploration continues in Chapter 4 by looking at four specific (but also overlapping) groups of single mothers. What are their special needs? What do they share? How do the answers shed light on general strategy? The answer emerges. One needs some combination of the third and fourth options: societal support of child rearing and support for entry and continuation of young mothers in the work force. But there will remain some categorical specifics for some single mothers, especially the adolescent mother.

The central issues, income and work, are explored in Chapter 5, which deals with the specifics of recommended policy and programs. In Chapter 6 we turn to the daily lives of single mothers and their children: time, social participation, daily routines. Much of this is in the province of private life, family, neighborhood, and informal associations—but there is a supportive role for society, and social infrastructure is essential. Child care is a major topic.

Chapter 7 reviews the general policy strategy proposed and discusses what is often called "prevention." The program specifics are also reviewed. We ask about prospects for overcoming political and cultural inhibition in the current environment. We conclude by suggesting that this area is sufficiently complex and so entangled in values and emotion as to defy significant progress unless it receives a broad band of interest and support. Humanitarian arguments aside, we also note the case from the perspective of national economic self-interest.

Chapter 1

MOTHERS ALONE: THEMES AND VARIATIONS

"Single-parent family" is almost a euphemism in the popular culture for "problem family," for some kind of social pathology. Yet describing someone as a "single parent" or a "single mother" provides very little information except that the family is not headed by a legally married, cohabiting husband and wife. The label does not, by itself, give a picture of the economic situation of the family, the health or well-being of the mother and children, the way the parent discharges her or his parenting and job responsibilities, or the threat the single parent may present to established social norms. All the label does is to serve as a kind of indicator of a possible problem. Moreover, the definition of "the problem" varies depending on who is involved, who is carrying out the analysis, and current societal preoccupations with the concept of the single parent. Here, for example, is a collection of alternative views of the "single-parent family problem" in the United States.

A problem of family breakdown and disorganization:

"Broken family" [means] more than just the divorced family. It means parents who live apart; parents who never married; and particularly, mothers who must raise their children with little or no assistance or support from a husband. . . . [It] means trauma both during and after the breakdown, trauma which long persists in various manifestations for each of the parents and children, manifestations which spread beyond the family to other relatives, friends, and associates.[1]

A problem of poverty:

. . . the single-parent family is the newly significant factor in the nation's high poverty figures and in growing social spending. It is

1

not that such families are poorer today (they are not), but that there are so many more of them swelling the ranks of the poor. . . . [H]ad we not seen the increase in single-parent families in the 1970s, and all other factors had remained constant, we might not have seen . . . such a high rate of poverty.[2]

A problem of and for blacks:

As much as we hear about the phenomenal growth in families headed by black females and the attendant rise in poverty, little is made of the "flip side" of this trend: the economic status of [black] men. . . . Four million out of nine million working age black men, or 46 percent, are jobless: unemployed, not participating in the labor force, or simply unaccounted for. The comparable figure for white men is 22 percent.[3]

A problem of teenage unwed mothers:

Families headed by teenage mothers are the most vulnerable of all families. . . . Indeed, if the trend if not reversed, we are likely to see a continuation of a substantial level of long-term dependency in this country, especially among black and other minority families.[4]

A problem of divorce:

While recent years have brought increased awareness of the feminization of poverty and the growth in single-parent female-headed households, what appears to be relatively unknown—or unacknowledged—is the direct link between divorce, the economic consequences of divorce, and the rise in female poverty.[5]

A problem of misguided welfare policies:

Welfare does not bribe *poor women to have babies, it* enables *them to do so. For the young woman who is not pregnant, "enabling" means that she does not ask, "Do I want the welfare check badly enough to get pregnant?" but rather, "If I happened to get pregnant, will the consequences really be so bad?"*[6]

A problem of societal change:

In the past five years some 200,000 single women in their thirties have chosen to become mothers. Do the numbers indicate isolated incidences of countercultural behavior or an emerging social trend?[7]

We may be seeing the end of the traditional family as we have known it and the emergence of a matrifocal family in which societies continue from generation to generation through women, with mothers and children living together while men move in and out of families, without any continued economic or emotional commitment or responsibility.[8]

A problem of the ghetto underclass and social dislocations:

The black delay in marriage and the lower rate of remarriage, each associated with high percentages of out-of-wedlock births and female-headed households, can be directly tied to the employment status of black males. Indeed black women . . . are confronting a shrinking pool of "marriageable" (that is, economically stable) men.[9]

The new "culture of poverty" . . . [communities] where 90 percent of the children are born into fatherless families, where over 60 percent of the population is on welfare, where the work ethic has evaporated and the entrepreneurial drive is channeled into gangs and drug-pushing.[10]

A problem of the "feminization of poverty":

The decade of the seventies was characterized by a double trend: More of the poor were women, and more women, especially those heading families with minor children, became poor. . . . The causes of women's poverty are different from those of men's poverty. For example, after a divorce, mothers must often bear the economic as well as emotional responsibility of childrearing, a burden that often impoverishes the family. U.S. welfare policies do not work for women because they have been based on the "male pauper" model of poverty and do not take account of the special nature of women's poverty.[11]

A problem of child poverty:

The term "feminization of poverty" is useful. It gets halfway to the point, but only halfway. It is not females who suddenly succumbed to poverty during this period but children, of whom slightly more than half are male (p. 95). . . . It is fair to assume that the U.S. has become the first society in history in which a person is more likely to be poor if young rather than old.[12]

A problem for children as they grow up:

Women who grow up in single-parent families are more likely to marry and bear children early, to have births before marriage, and to have their own marriage break up. . . . [These] intergenerational consequences are not due entirely to differences in family socioeconomic status.[13]

A problem of assumed deviancy:

In whatever ways they differ, however, all single parents suffer from public images of the ideal family. . . . A good deal more thought is

*required about the issues related to single parents. . . . [I]ssues
change focus if one views single parenthood as a normal and
permanent feature of our social landscape.*[14]

Clearly, many different problems are being identified, but not
all characterize every single mother and her children. Some problems, such as poverty, the economic consequences of divorce,
stress, and managing parenting and child rearing, are problems
experienced directly by the women and children. Others, such as
the potential burden for public expenditure, the assault on accepted values concerning behavior, and the long-term consequences for children, are particular concerns for society as a whole.
Opinions as to which problems should occasion public response
and which are private concerns also vary. Moreover, perspectives
on what constitutes a "problem" in this arena have changed over
time as well.

As we will see in Chapter 2, historically the concern was with
single mothers who were widows and with the relatively small
numbers of young women who bore children out of wedlock and
became public charges. Poverty was the issue for the first group,
and stigma, as well as poverty, was the problem for the second.
The poor unfortunate children of widows were often viewed as
having the potential to rise above their misfortune and even out-
achieve their more fortunate peers with two parents; in contrast,
the children of unmarried mothers were viewed as never likely to
recover from the situation of their birth.

Obviously, the improvement in contraceptive technology and
the existence of legalized abortion mean that unmarried women
having children today are very different from what they were in
earlier years. In some sense they are making a deliberate choice.
Yet the most superficial assessment reveals how different that
choice—and its consequences—are for a 15-year-old girl who has
just finished junior high and lives with her 32-year-old mother and
a younger brother and is supported by "welfare" versus a 36-year-
old female professor or lawyer who has a successful career, a good
income, and owns her own home.

Further, the income protection available to widows has improved substantially over time. Most now qualify for survivors'
insurance benefits through social security. Widows with young
children still may be at substantial risk of poverty, but far less so
than in earlier years. Moreover, widows with young children are a
small and declining group as longevity increases for all. In contrast,
there is no social insurance protection for children—let alone their

mothers—at the time of divorce; and divorce is a growing phenomenon, increasing especially for women with young children.

Finally, attitudes toward men's and women's roles and life-styles have changed. Women today are more likely to work and to support themselves. Nevertheless, economic problems remain for many, especially single mothers. First, women's salaries, although rising, are still lower than men's. Second, women with children, including single mothers, are likely to have primary responsibility for child care and child rearing; thus, their ability to work long hours or to change places of work is severely constrained. Third, it is becoming increasingly hard to support a family with only one average wage, whether in a single-parent family or a two-parent family. Society may not frown on these women as much as earlier, but life is not much easier for them.

Today, many new problems associated with being a single parent, particularly a single mother, have emerged. Whether all single-parent families have or constitute problems is not all clear. Societal concern for these problems, as well as an intensified search for solutions, has grown, even though uncertainty remains over whether the focus should be on some or all these developments as "problems of single-mother families" or whether they should be attacked from some other perspective. First we must look at the families and the women who head them.

The Phenomenon

We begin with numbers, percentages, and trends. The past decade has yielded a better picture, even if some gaps remain. The numbers must be attended to because they hold lessons for the choice of policies.

Almost 90 percent of all single-parent families are headed by women. Perhaps as a consequence, when people talk or write about mother-only families—lone mothers, single mothers, solo mothers, sole mothers, female-headed families with children, whatever the term—it is as if the families were all the same. Yet the reality suggests instead an extraordinary diversity—a diversity that may affect families' views of their experience as well as societal perceptions and attitudes toward them. Similarly, the diversity may influence the variety of public policies that address these families and their needs, and the consequences for them.

Most reports about single-mother families deal with out-of-wedlock teenage mothers or with AFDC (Aid to Families with Dependent Children) "welfare" mothers and suggest that the phenomenon is largely one of black, unwed mothers with large families. A parallel discussion focuses on divorced mothers as a largely middle-class problem. When describing the consequences for children, most reports do not separate out the particular experiences of children differentiated by different types of single mothers.

Here, we begin with the diversity. It is evidenced by the lack of a uniform set of characteristics describing the women or the existence of major subgroups and their numerical significance. We discuss the differences in single women by marital status. We look at their economic situation and discuss who is poor and which mothers are in the labor force. We pay attention to how old these single mothers are and how many children they have, and of what ages. We look at their race and ethnic backgrounds. Later, we review what is known about the consequences for children of growing up in such families.

Variations by Race, Ethnicity, and Marital Status

The growth in one-parent families with children, particularly mother-only families, has been one of the most dramatic changes in family composition of the last two decades. Doubling since 1970, the rate of growth was most dramatic in the early 1970s but increased somewhat again in the 1980s. Single mothers (divorced, separated, widowed, never married) accounted for 26 percent of all families with children in 1986—more than double the rate in 1970 (see Table 1–1).[15] In 1970 there were 3.8 million single-parent family units with children under age 18; in 1986 there were 8.9 million (see Table 1–2).

From 1940 to 1970, single-parent families with children constituted a consistent and stable proportion of families with children—about 10 percent. An emerging change in the composition of these families as widowhood declined and divorce increased was masked by the apparent stability in the rate, sustained with only modest growth until the end of the 1960s. Indeed historians suggest that the percentage of single-parent families actually declined from a much higher rate from the 18th century to the middle of the 20th, as mortality rates declined. The dramatic increase in female-headed families with children that occurred in the 1970s was a consequence of a divorce rate that rose to unprecedented heights while mortality rates for adults in their middle years continued to decline.

Public perceptions of single-parent families changed during these years because we went from a situation in which widows

Table 1-1 **Family Groups with Children, by Race: 1970–1985 (numbers in thousands)**

Family Groups with Children under 18 Years Old	1985		1980		1975		1970		Percent Change		
	No.	%	No.	%	No.	%	No.	%	1980–85	1975–80	1970–75
All races											
Family groups with children	33,353	100.0	32,150	100.0	31,087	100.0	29,631	100.0	3.7	3.4	4.9
Two-parent groups	24,573	73.7	25,231	78.5	25,426	81.8	25,823	87.1	2.6	0.8	1.5
One-parent groups	8,779	26.3	6,920	21.5	5,661	18.2	3,808	12.9	26.9	22.2	48.7
Maintained by mother	7,737	23.2	6,230	19.4	5,110	16.4	3,415	11.5	24.2	21.9	49.6
Maintained by father	1,042	3.1	690	2.1	552	1.8	393	1.3	51.0	25.0	40.5
White											
Family groups with children	27,629	100.0	27,294	100.0	26,731	100.0	26,115	100.0	1.2	2.1	2.4
Two-parent groups	21,873	79.2	22,628	82.9	22,926	85.8	23,477	89.9	3.3	1.3	2.3
One-parent groups	5,757	20.8	4,664	17.1	3,805	14.2	2,638	10.1	23.4	22.6	44.2
Maintained by mother	4,912	17.8	4,122	15.1	3,361	12.6	2,330	8.9	19.2	22.6	44.2
Maintained by father	844	3.1	542	2.0	443	1.7	307	1.2	55.7	22.3	44.3
Black											
Family groups with children	4,659	100.0	4,074	100.0	3,848	100.0	3,219	100.0	14.4	5.9	19.5
Two-parent groups	1,856	39.8	1,961	48.1	2,063	53.6	2,071	64.3	5.4	4.9	0.4
One-parent groups	2,802	60.1	2,114	51.9	1,785	46.4	1,148	35.7	32.5	18.4	55.5
Maintained by mother	2,641	56.7	1,984	48.7	1,687	43.8	1,063	33.0	33.1	17.6	58.7
Maintained by father	160	3.4	129	3.2	99	2.6	85	2.6	24.0	30.3	16.5

Note: Family groups consist of family households, related subfamilies, and unrelated subfamilies.
Source: U.S. Bureau of the Census, "Household and Family Characteristics: March 1985," *Current Population Reports*, series P-20, no. 411 (Washington, D.C.: U.S. Government Printing Office, 1986).

Table 1-2 One-Parent Family Groups, by Race and Marital Status: 1970–1986 (numbers in thousands)

Subject	1986		1980		1970	
	No.	%	No.	%	No.	%
All Races						
One-parent family groups	8,930	100.0	6,920	100.0	3,808	100.0
Maintained by mother	7,842	87.8	6,230	90.0	3,415	89.7
Never married	2,276	25.5	1,063	15.4	248	6.5
Spouse absent	1,724	19.3	1,743	25.2	1,377	36.2
Separated	1,506	16.9	1,483	21.4	962	25.3
Divorced	3,294	36.9	2,721	39.3	1,109	29.1
Widowed	546	6.1	703	10.2	682	17.9
Maintained by father	1,088	12.2	690	10.0	393	10.3
Never married	205	2.3	63	0.9	22	0.6
Spouse absent*	218	2.4	181	2.6	247	6.5
Divorced	571	6.4	340	4.9	(NA)	(NA)
Widowed	94	1.1	107	1.5	124	3.3
White						
One-parent family groups	5,964	100.0	4,664	100.0	2,638	100.0
Maintained by mother	5,070	85.0	4,122	88.4	2,330	88.3
Never married	885	14.8	379	8.1	73	2.8
Spouse absent	1,129	18.9	1,033	22.1	796	30.2
Separated	972	16.3	840	18.0	477	18.1
Divorced	2,676	44.9	2,201	47.2	930	35.3
Widowed	380	6.4	511	11.0	531	20.1

Maintained by father	894	15.0	542	11.6	307	11.6
Never married	135	2.3	32	0.7	18	0.7
Spouse absent*	168	2.8	141	3.0	196	7.4
Divorced	513	8.6	288	6.2	(NA)	(NA)
Widowed	78	1.3	82	1.8	93	3.5
Black						
One-parent family groups	2,752	100.0	2,114	100.0	1,148	100.0
Maintained by mother	2,597	94.4	1,984	93.9	1,063	92.6
Never married	1,355	49.2	665	31.5	173	15.1
Spouse absent	546	19.8	667	31.6	570	49.7
Separated	510	18.5	616	29.1	479	41.7
Divorced	561	20.4	477	22.6	172	15.0
Widowed	133	4.8	174	8.2	148	12.9
Maintained by father	155	5.6	129	6.1	85	7.4
Never married	60	2.2	30	1.4	4	0.3
Spouse absent*	40	1.5	37	1.8	50	4.4
Divorced	47	1.7	43	2.0	(NA)	(NA)
Widowed	7	0.3	19	0.9	30	2.6

*Data for 1970 include divorced fathers.

NA Not available.

Note: Family groups comprise households, related subfamilies and unrelated subfamilies.

Source: U.S. Bureau of the Census, "Household and Family Characteristics: March 1986," *Current Population Reports*, series P-20, no. 419 (Washington, D.C.: U.S. Government Printing Office, 1987), table G. p. 10.

dominated to a category consisting overwhelmingly of the divorced
and separated, including as well a large and growing number of
unmarried mothers. The large proportion of divorced women are
far more likely than widows to have younger children, and the
increasing numbers of unmarried mothers are even more likely to.
Thus, younger and younger children are now experiencing growing
up with only one parent. Moreover, as widowhood has declined
and the other social categories have grown, racial and ethnic
variations have become more salient, too.

Significant racial and ethnic differences exist among single-
mother families. The rate for black families has increased by almost
75 percent since 1970, when only one-third of black families were
headed by single mothers. The rate among white families has
increased as well, more than doubling since 1970, but it is still
nowhere near as high as among blacks. Over 20 percent of white
families with children currently are maintained by one parent,
while close to 60 percent of black families with children are now
headed by mothers.

As noted, marital status among these families has changed
significantly during these years as well. Divorced families constituted the largest group, both in 1986 and in 1970, but the
proportions increased from 32 percent of all single-mothers in 1970
to 42 percent in 1986. Separated mothers accounted for almost 19
percent of single-mother families in 1986, which represents a
significant decline from the 28 percent in 1970. Clearly, some of
the increase in divorce is accounted for by the decline in separation
as divorce became easier in the 1970s. Widows declined in importance dramatically, from 20 percent in 1970 to 7 percent in 1986.
On the other hand, never-married mothers increased significantly
in these years, in fact more than quadrupling, from 7 percent of all
lone mothers in 1970 to almost 30 percent in 1986.

These rates vary significantly by race and ethnicity, also. Among
whites, divorced families are by far the most numerous, accounting
for more than half of the mother-only families (see Table 1–2).
Separated couples account for almost 20 percent, and never-
married mothers, 17 percent. In contrast, among blacks, never-
married mothers are the largest group, accounting for half of all
black families with children in 1986, and more than half of those
headed by lone mothers. Separated mothers account for about the
same proportion as whites—just under 20 percent—while divorced
families account for far fewer than among white—just a little more
than separated mothers. Families headed by widowed mothers
accounted for a very small proportion of these families—about 7
percent for both whites and blacks. About 29 percent of Hispanic

families with children were maintained by lone mothers in 1986. Hispanic single mothers are most likely to be separated, although there are also high proportions of divorced and never-married mothers, too.

Finally, there were over 600,000 cohabiting couples with children under age 15 in 1986, constituting only about 2 percent of the total number of families with children, but 7 percent of those not living in husband/wife families (see Table 1–3). Childbearing and rearing by cohabiting but not legally married couples has tripled since 1970, but the rates are still so small as to leave this as a relatively insignificant family type. Although the rates clearly are increasing (from 1.3 percent in 1980 to almost 2 percent in 1986), this is nowhere near the 10 to 15 percent of families with children in several Scandinavian countries, nor near even the lower but still significant rates in countries such as France. Exactly how many of our single-parent never-married mothers are in fact part of a cohabiting couple is not known; for census purposes, at least, these mothers define themselves as single.

Children in Single-Parent Families

It is helpful also to look at this development from the child's perspective. Almost one-quarter (24 percent) of all children under 18 (14.8 million children) lived with one parent in 1986, compared with 9 percent in 1960 (see Table 1–4). Twenty-one percent lived

Table 1–3   Unmarried-Couple Households, by Presence of Children: 1960–1985 (numbers in thousands)

Year	Total	Without Children under 15 Years	With Children under 15 Years
1985	1,983	1,380	603
1984	1,988	1,373	614
1983	1,891	1,366	525
1982	1,863	1,387	475
1981	1,808	1,305	502
1980	1,589	1,159	431
1979	1,346	985	360
1978	1,137	865	272
1977	957	754	204
1970	523	327	196
1960	439	242	197

Source: U.S. Bureau of the Census, "Marital Status and Living Arrangements: 1985," *Current Population Reports*, series P-20, no. 411 (Washington, D.C.: U.S. Government Printing Office, 1986), Table A-14, p. 76.

Table 1–4 Living Arrangements of Children Under 18 Years Old: 1986, 1980, 1970, and 1960 (numbers in thousands)

Living Arrangements	1986	1980	1970	1960	Percent Distribution			
					1986	1980	1970	1960
All Races								
Children under 18 years	62,763	63,427	69,162	63,727	100.0	100.0	100.0	100.0
Living with—								
Two parents	46,384	48,624	58,939	55,877	73.9	76.7	85.2	87.7
One parent	14,759	12,466	8,199	5,829	23.5	19.7	11.9	9.1
Mother only	13,180	11,406	7,452	5,105	21.0	18.0	10.8	8.0
Father only	1,579	1,060	748	724	2.5	1.7	1.1	1.1
Other relatives	1,348	1,949	1,547	1,601	2.1	3.1	2.2	2.5
Nonrelatives only	272	388	477	420	0.4	0.6	0.7	0.7
White								
Children under 18 years	50,931	52,242	58,790	55,077	100.0	100.0	100.0	100.0
Living with—								
Two parents	40,681	43,200	52,624	50,082	79.9	82.7	89.5	90.0
One parent	9,303	7,901	5,109	3,932	18.3	15.1	8.7	7.1
Mother only	8,021	7,059	4,581	3,381	15.7	13.5	7.8	6.1
Father only	1,282	842	528	551	2.5	1.6	0.9	1.0
Other relatives	747	887	696	774	1.5	1.7	1.2	1.4
Nonrelatives only	200	254	362	288	0.4	0.5	0.6	0.5

Black[1]							
Children under 18 years	9,532	9,375	9,422	8,650	100.0	100.0	100.0	100.0
Living with—								
Two parents	3,869	3,956	5,508	5,795	40.6	42.2	58.5	67.0
One parent	5,058	4,297	2,996	1,897	53.1	45.8	31.8	21.9
Mother only	4,827	4,117	2,783	1,723	50.6	43.9	29.5	19.9
Father only	231	180	213	173	2.4	1.9	2.3	2.0
Other relatives	542	999	820	827	5.7	10.7	8.7	9.6
Nonrelatives only	63	123	97	132	0.7	1.3	1.0	1.5
Hispanic[2]								
Children under 18 years	6,430	5,459	[3]4,006	(NA)	100.0	100.0	100.0	(NA)
Living with—								
Two parents	4,275	4,116	3,111	(NA)	66.5	75.4	77.7	(NA)
One parent	1,955	1,152	(NA)	(NA)	30.4	21.1	(NA)	(NA)
Mother only	1,784	1,069	(NA)	(NA)	27.7	19.6	(NA)	(NA)
Father only	171	83	(NA)	(NA)	2.7	1.5	(NA)	(NA)
Other relatives	162	183	(NA)	(NA)	2.5	3.4	(NA)	(NA)
Nonrelatives only	38	8	(NA)	(NA)	0.6	0.1	(NA)	(NA)

Note: Excludes persons under 18 years old who were maintaining households or family groups.
[1]Nonwhite for 1960.
[2]Persons of Hispanic origin may be of any race.
[3]Persons under 18 years.
Source: U.S. Bureau of the Census, "Marital Status and Living Arrangements: 1986," *Current Population Reports*, series P-20, no. 418 (Washington, D.C.: U.S. Government Printing Office, 1987), table E. p. 8.

alone with their mothers, as compared with 8 percent in 1960. Among white children, the proportion in single-parent families is 18 percent, double that in 1970; among blacks, more than half (53 percent) of all children live in such families, two-thirds more than in the 1970s. Among Hispanic children, 30 percent lived with one parent.

As we would expect, having looked at the situation of their mothers, more than half the children in white one-parent families live with a divorced mother. The proportion of children living with separated mothers has remained relatively constant, but the proportion of white children with never-married mothers, now close to 15 percent, has more than doubled just since 1980, having doubled in the 1970s as well.

Almost half of all black children in single-parent families live with a never-married mother. The proportion living with a separated mother has declined by more than half, while about one-quarter live with a divorced mother—about the same number as in 1980 but 50 percent more than in 1970, and a smaller proportion of the whole group. Among Hispanics, although about one-quarter live with never-married mothers, more than one-third live with a separated mother.

In reviewing what is happening to mother-only families and to their children, what seems most important is the dramatic increase in divorce that occurred among white families in the 1970s and the equally dramatic increase in never-married families that has occurred among blacks since then, and may now be occurring among whites as well. These data raise new questions about what may be happening to marriage and family life in the United States.

These are not exceptional experiences on the American scene. Norton and Glick, on the one hand, and Bumpass, on the other, report the probability that as many as 50 to 60 percent of children born in the mid-1980s will experience a period living in a single-parent family before age 18. Some experts have made higher estimates. Bumpass also calculates that more than half the children who remain with their mothers following parental divorce will live at least five years in such a family. The estimate follows from a computation of current divorce, remarriage, and nonmarital birth rates. Norton and Glick, in 1985, found that 12 percent of children would be in one-parent families because of birth outside of marriage, 40 percent because of divorce, 5 percent because of long-term separation, and 2 percent because of death. If one looks at the experiences from the mother's perspective, they project that 37 percent of women who were in their late 20s in 1984 can be expected to maintain a one-parent family with children under age

18: 8 percent because of nonmarital births, 23 percent because of divorce, 4 percent because of widowhood, and 2 percent because of separation.[16]

The Economic Problems of Mother-Only Families

The economic situation of mother-only families with children is precarious at best. These families experience high rates of poverty and relatively low income. Divorced mothers face the problem of adapting to a lower standard of living, even if they are not "poor" in absolute terms.

Poverty or Low Income

Median family income for single-mother families was less than one-third the income of husband-wife families in 1985 ($9,858 as compared with $32,558). Only a little of this enormous difference is accounted for by the presence of two earners in many husband/wife families. Thus, for example, median family income in two-parent families when both parents are employed was about $38,000 in 1985; however, in traditional husband/wife families with only a male wage earner, median family income was $30,000—still more than three times the income of women heading families alone. Single-parent, father-only families have much lower incomes than male-headed, two-parent families with one wage earner, but still more than twice the income of mother-only families ($20,719). Obviously, the number of wage earners alone does not account for all the difference.

A second important factor contributing to the income gap between mother-only and father-only families (and to part of the contrast with husband/wife families with only one wage earner) is the difference in labor force status of single mothers as contrasted to single (and married) fathers. Although median family income for all single-mother families with children is about half that of father-only families, once we examine the labor force status of these mothers, some of this discrepancy is explained. Thus, working single mothers, including those working part-time as well as full-time, have a median family income of $15,420, about 75 percent that of working single fathers. In contrast, for such families when mothers are not in the labor force, median family income declines to a frighteningly low $4,913.

For young families—families with children under age 6—the situation is even worse. Median family income for lone mothers with young children was $6,346 in 1985, well below the poverty threshold for that year, as compared with $16,156 for father-only families and $28,775 for husband-wife families.[17] (The poverty threshold for a family of four was $10,984 in 1985, and $8,573 for a family of three—the typical single-mother family, with two children.)

Almost 60 percent of the children living in mother-only families are poor, more than five times the proportion in husband-wife families (11 percent); and close to 75 percent of children under age 6 in such families are poor. The high poverty rate among children in mother-only families has persisted for more than 20 years, except in 1979, which was the only year the rate dropped below 50 percent. Among black children the poverty rate has been about 67 percent throughout the same period.

When corrected for inflation, the median family income of children living in two-parent families rose from 1964, was relatively stable in the 1970s, and fell slightly during the first half of the 1980s. For children living in mother-only families, however, income was low but stable through the 1970s and then declined in the early 1980s (see Table 1–5).

Median family income for mother-only families was below the poverty threshold in 1985 and has been below it consistently over the last two decades. In 1984, half of all mother-only families were poor: 40 percent of the whites and 61 percent of the blacks. The rate is still higher for women with children under age 6—almost two-thirds.[18] For mothers not in the labor force, family income was half or less than half of the poverty line. Only if single mothers are employed is there even a possibility of income over that level.

Duncan and Hoffman highlight the financial trauma for women and their children following divorce. Duncan and Rodgers document the far more extensive and persistent poverty effects of being born to an unwed mother. Forty percent of mother-only families, one year after divorce or separation, had family incomes cut by more than one-half, whereas only 16 percent of men experienced such a drop. Even after five years, one-third of the women heading families who remained unmarried still had incomes less than one-half of the pre-divorce level. However, "a higher fraction . . . of the years of childhood poverty were linked to birth to an unwed mother than to a marital disruption."[19]

Mother-only families constitute almost 60 percent of all poor families with children. Moreover, the growth in this family type, coupled with the decline in poverty among husband-wife families and the aged and disabled, is what has led to the growing trend toward the "feminization of poverty."[20] According to Garfinkel and

Table 1–5   Median Family Income of Children Living in Families

	1964	1970	1975	1979	1980	1981	1983	1984	1985
Current dollars									
All types of families	$6,711	$10,227	$13,915	$19,732	$20,939	$22,041	$23,306	$25,334	$26,720
Husband-wife families	NA	11,041	15,534	22,258	23,846	25,636	27,190	29,831	31,451
Mother-only families	NA	4,145	5,501	7,734	7,938	8,653	8,563	9,162	9,472
Constant (1985) dollars									
All types of families	$23,275	$28,333	$27,813	$29,244	$27,336	$26,071	$25,165	$26,238	$26,720
Husband-wife families	NA	30,588	31,049	32,988	31,131	30,323	29,359	30,895	31,451
Mother-only families	NA	11,483	10,995	11,462	10,363	10,235	9,246	9,489	9,472

Note: Data are for related children under 18, that is, biological, step-, and adopted children of the householder, and any other children related to the householder by blood, marriage, or adoption. The medians are based on children. That is, each child is characterized by the income of its family, and the median for all children is computed. Thus, of all children living in families in 1981, half were in families with an income greater than $22,041, and half were in families with a lower income. Mother-only families are those having a female householder with no husband present. Constant dollars are calculated on the basis of the Consumer Price Index, U.S. Bureau of the Census, unpublished data for 1985.

Source: Compiled by Child Trends, Inc., Washington, D.C., from data in U.S. Bureau of the Census, *Current Population Reports*, series P-60, no. 47, table 5; no. 80, table 19; no. 105, table 24; no. 132, tables 16, 17, 30; no. 137, table 27; no. 146, table 27; no. 151, table 19; P-23, no. 114, table 42; and unpublished data from the U.S. Bureau of the Census.

McLanahan, about half of the feminization of poverty since 1967 was due to increases in the number of mother-only families and half to improvement in the living standards of other groups.[21]

Among the most important findings of a long-term, ongoing study of a panel of American families is that a change in family composition (separation, divorce, marriage, remarriage, becoming a parent) is the most important factor in determining the economic well-being of families.[22] After this, the next most important factor is the labor market decisions of a family—whether one or more members will enter the labor market or withdraw. Recent research by Mary Jo Bane has shown that a significant factor in the poverty of mother-only families is "event-driven poverty"—that is, poverty that occurs as a result of either a change in family composition or loss of earnings.[23] Bane's analysis of the data, however, led her to conclude that although an external event is important in the poverty of most white mothers, especially divorce, such events are less important for black mothers. Most black single mothers were poor even before they became mothers. Thus, Bane concludes that much of the poverty of black mother-only families is "reshuffled" poverty: poor women who form new families that are still poor or poor families that break up and form new or different but still poor families. The poverty problems of divorced women who become temporarily poor as a result of divorce differ from those of women who may have been poor all their lives and now are both poor and single parents. Each may require a different type of solution, although the latter will be more difficult to solve.

Inadequate or Nonexistent Child Support

The lack of financial support from the absent parent, usually the father, is a major factor in child poverty and in the economic problems of mother-only families. Of all women potentially eligible to receive child support in 1985, only 61.3 percent were awarded it.[24] Of those expected to receive it, 74 percent (slightly higher than the 72 percent in 1981 but below the 76 percent in 1985) actually received some payments. Less than half received the full amount, and over one-quarter received nothing in 1985. In effect, even among those who were supposed to receive child support, less than half received any. The aggregate amount of child support payments due in 1985 was $10.9 billion, but actual payments received amounted to only about $7.2 billion.

The proportion of women awarded support payments was about twice as high for whites (71 percent) as for blacks (36 percent). Among those awarded support, a similar proportion of whites and blacks received it, but the average support payment received by blacks was only three-quarters that received by whites. Women with college degrees were more likely to have been awarded support payments and to have received them. Similarly, women with earnings were more likely to have been awarded and received support, and women receiving child support were more likely to be in the work force. Almost 40 percent of poor single mothers were supposed to receive child support in 1985, and of these only 66 percent received any payments. In effect, almost three-quarters of all poor single mothers received no child support payments. Never-married mothers were by far the least likely to be awarded child support payments; once awarded support, however, they were about as likely as divorced mothers to receive it.

The average amount of child support received in 1985 was $2,215, which is less than the amount received in 1983 after adjusting for inflation and significantly less than the average monthly AFDC benefit. About two-thirds of divorced, separated, or never-married women stated that they wanted support payments but could not obtain an award. As indicated above, never-married mothers were the least likely to receive an award; their child support, moreover, was likely to be less than half that received by divorced mothers ($1,147 as contrasted with $2,538). Women receiving government cash benefits were less likely to have child support for their children and less likely to receive payments once awarded. Their average payment was lower ($1,740 versus $2,520).

Obtaining support awards, setting the level of support appropriately, and enforcing support obligations are all critical aspects of assuring children adequate financial support. New data suggest that most absent fathers either pay no support, or if they pay any, pay most of their obligations.[25] The most important issue, apparently, is to establish an award at an adequate level and then enforce it (see Chapter 5). Assuring a minimally adequate benefit for children when the father's capacity is limited remains an important problem that has not yet been adequately addressed in this country.[26]

Child support is clearly an essential component of family income for single mothers. Nevertheless, the Census Bureau's analysis indicates that even if all the poor single mothers awarded support had received it, there would have been no significant change in their poverty rate. A child support system cannot by itself provide enough income for families to manage unless they have other resources, even among those receiving support let alone for those who do not.

As of spring 1986, only about 14.6 percent of the 19.2 million ever-divorced or currently separated women were awarded or had an agreement to receive alimony or maintenance payments. The proportion was lower for women under age 40, women who had four or more children, women who were never married, women who were divorced or separated after 1970, women who worked in the five years prior to separation, and black women. The mean total money income of women receiving alimony in 1985 was $17,781—about 20 percent higher than the mean income of those women who received child support that same year. In effect, the roughly 15 percent of single mothers who receive alimony remain an especially advantaged, small subgroup of single mothers, despite the fact that what they receive may still constitute a significant decline in income from their earlier status.

Labor Force Status

Since only earnings provide adequate income for mother-only families, labor force participation and employment status are obviously of critical importance. Yet here, too, the patterns are neither uniform nor consistent across all types of single mothers.

While labor force participation rates (LFPR) for married women with children, living with their husbands, rose by more than 50 percent between 1970 and 1986 (from 39.7 to 61.3 percent), the rate for women heading families alone increased only a little more than 10 percent (from 59 to 67.5 percent); (however, the proportion employed who worked full-time increased significantly).[27] Historically, black single mothers always had high labor force participation rates; however, most of the recent increase was among white lone mothers. White single mothers had a LFPR of 71 percent in 1986, while that of black single mothers was significantly lower (61 percent); it was still lower for Hispanic mothers.

Labor force participation rates vary by the marital status of the mother as well. Divorced mothers have the highest rates (82 percent in 1986), with relatively modest racial differences (83 percent for whites versus 76 percent for blacks). In contrast, never-married women have the lowest rate—far lower than married women (about 53 percent)—and it is the same for both whites and blacks. A 1987 Bureau of Labor Statistics report reveals some of the problems faced by these women when they enter—or try to enter—the work force.[28] Never-married mothers are disproportionately young, black, likely to have preschool children, and likely to have limited education. More specifically, 43 percent of these mothers were under age 25 in 1987, and 70 percent had preschoolers. These figures are in contrast to married mothers, where the comparable proportions were 9 and 49 percent. (About two-thirds of these young women maintain their own families.) As a consequence, obtaining a job, earning a decent wage, and managing full-time work are all especially difficult for many of these women.

Separated and widowed mothers, with relatively similar rates, are between the divorced and never-married in labor force involvement.

Understandably, the age of the children affects labor force participation, too, as does the number of children. Almost 80 percent of single mothers with school-aged children are in the labor force versus about 60 percent of those with children under age 6. Similarly, LFPRs range from 80 percent of those with only one child to 52 percent of those with four children. Given the relatively few families with four or more children, the age of the child is more likely to create a barrier than the number of children.

Single mothers who are in the labor force, however, are likely to work full-time rather than part-time and are far more likely than married mothers to work full-time. About two-thirds of married mothers who work—both those with school-aged children and those with preschool-aged children—work full-time. Among single working mothers, regardless of marital status and race, more than 80 percent work full-time, including more than 75 percent of those with children under age 6.

Single Working Mothers and Their Wages

Single working mothers had median incomes in 1985 equal to about 75 percent of the incomes of families headed by sole fathers and half the incomes of traditional husband/wife families with one wage earner. A small part of this gap can be accounted for by the probability that some of these mothers work part-time or part-year (although the overwhelming majority work full-time all year round). A larger part of the gap may be accounted for by the male/female wage gap, which for some years left the average full-time working woman with a salary of about 59 percent of that of a working man. According to a Rand report, some dramatic improvements in women's wages have taken place since 1982.[29] In 1980, working women's hourly wages were 60 percent of men's; by 1984, the figure had risen to 64 percent, "the largest and swiftest gain" during the 20th century. Recent Bureau of Labor Statistics (BLS) data suggest that women's wages as a percentage of men's have risen still further and reached 70 percent in 1986. Although the Rand report estimates conservatively that by the end of the century women's wages will constitute at least 75 percent of men's wages, there is still another decade to go before that level is achieved, and even then, women supporting their families alone could still be disadvantaged. Moreover, as the Rand report and many others have pointed out, wages reflect education and work experience. Thus, once again, there will continue to be differences in earnings of single mothers, especially among the never-married.

The Multiple Burdens on Many Lone-Mother Families

Data from family service agencies and family counseling services indicate that lone mothers are far more likely than other women to experience stress and to need and seek help.[30] The social isolation experienced by many of these mothers only exacerbates the problems created by lack of money. Single mothers have to contend with constant time and energy pressures as well as economic strain (see Chapter 6). For the most part, not only are two-parent families often assured of two sources of income; they also have available two rather than one pair of hands for household and child care tasks, two sets of relatives to help out in emergencies, and two heads when urgent decisions must be made. Single mothers have less than their married sisters of almost everything except, perhaps, problems and a degree of autonomy in some instances. They have less money, less time, less energy, fewer skills, and less support, both in and out of the home.[31]

Children growing up in most, but not all, mother-only families often face multiple burdens. Many of them are likely to be poor and from low-status minorities (black and Hispanic), most receive little or no support from their fathers; nor do they see their fathers very often. In some categories of mother-only families, the children's mothers are likely to be very young, unemployed, and to have limited education and skills. Most children growing up in mother-only families are likely to be dependent on AFDC, the most stigmatized public assistance program; in fact, about 90 percent of poor mother-only families—including significant numbers of divorced and separated mothers—receive AFDC benefits, or "welfare." Finally, because of the dramatic increase in the numbers of mother-only families, far more children are likely to experience these problems than previously.

Researchers studying the effects on children of living in a mother-only family often confound the effects of poverty with those of father-absence. Moreover, since not all types of father-absence are the same, this too can lead to differential results.

Given all the variables potentially involved, it is doubtful that any one series of generalizations will hold up to rigorous scrutiny. For one thing, there are many child problems in intact families, rich and poor. Some intact families are characterized by uninformed, neglectful, abusive, conflict-ridden, irresponsible, or impoverished parenting—and may experience serious external stress (accidents, discrimination, neighborhood conflict, lack of decent housing). One need only examine the statistics for delinquency, drug problems, truancy, mental health problems, poverty, child placement, or abuse to know that children from many types of families are at risk. Small wonder that considerable research suggests that as the variables balance out there are perhaps no more sustained negative effects from the single-parent family status per se than from other negative effects elsewhere.

Obviously, some caveats are necessary. Intact families who function well, are not seriously deprived, and do not face unmanageable external stress are expected on average to produce more successful children—and they do, as seen in college enrollment, occupational histories, and adult careers. On the other hand, the odds of having some problems or many problems are very high for children from some identifiable single-parent subgroups.

McLanahan and Bumpass reach a more general negative conclusion. They find that "women who grow up in single-parent families are more likely to marry and bear children early, to have births before marriage, and to have their own marriage break up."[32] They also suggest that intergenerational consequences are not due entirely to socioeconomic differences, although they qualify this somewhat by stating that they were not able to control directly for family income. They attribute this development to the role-model theory, which argues that children develop their ideas of what is acceptable from what they observe in their parents.

The extremes seem clear—hence the talk of "problems" for children (it should be *some* children) in single-parent families. The middle is "iffy" and "it depends"—hence the statement that some single-parent families do not represent sources of inevitable child difficulties. For some children, the family breakup may even result in liberation from a difficult environment and creation of a more supportive parent-child milieu.

For many children, however, the single-parent family is a handicapping and destructive environment. Having an unwed teen mother does appear to have negative effects on a number of outcomes for the child, in particular intelligence, achievement, and some aspects of socioemotional development.[33] These results do not decrease over time. However, the research also indicates that the direct effects of having a young mother are very small; most are mediated by other variables. Thus, for example, if the young mother remains with her parents and later marries, many of the negative effects are attenuated. On the other hand, if she lives by herself, remains single, and has subsequent additional out-of-wedlock births, the effects are likely to be worse.

Hofferth points out that one of the most consistent findings concerning the impact of the mother's age on child outcomes is that the education of the mother has a significant impact on the intelligence and achievement of her child. Thus, not only does lack of school impede the teenage mother's own future prospect for employment, economic well-being, and achievement; it also has severe negative effects on her children. Whether this impact is brought about through parenting behavior or some other factor is not yet clear.

Moore analyzed the data from the first two waves of the National Survey of Children, both when children were aged 7–11 in 1976 and when they were 11–16 in 1981.[34] She focused specifically on the effects of early childbearing on the children of teenage mothers. Her analysis indicated that "the children of adolescent mothers experienced significant social and economic disadvantages." They are more likely to live in poor families and to be raised by poorly educated parents. They are more likely to have more siblings and to live with only one biological parent. Black children are more likely to be on welfare. All are more likely to do less well in school, and the white children are more likely to run away, get into fights, steal, smoke, and to get into trouble in school. Girls are more likely to expect to be a teen parent themselves (and to be good predictors!), and boys are more likely to have engaged in antisocial behavior. Of particular importance, children of teen mothers who dropped out of school before pregnancy are more likely to have school problems; in addition, early school problems are likely to predict later acting out behavior.

Moore says that, "In general, the effects of early childbearing are more negative for whites than for blacks. However, the black children are so disadvantaged as a group that the negative effects associated with race frequently dwarf the negative effects associated with early childbearing."[35]

Heatherington, drawing on her own longitudinal studies with a relatively small group of white middle-class families and her integration of the research literature, offers a clear summary of the state of understanding as to the effects of divorce on the adjustment of children. We have deleted her extensive research citations:[36]

> *It has been found that in the period immediately surrounding separation and divorce most family members experience emotional distress and disrupted functioning. However if the aftermath of divorce is not compounded by continued or additional stressors both parents and children are able to adapt to their new life situation within two to three years following divorce. The adverse effects of divorce are more intense and enduring for boys than for girls although there have been some reports of delayed effects in the form of rebellious behavior, depression and disruptions in heterosexual relations emerging in adolescent girls. Moreover when differences between children in divorced and nondivorced families are found they are most likely to be obtained in externalizing disorders involving poor impulse control, aggression, and noncompliance and in achievement deficits rather than in internalizing disorders or disruptions in self-esteem. Finally, when such behaviors occur they tend to be found not only in the home but also in the school and in peer relations and are correlated with inept parenting on the part of the custodial parent. It should be kept in mind that most of the studies of divorce involve mother custody homes and it has been found that elementary school aged children manifest fewer behavior problems when they are in the custody of a parent of the same sex.*

Looking at Heatherington's research and other current work as well, Hofferth and Evans summarize their best judgment: "Recent studies add to a growing body of research that suggests substantial long term effects of experiencing a divorce or separation on educational attainment, later economic well-being, and early family formation." The National Survey of Children, also cited by Heatherington, offers a large, representative sample. It too concludes that marital disruption is associated with a range of negative outcomes for children but that the post-divorce experience can affect the outcomes. Moreover, marital conflict in intact homes, especially if persistent, may have as equally harmful effects as divorce itself. Maintaining good relationships with parents can reduce the effects of conflict or disruption.[37]

Divorce also has serious economic impacts, which may both contribute to and be independent of the emotional consequences. Certainly, one of the immediate experiences is a series of important economic problems that may be experienced by children as a daily cutback in allowances and resources and in a disruption of housing arrangements, even removal from their familiar neighborhoods. Some then experience recovery, as arrangements are made for support by the noncustodial parent and/or as the custodial parent, the mother, goes out to work. Some 41 percent of divorced families receive child support (as contrasted in 1983 with 5 percent of the never-married and 20 percent of the separated). Three-quarters are in the paid labor force. Table 1–6 provides dramatic data that show that while only the widowed among all single-parent families are better off than the divorced, as of March 1985, a single-parent divorced family still had only 40 percent of the income of the average two-parent family. Most experience a significant living standard decline—whatever the balance between the emotional relief and stress of the divorce per se. (More will be said about the effects of divorce on children and their parents in Chapters 4 and 6.)

Why So Many Single Parents?

Inevitably, the question arises: Shouldn't society seek to stop all this, to avoid the creation and perpetuation of single-parent families? In turn, the inquiry must then face the question, "Why?" What is the source of this phenomenon? Can it be stopped?

The full answer—the basic response—merits a volume and goes beyond our search for policy and programs. It deals with social change in the most profound sense—the development of an economy which largely separates household from work; shifts within the manufacturing and service sectors to forms of employment in which women are obviously as proficient as men; and trends in the macro- and microeconomies of country after country so that two salaries are required for economic survival in a family (absent one quite high earner) and to provide the housing and amenities which societal norms define as desirable and comfortable.

Partially as cause, and certainly, also, as result, is the movement for gender equality and equity. Whether in politics, management, ordinary work, or in home roles, women are demanding independence and equality to replace dependence and subservience. The transition, which is supported by federal and state laws on rights and opportunity and by state family law as well, is hardly complete. The evidence of continuing discrimination, inequality, and secondary status remains considerable. Yet the change also has been dramatic. Inevitably, the family, the most central of primary institutions, responds to the requirements of the wider changes in economy, polity, and culture, and in turn shapes them.

Divorce, separation, cohabitation, new sexual patterns, child-bearing outside of marriage, changes in fertility, and all the other related demographic and social shifts must be looked at in this context. Changes in family law that have created "no-fault" divorces of several varieties have made it easier to end a marriage. Some tendency to define cohabitation as though it is economically the equivalent of legal marriage has encouraged new forms of household formation.

Mary Ann Glendon, for example, points out that between 1969 and 1985, divorce laws in almost every western industrialized country, including the United States, were altered to make divorce easier by expanding no-fault grounds and accepting or simplifying divorce by mutual consent.[38] She adds, moreover, that "most American states have gone further than any country except Sweden in making marriage freely terminable, but that the United States has lagged behind several other nations to which we often compare ourselves in dealing with the economic aspects of marital dissolutions."

In most American states, as in Sweden, a "right" to divorce may be said to exist, at least in the popular sense. In effect, divorce has been made easier in the United States, but policies have not responded to the economic consequences for women and minor children in particular, by setting more rigorous and adequate support obligations and/or providing more generous supplementary support by government.

When we turn, eventually, to the "prevention" question, we shall face the inevitability and unpredictability of the fundamental social changes—or, at least, argue that they are the arenas for political debate and choice well beyond our scope, as we concentrate on single-parent families. They are probably well beyond social engineering in any democratic society. But family law and the law of child support, in particular, are certainly within the policy domain here relevant for exploration and analysis.

Even if we were to join the policy debate, we could not ignore the more particular explanations, going beyond the large-scale societal shifts with regard to specific subgroups of single-mother families. The four major groups specifically discussed in Chapter 4 are mothers-by-choice, displaced homemakers, adolescent mothers, and "welfare mothers," a cross-cutting category. For the present, however, it is necessary to acknowledge a school of thought which has gained some vogue over the past decade with its claims that increases in child poverty (and much more by the way of urban social pathology as well) must be attributed to changes in family structure and composition and that, in turn, the availability of "welfare" payments through the Aid to Families with Dependent Children program is a major incentive to set up and sustain such families.[39] We are impressed with the weight of the analytic social science studies which compare teenage and other

Table 1–6 Social and Economic Profile of Children in Two-Parent and Single-Parent Families, March 1985

	Two-Parent Families	Mother-Only Families					All Father-Only Families
		All Mother-Only Families	Divorced Mother	Never-Married Mother	Separated Mother	Widowed Mother	
Number of children under 18 (in thousands) living in each type of family as of March 1985	46,149	13,081	5,280	3,496	2,962	939	1,554
Family Characteristics		*(Percentages and other statistics are child-based)*					
Parent Education Level							
Parent has less than a high school education	19%	35%	23%	47%	43%	38%	25%
Parent finished 4+ years of college	25	7	10	2	6	9	17
Parent Employment Status							
Not in labor force	8	39	25	54	45	43	13
Employed full-time	83	40	55	25	33	35	70
Unemployment rate	5.3	16.2	10.5	26.6	19.7	13.8	11.6

Family Income							
Mean income in 1984	$33,182	$10,694	$13,281	$6,225	$9,407	$17,407	$22,164
Assistance from Absent Parent							
% receiving child support (March 1983 data)	—	23%	41%	5%	20%	—	2%
Public Assistance							
Receiving Aid to Families with Dependent Children (March 1983 data)	3	37	27	57	44	11	6
Living in publicly subsidized housing	2	13	8	24	11	6	3
Parent Age							
% with mothers less than 25 years old (March 1983 data)	8	17	6	42	14	3	—
Ethnic Composition							
% of children in group who are black (March 1983 data)	8	37	20	67	35	25	18
% of children in group who are Hispanic	9	12	8	11	20	11	9
Extended Family							
Adult relative other than parent(s) who lives in household	16	28	23	35	25	40	22

Source: Child Trends, Inc., Washington, D.C.

out-of-wedlock pregnancy rates with state and national AFDC coverage, expenditures, levels of generosity, and trends and which look at the family backgrounds of AFDC mothers.[40] It is difficult to examine these data and then argue simplistically that people typically have babies in order to become eligible for AFDC, although certainly some young mothers do testify to such motivation.

More convincing but hardly definitive is a second, fall-back, hypothesis of Charles Murray, one of the proponents of the original view. It is not, he holds, that young mothers necessarily are "bribed" by "welfare" to have babies out of wedlock, but they rather are "enabled" to. That is, with AFDC available, if a young woman has a baby, she may be assured of receiving some modest support. Perhaps most important, becoming a parent might make it possible, albeit at a very modest scale (at least it did during the 1970s), for a young woman to set up an independent household; for some, this may have been an important factor in a decision to carry an unintended pregnancy to term and to keep a child after birth.[41]

Other research, from a range of investigators, summarized in clear and helpful detail by Garfinkel and McLanahan, supports the view that while the availability of welfare benefits "is a minor cause of the growing number of single-mother families" (as put by the editors of their volume, John Palmer and Isabel Sawhill), nonetheless the availability of welfare benefits has a major impact on living arrangements chosen by young single mothers when they decide whether to attempt to set up independent households or to live with their own parents. Welfare availability could be said to enable some young mothers to forego marriage to the fathers of their out-of-wedlock children, to help some divorced women forego remarriage, to permit some pregnant young women to avoid either abortion or placement of their babies for adoption. While the studies with such conclusions are impressive, none of the theses is "proven," and sometimes the direction of causality is not completely clear.[42]

Wilson and others believe that these may be the immediate dynamics, but that the higher rate of out-of-wedlock births and single parenthood in the black community has a yet more basic explanation. They point out that black males between the ages of 25 and 44 have largely "disappeared" as potential husbands during the last two decades as a result of unemployment and other developments in the black community.[43] They hold that the rate of formation of black never-married families increased not just because fewer black women chose to marry or remarry after divorce.

Rather the most important conclusion of these observers is that the marriage rate for black women declined because of the growing unavailability of marriageable, employed black males—not the availability of welfare. Many observers have joined Wilson in the general approach but, again, one cannot claim either rigorous proof or full consensus.

The recent Garfinkel and McLanahan synthesis is, for the present, the most useful point of departure for policy. They note that increased labor force participation by women will increase the proportion of women who do not marry or who divorce. Women who have greater economic independence are more likely to leave a bad marriage; they are also more likely not to marry at all. What they now view as "marriageable" males are harder to find. And there is less incentive for them to compromise.[44] This theory may also account for the growth in the number of single-mother families "by choice"—older, often professionally successful women who decide to bear and rear children on their own (see Chapter 4).

When popular movie, music, and media stars regularly have children out-of-wedlock and tell their glamorous stories to the media, and even more frequently get divorced, it is difficult to claim that there has not been a major change in the culture. Changes in teenage sexuality cannot be far behind. The impacts on the poor who lack access to glamour or even opportunity are out of control. Certainly, also, changing attitudes toward single parenting have made it easier for women to live alone and to raise children alone.

Society cannot avoid the question, Should we act? Or, more precisely, since there is little in the way of public policy in such areas as income maintenance, employment, health, education, or housing which will not affect the well-being of families and children, whether or not there is explicit policy, what is an appropriate response here that considers the single-parent phenomenon and the people involved?

Diversity—And Themes

Family structure may be all that one-parent families have in common, but that can hardly be insignificant! Many share other problems: poverty, lack of job skills, poor education. Large numbers are isolated. Some are stigmatized. Others are secure, self-directing, and don't want to be set apart. Many are in rapid transition, en route to remarriage or new careers. They will not remain in the single-parent status.

The policy task is to identify when and where policy and programs should be addressed to these families or some subset of them as though they constitute one group—and when not. When is a policy targeted on one-parent families useful, and when is it counterproductive? What should such policies and programs be? We find it essential to caution against forgetting the diversity, lest society make serious mistakes. And we note below that the categories of single mothers are cross-cutting and overlapping.

1. *Widows* are a small and declining group of single mothers (7 percent in 1986) and constitute a declining proportion among the poor. They are a protected group, since they are overwhelmingly likely to receive survivor benefits; nonetheless, some widows with young children are poor. Any attention they need beyond their pension protection would hardly be identical to that needed by the adolescent out-of-wedlock mother.

2. Some researchers are convinced that not only do *divorced women* (42 percent of single mothers in 1986) suffer an immediate and major decline in income but that men experience an improvement; others report a decline for both but a substantially greater one for women.[45] In addition, divorced women are often faced with the need to reenter the labor market if they have been home for a while, and to cope with a variety of stresses as they adapt to a situation that they may not have expected or wanted, or even if they wanted, were not prepared for. Many, of course, remarry after some years but some do not. Questions have been raised about ways to provide transitional help to these women, at least until they can work, and about ways to assure them of at least some minimum child support. Separated single mothers (19 percent of the group) share many of these problems with the divorced and also face some disadvantages of an unsettled legal status. Again, their needs would appear to be different from those of many of the never-married mothers.

3. *Never-married mothers* (29 percent of the single-mother group) are likely to be younger, less educated, have younger children, have less work experience, and to be poorer. However, here it becomes important to distinguish between the very young teenage mother and the older well-educated and established woman who makes a deliberate decision to parent and who is able to support her child financially. Also important here is to distinguish those women who were poor even before becoming single mothers and who can anticipate a long spell of poverty from those who have modest support and are likely to be able to manage adequately. What kind of help can be provided the first category

of mothers? Will providing financial help create an incentive for further growth in this life-style? Or, is this a trend that is now occurring regardless of policy interventions? If so, what are the implications and what, if anything, can or should be done?

4. The *working single mother* and the nonworking single mother also need to be distinguished, regardless of marital status. Everything we know about mother-only families suggests that the only way out of economic deprivation is through a job. Yet not every job provides income above the poverty threshold. Is a job the solution for the economic problems of these mothers? What kind of job, with what wage, and what happens when wages are low? How are single mothers to manage family life when they work?

5. *Teenage mothers* have special problems: physical and emotional immaturity, limited capacity to nurture and parent a child let alone support that child and themselves financially, and inadequate education and training. Ideally, we would want to prevent young adolescents from becoming parents prematurely, but once they are parents, they and their children need help, too. How can this be done and how can a repeat pregnancy be avoided?

We have not listed the *welfare mother* as a separate type because she is often separated, divorced, never married, or a teen mother. "Welfare" is one program option, not a demographic category, yet it dominates the public perception and makes policy difficult. We shall pursue this further in Chapter 2 and Chapter 4.

In this book we take a more extensive look at what the experience is like for different types of mother-only families and what could be done to improve the situation for the mothers, their children, and society at large. Clearly, it is a tough life for mothers on a day-to-day basis, and a depriving life for many of their children. Society cares, too, perhaps most, about the costs of the public aid for those who need help. Moreover, even with regard to many of those who can manage on their own, society may view their behavior as an affront to established and prevailing values.

What does appear clear is that the fact of diversity rules out any assumption that a strategy targeted on all the poor will immediately and adequately address all types of single mothers and their needs. Nor could one categorical program specific to "the single mother" encompass so wide a range of circumstance and need. In other words, Options 1 and 2, alone, will not suffice. Indeed, as will be seen in the next chapter, the United States has tried such approaches and experienced considerable frustration with them.

Endnotes

1. Senator Jeremiah Denton, Opening Statement, *Broken Families*, U.S. Senate, Committee on Labor and Human Resources, Subcommittee on Family and Human Services, Hearings, March 22 and 24, 1983 (Washington, D.C.: Government Printing Office, 1983).
2. Bruce Chapman, then Director of the U.S. Census Bureau, "Seduced and Abandoned: America's New Poor," *The Wall Street Journal*, 5 October 1982.
3. Tom Joe and Peter Yu, "Black Men, Welfare and Jobs," *The New York Times*, 21 August 1984.
4. Blanche Bernstein, "Welfare Dependency," in *The Social Contract Revisited*, ed. D. Lee Bawden (Washington, D.C.: The Urban Institute Press, 1984), 148–149.
5. Lenore J. Weitzman, *The Divorce Revolution: The Unexpected Social and Economic Consequences for Women and Children in America* (New York: Free Press, 1985), xiv.
6. Charles Murray, "No, Welfare Isn't Really the Problem," *The Public Interest*, no. 84 (Summer 1986): 311.
7. Sharyne Merritt and Linda Steiner, *And Baby Makes Two: Motherhood without Marriage* (New York: Franklin Watts, 1984).
8. Participant at International Working Party on the Future of the Welfare State, Aspen-Berlin Program, West Berlin, FRG, June, 1985.
9. William Julius Wilson, *The Truly Disadvantaged* (Chicago: University of Chicago Press, 1987), 145.
10. Mickey Kaus, "The Work Ethic State," *The New Republic*, 7 July 1986. See also, Nicholas Lemann, "The Origins of the Underclass," *The Atlantic*, July and August 1986.
11. Diana Pearce and Harriette McAdoo, "Women and Children: Alone and in Poverty" (Washington, D.C.: Women's Research and Education Institute, 1982), 1.
12. Daniel Patrick Moynihan, *Family and Nation* (New York: Harcourt Brace Jovanovich, 1986), 112.
13. Sara McLanahan and Larry Bumpass, "Intergenerational Consequences of Family Disruption" (Madison: University of Wisconsin, Institute for Research on Poverty, DP# 805–86, 1986).
14. Alvin L. Schorr and Phyllis Moen, "The Single Parent and Public Policy," *Social Policy* (March/April 1979): 15–21.
15. See U.S. Bureau of the Census, "Marital Status and Living Arrangements: March 1985"; "Household and Family Characteristics: March 1985"; "Marital Status and Living Arrangements: March 1986"; and "Household and Family Characteristics: March 1986," *Current Population Reports*, series P-20, Nos. 410, 411,418, and 419 (Washington, D.C.: Government Printing Office, 1986, 1986, 1987, 1987). Some of the reported increase results from a technical change in how these families were counted, but most reflects a true increase.
16. Arthur J. Norton and Paul C. Glick, "One-Parent Families: A Social and Economic Profile," *Family Relations*, Special Issue on "The Single-Parent Family," vol. 35, no. 1 (January 1986): 9–17. See also, Larry Bumpass, "Children and Marital Disruption: A Replication and Update," *Demography*, vol. 21, no. 1 (February 1984): 71–82; Sheila B. Kamerman, "Young, Poor and

a Mother Alone," in *Services to Young Families,* ed. Harriette McAdoo and T. M. Jim Parham (Washington, D.C.: American Public Welfare Association, 1985).

17. Unpublished data from March 1986 survey by the U.S. Department of Labor, Bureau of Labor Statistics.

18. U.S. Bureau of the Census, "Characteristics of the Population Below the Poverty Level: 1984"; "Poverty in the United States: 1985," *Current Population Reports,* series P-60, nos. 152, 159 (Washington, D.C.: Government Printing Office, 1986, 1987).

19. Greg J. Duncan and Saul D. Hoffman, "A Reconsideration of the Economic Consequences of Marital Dissolution," *Demography* 22 (November 1985): 495–98; Greg J. Duncan and Willard Rodgers, "Lone-Parent Families and Their Economic Problems: Transitory or Persistent?" Paper 4, *Lone Parents: The Economic Challenges of Changing Family Structures* (Paris: Organisation for Economic Co-operation and Development, 1987), 13.

20. Diana Pearce, "The Feminization of Poverty: Women, Work and Welfare," *Urban and Social Change Review* (February 1978): 28–36.

21. Irwin Garfinkel and Sara S. McLanahan, *Single Mothers and Their Children: A New American Dilemma* (Washington, D.C.: The Urban Institute Press, 1986).

22. James Morgan et al., Panel Study of Income Dynamics, *Five Thousand American Families* (Ann Arbor, Mich.: Institute of Social Research, 1947–1987, multiple volumes). Duncan and Rodgers argue that in one sense structural factors are less important than labor market factors in accounting for poverty: "Labor market events are more frequent than family composition events" (p. 21, see Note 19).

23. Mary Jo Bane, "Household Composition and Poverty," in *Fighting Poverty: What Works and What Doesn't,* ed. Sheldon H. Danziger and Daniel H. Weinberg (Cambridge, Mass.: Harvard University Press, 1986), 230–31. See also, Margaret Weir, Ann Shola Orloff, and Theda Skocpol, eds., *The Politics of Social Policy in the United States* (Princeton, N.J.: Princeton University Press, 1988).

24. U.S. Bureau of the Census, "Child Support and Alimony: 1983"; "Child Support and Alimony, 1985," *Current Population Reports,* series P-23, nos. 148, 152 (Washington, D.C.: Government Printing Office, 1986, 1987).

25. James L. Peterson, "Post-Divorce Event and the Provision of Child Support Payments" (Washington, D.C.: Child Trends, Inc., forthcoming).

26. Alfred J. Kahn and Sheila B. Kamerman, *Child Support: From Debt Collection to Social Policy* (Newbury Park, Calif.: Sage, 1988).

27. Department of Labor, Bureau of Labor Statistics.

28. Department of Labor, Bureau of Labor Statistics, Report 740, "Employment in Perspective: Women in the Labor Force," First Quarter 1987, Washington, D.C.

29. James P. Smith and Michael P. Ward, *Women's Wages and Work in the Twentieth Century* (Santa Monica, Calif.: Rand, 1984), ix.

30. Alfred J. Kahn and Sheila B. Kamerman, *Helping America's Families* (Philadelphia: Temple Uiversity Press, 1982); Sheila B. Kamerman, *Parenting in an Unresponsive Society* (New York: Free Press, 1980).

31. See Kamerman, *Parenting in an Unresponsive Society,* and Claire Vickery,

"Economics and the Single-Mother Family," *Public Welfare*, vol. 36, no. 1 (Winter 1978): 18–21.

32. McLanahan and Bumpass, "Intergenerational Consequences of Family Disruption."

33. Sandra L. Hofferth, "The Children of Teen Childbearers," in *Risking the Future: Adolescent Sexuality, Pregnancy, and Childbearing*, vol. II, ed. S. L. Hofferth and Cheryl D. Hayes (Washington, D.C.: National Academy Press, 1987), 174–208.

34. Kristin A. Moore, "The Children of Teen Parents" (Washington, D.C.: Child Trends, 1986).

35. Ibid., p. 6.

36. E. Mavis Heatherington, "Parents, Children and Siblings: Six Years After Divorce," in *Relationships Within Families: Mutual Influences*, ed. R. A. Hinde and J. Stevenson-Hinde (New York: Oxford University Press, 1988).

37. Sandra L. Hofferth and V. Jeffrey Evans, "The State of the Child and the Debate over Resource Allocation in the U.S." (Paper prepared for presentation at Joint Seminar on Life Course, Family and Work, Oslo, Norway, February 1987); James L. Peterson and Nicholas Zill, "Marital Disruption, Parent-Child Relationships, and Behavior Problems in Children," *Journal of Marriage and the Family*, vol. 48, no. 2 (May 1986): 295–307.

38. Mary Ann Glendon, *Abortion and Divorce in Western Law* (Cambridge, Mass.: Harvard University Press, 1987).

39. Charles Murray, *Losing Ground* (New York: Basic Books, 1984); and Lawrence Mead, *Beyond Entitlement* (New York: Free Press, 1986). Also, see Bruce Chapman, *U.S. Senate, Hearings, Broken Families*, part I.

40. David T. Ellwood and Mary Jo Bane, "The Impact of AFDC on Family Structure and Living Arrangements," in *Research in Labor Economics*, vol. 7, ed. Ron G. Ehrenberg (Greenwich, Conn.: JAI Press, 1985). See also, Garfinkel and McLanahan, *Single Mothers and Their Children*.

41. Murray, "No, Welfare Isn't Really the Problem."

42. Garfinkel and McLanahan, *Single Mothers and Their Children*, 55–63.

43. William J. Wilson and Kathryn M. Neckerman, "Poverty and Family Structure," in *Fighting Poverty: What Works and What Doesn't*, ed. S. H. Danziger and D. H. Weinberg (Cambridge, Mass.: Harvard University Press, 1986), 232–59. William J. Wilson, *The Truly Disadvantaged* (Chicago: University of Chicago Press, 1987). For an introduction and a review of the recent debate, see Robert D. Reischauer, "America's Underclass: Other Viewpoints," *Public Welfare*, vol. 45, no. 4 (Fall 1987), 26–37. Also, Sara McLanahan, Irwin Garfinkel, and Dorothy Watson, "Family Structure, Poverty, and the Underclass," Discussion Paper 823–87 (Madison, Wisc.: Institute for Research on Poverty, 1987).

44. Garfinkel and McLanahan, *Single Mothers and Their Children*.

45. Weitzman, *The Divorce Revolution;* Duncan and Hoffman, "A Reconsideration of the Economic Consequences of Marital Discord." However, on the impact of child support on noncustodial families, see Ann Nichols-Casebolt, "The Economic Impact of Child Support Reform on the Poverty Status of Custodial and Noncustodial Families," *Journal of Marriage and the Family*, vol. 48, no. 4 (November 1986): 875–80.

Chapter 2

LOOKING BACKWARD: THE SEARCH FOR PERSPECTIVE

If our society is to act wisely as it responds to or decides to ignore the complex worlds of the several types of mother-only families and their children, it will need all the facts and background it can muster. As options for action are lined up, it is useful to recall that we are not without experience.

The media, agendas of professional meetings, and political debate all serve to remind us that the question of public response to single mothers and their children is deeply involved in strongly held values and in the traditional stakes of agencies, organizations, departments, and professions. There are viable policy traditions and program modes that go back quite far in history, along with many others that certainly are not and have not been defensible for a long time.

In the search for perspective, even the question of what is relevant becomes complicated. In some sense, the history that people choose to look at and to tell us about is not unrelated to what they prefer to do. The fact is that the full story is not simple, although some participants in the debate would have us believe that it is. In our own view, a number of strands must be joined for a complete appreciation of current choices.

Poor Law as Classification

The history of policy toward single-mother families obviously must encompass the history of direct financial aid to the poor,[1] but we would direct attention, as well, to the development and changing emphases of child welfare service programs. Neither of these can be fully understood without at least brief mention of the earlier evolution of less differentiated public responsibility and response to many categories of the needy, the deviant, and the troublesome.[2]

This story, in its full complexity, has a very long timeline. For our purposes, the 17th century is early enough. Several hundred years of trial-and-error experimentation had yielded the Poor Law in England, and the United States was to live with its elaborations and influences until late in the 19th century. In fact, much of the Poor Law is still with us, and the treatment of single mothers is a part of this history.

The growth of towns, trade, and manufacturing required labor force mobility and land enclosure. If the response to the resulting stress had been only Christian charity, there would have been no pressure for the painful economic and institutional changes that were to occur. If, on the other hand, there had been no charity at all, the public resistance could have been powerful.

The Poor Law compromise was a turning point; it invented modern welfare, in a sense. The local parish, as the responsible unit, had to guarantee either "outdoor relief" (assistance while one remained in the community) or "indoor relief" (care in an institution) to those in need, but only after the primacy of family and relatives' responsibility was taken into account and, then, after assurance that the employable would be put to work if possible. Permission was given to levy a special local tax for this purpose— an important step in a world with little precedent for local authority taxation. The locality was required to make some provision for the poor who had no other recourse; so, in a sense, it was a primitive assertion of the right to aid.

While we shall describe Poor Law as though it was an unvaried program and coherent from the start, there were, of course, changes and differences in emphasis and implementation over the years and by place. From the point of view of our exploration, the notion of differentiation among categories of the poor—a classification system—was a critical component. Young children and their widowed mothers, who were deemed "virtuous" and "efficient," to use the terms of the day, were one of the most privileged subgroups. For the policy to achieve its major objectives, most of those who came to ask for help were put to work, preferably in the evolving private economy, but, if necessary, by public authorities. These people were not given "outdoor relief"—in our terms, cash and in-kind assistance—which would have made it possible for them to live in their own homes. Nor were they permitted to beg; giving alms was viewed as creating as much of a "work disincentive" then as welfare is today. (The actual enforcement of the prohibition against begging varied considerably over the years, depending both on local circumstances and other developments.) The main point is that the police power of the state backed up labor market policy; the able-bodied poor were expected and required to work. Charitable impulses were channeled to those considered to be "impotent" or unemployable and thus worthy of protection against the harsher alternative.

Who, then, were the "impotent" poor who could be aided while at home, allowed to have outdoor relief, and not be defined as employable? First, there were the very old, with no family left—a rare circumstance. Then (and now, we approach the single-mother story), there could be outdoor relief for the virtuous widow and her children, usually meaning a widow whose husband had been a responsible, self-supporting, respected member of the community. Finally, depending on time and place, there were some categories among the handicapped and homeless who were not objects of public anger or punitive feeling and might be helped at home; these latter were few in number.

It must be stressed that family and relative responsibility came first. Neighborly help was next. Public help was very limited and seldom long term. The community was expected to do the economical thing: create or—with other nearby communities—sponsor various forms of the poorhouse (almshouse) if that was an advantageous way to cope. Almost all except the most advantaged were offered this type of "indoor" relief.

Work was the general answer. When men and women came for aid, the poor law authorities tried to find them work or to contract their labor. If jobs were not available, indenture was the alternative: The authorities would auction off the worker to the lowest bidder; the successful bidder would meet the costs out of the labor of the now-indentured worker. A small subsidy might be needed to ensure complete transfer of responsibility for a poor person's food, shelter, and clothing.

In a world in which even the youngest children were part of the household economy in all but the wealthiest families, very young children were also indentured. Thus, if a family came for help, it was quite possible that each member of the family would end up in a different household in a different place. Children might leave their parents forever. Poverty broke up families.

In this world single-parent families had few protections. A favored widow and her children could be given outdoor relief under Poor Law, and they sometimes were, particularly in small towns where people knew one another. She might be protected, particularly if her departed husband had been considered a leading citizen, virtuous, and respected. In deciding who was virtuous and who lacked virtue among those seeking aid, Poor Law defined the latter as exploiting the community or as a burden upon it. The former were seen as in need because of what might be thought of as "acts of God," whereas the latter's turn to the community was viewed as a demonstration of their complicity in "acts of moral failure." Such distinctions, of course, made the policy more comfortable.

Widow or not, long-term need usually led to work placement for the mother and her children if she did not herself find some work, or at least enough for partial support. If the children were too young for indenture and could not be separated from their mother, the choice—in the absence of adequate outdoor relief—was the poorhouse, an institution that housed those who could not or would not work; the aged, ill, and handicapped whom the community would not support at home; and many petty offenders. Mixed in with this group were women who today would be described as unwed mothers, prostitutes, divorced, separated, "unworthy" widows, and many others for whom the community had simply exhausted whatever resources it had been willing to share earlier. Readers of *Oliver Twist* will recall the ambience of this kind of almshouse. Well into the 19th century it was reported that 90 percent of the infants and toddlers for whom this became a shelter faced certain death. Such an existence was a harsh regime by today's standards, but not so in a world of strong moral judgments, minimal government, limited concepts of citizen rights, and a general poverty that was experienced by all but the most fortunate.

Many of those in need clearly were victims and could be recognized as such in a world of small towns, intimate neighborliness, and small churches. Here were people who were virtuous, met their obligations, but were now in trouble. How could society around them—moral people, religious people, humanitarians—tolerate so punitive a regime? There was, of course, the view that poor communities had no alternatives. There were a number of other reasons as well. First, there was the known help by extended family and neighbors. People helped one another as much as they could, certainly over the short run and especially in the face of a natural catastrophe, fire, spoiled harvest, or injury. There also was the mutual aid, symbolized in mid-19th century United States by the "barn raising." On these two levels—extended family and neighbors, and mutual aid—one did all one could. Then, there also was church charity. To the extent that intimate knowledge of and shared experience with their neighbors made people uncomfortable about letting poor law authorities deal with their neighbors in need who did not deserve harshness, these were real alternatives, and many needy people were never subject to the Poor Law.

England, more densely settled and with many larger cities, was on a faster track, so these poor law policies were experienced in their harshest form by large numbers. But in the United States, almost any town could meet to individualize its decisions about specific families until late in the 18th century. The full harshness of Poor Law was not applied in the United States on a significant scale until cities had become so large and impersonal that the injustice of punitive alternatives was not obvious to one's neighbors and church. Now the able-bodied poor, no matter what their past histories and true virtues, could be treated no better then petty criminals unless the authorities could send them—or put them— to work. In these larger settlements, almshouses or poorhouses were more economical than outdoor relief, even for those who in an earlier era might have been aided at home. The new and larger almshouses from the early 19th century housed a greater range of petty criminals, prostitutes, and the disturbed, who might be sharing the facility with the able-bodied for whom there was no work, along with the impotent poor whom nobody wanted to aid at home, and assured a regime of horror, danger, contagion and, for infants, almost inevitable death.[3]

The Safety Valves

As mercantilism was replaced by laissez-faire capitalism and social institutions adapted to create a free labor market (the "task" of the economy from the early 19th to the early 20th century),[4] this entire process of poor law policy development accelerated. Both the size of towns and cities and the numbers involved in poor law measures led from quantity to a change in quality. In England, the next level of administrative harshness and "efficiency" was introduced formally by the 1832 Poor Law Commission, and reinforced by the commission's 1834 report and subsequent legislation in the late 1840s.[5] In the United States, while the same elaboration of poor law policies was well underway in the 1820s, it was played out most fully after the Civil War.

As already suggested, there had been many lapses and escape routes from Poor Law throughout earlier centuries, since sentiment and charity sometimes overcame public policy. Sentiment and charity now became unacceptable in the public policy arena, and alms giving was outlawed firmly. If the able-bodied poor could not find work or be indentured, the public would put them to work to earn their keep—but in an almshouse or workhouse. According to Brown, by the 19th century the almshouse had effectively superseded farming out and indenture generally; outdoor relief, considered costly and wrong, was mostly a temporary or emergency device. There were to be no attractive alternatives to work in the emerging industrial system. Whenever relief in cash or kind was to be given, even to "deserving" categories or for good public reason, it was to be at a level below the least satisfactory of available wage rates (the doctrine of "less eligibility").[6]

The story has been well told by specialists of how the workhouse, designed as the ideal solution for the employable who insisted on requesting aid, could never succeed.[7] The able-bodied (mostly men through this period) were to prove their readiness to work here ("the work test") and, in any case, to pay their keep. Yet, if the workhouse were to employ the able-bodied efficiently so that they would not be burdens, it would be competing "unfairly" with market producers. If the workhouse wanted to become a profitable factory, it had to be selective in its workers. If it avoided unfair competition or preselection of its inmates, the workhouse was just one more costly mixed almshouse. So it was periodically to be investigated and "reformed."

We have already suggested that almost from the beginning the Poor Law was to have an effective safety valve of charity, humanitarianism, and primary group response. As it entered its most extreme laissez-faire stage in the post–Civil War period, its counterpart was the much expanded middle-class humanitarianism and religious charity of the 19th century. The devices, reforms, and innovations came in waves, as did the plateauing of poor law implementation (and, then, more vigorous efforts, variously affected by economic conditions, waves of immigration, and the coming of new political leadership). The fate of children was dependent on some of these alternatives, most of them private.

The early 18th-century version of Poor Law was both sustained and softened by various religious strains in the American ethic. Calvinist notions of predestination and broader Christian understanding that there were always poor in the society, as indicated in the Old and New Testaments, suggested an accommodation through charity for those who should not be punitively mishandled by poor law authorities. Late in the century there was Social Darwinism, "puritanism without a conscience," which defined any possible alternative public policies that might take good care of the poor as basically hopeless ideas and doomed to be self-defeating.

The castoffs of the society were described by this doctrine as the price to be paid for an essentially benign natural evolutionary process through which the capable succeeded, the society prospered and improved, and the "doomed" whom it helped were simply burdens assumed if absolutely necessary. (Besides, many observers in the 1870s and 1880s were certain that large government was inherently corrupt and inefficient.) Yet humanitarian and religious people saw all about them individuals for whom such policies could only be unfair. Here were obviously "good people," "moral people," and "victims" in the modern sense all being punished for misfortune.

The classification tradition, always present in Poor Law, was now to be elaborated and refined, again and again. The "impotent" and "able-bodied" of the 17th century became the "worthy" and "unworthy," the "helpable" and the "shiftless," the "deserving" and the "undeserving," and finally, the "normal" and the "multiproblem." (Most recently, they have been labeled "the underclass".) Especially important, fewer categories of difficulty would be assigned to the class of "moral culpability" and more to "acts of God," as religious and humanitarian impulses and more rigorous understanding of some categories of problems began to prevail later in the century. A larger "umbrella" would protect some people from the most punitive options of the Poor Law, as experience, understanding, empathy, and—much later—social science began to testify to the inappropriateness of the punitive almshouse, the workhouse, and indenture for some people. The traditional solutions were no longer appropriate once one understood these people better.

Such developments inevitably are uneven. The United States is a large country in which economy, industrialization, wealth, city growth, and the sophistication of public administration have over the decades varied by place and interacted with different religious, ethnic, regional, and political traditions. Yet the pattern was there. The poor law "mass" was increasingly differentiated. Nonsectarian and religious charities, many types of specialized institutions, and even some public facilities offered alternatives. We merely suggest the range—because of the eventual importance of the process to single mothers and their children.

Late in the 18th century and early in the 19th, Societies for the Prevention of Pauperism appeared in the Northeast, pioneering an individualized, outdoor, family help, combined with advice from successful citizen volunteers, giving the "helpable" a fresh start—and protecting the family. At the same time, some religious groups and a few public authorities began to institutionalize orphans in settings apart from adults and, by the standards of the day, were protective. The children placed in these institutions were orphans of soldiers or sailors, from among the "deserving." Early in the 19th century, when the true horrors of the mixed almshouse were yet to be fully experienced in the United States, a House of Refuge for juvenile delinquents opened in New York City. The New England "renaissance" of the 1830s inspired the creation of specialized schools for handicapped children, even though two decades later the streets of large cities throughout the country were still home to hundreds of abandoned children.[8] Prison reform and abolitionism also spread in this New England environment. Then, in the early 1840s, Dorothy Dix began her efforts to remove the mentally ill from mixed almshouses, jails, and attics to humane state hospitals. In several states reformers attacked the almshouses for what they did to children and urged creation of special institutions for children. Such institutions began to open and were called various names, such as state public schools in Massachusetts and orphan asylums in many other places. The differentiations continued so that the various categories of poor, deviant, and handicapped eventually all had their more humane reforms, some more successful than others. By the end of the century the almshouse had evolved into the county old age home, with its previous population having been dispersed into specialized institutions.

In another wave, in the middle of the 19th century, the more "hopeful," "deserving," or "helpable" among the urban poor could turn to the new Associations for Improving the Conditions of the Poor (AICP). These individualized, volunteer-staffed city charity societies coordinated help, led some city reforms, and offered to some an alternative to the public harshness. Their roles should not be misunderstood. For the poor and unfortunate who would comply, take advice, conform, there was help, particularly transitional help for a family and sometimes long-term help for a widow and child. But this, too, was a powerful form of social control, in which the dominant morality of the day was enforced in the name of saving the fortunate whom they would help from the harsher alternative of the public almshouse. The AICP worked for a while, but its mission had to be renewed in the last decade of the century by a new organization, the Charity Organization Societies (COS). It was from these societies that the concepts of modern social work emerged. First came the creation of a corps of volunteers, then paid friendly visitors, who would mobilize community resources around the family's needs, while giving advice, guidance, and instruction concerning the route to self-sufficiency and respectability. This, too, was enforcement of community norms and social control, of course, as are all such institutional responses to some degree. Nonetheless, those in need who were deemed deserving were offered alternatives more adequate and more hopeful than what could be expected from most public authorities at this time.

Indenture, Outdoor Relief, Institutions, and Foster Homes

As social welfare programs evolved, widows and children were the recipients of humanitarian impulses, because from the very beginning they had been classified as deserving and worthy of special protection. The absence of what we might think of today as a reliable public assistance program had left many of them vulnerable. Early in the 19th century they were subject to indenture—unless saved by local charities and neighbors or the ability of the mother to work. And, as indicated, if the mother was not an especially favored widow, she and her children were relegated to the mixed almshouse, along with the other single mothers and their children—the people in the rejected categories. But we have also noted that from the late 18th century, and certainly from the early 19th century, some categories of children, particularly orphans of soldiers, sailors, and others, could enter the small number of favored religious or public institutions. (Only about 100 of these are listed as late as 1850.) Some single mothers worked, placed one or two children, and kept some at home, doing what they could. The exceptions—those given outdoor relief by private charities—were lucky although not numerous, even when, late in the 19th century, some public authorities joined in funding the help as well.

In the mid-19th century, there was another important development. Charles Loring Brace in New York, Hastings H. Hart in Minnesota, and Martin Van Buren Van Arsdale in the Midwest promoted the idea of the free home—what was to become the modern foster home and the major alternative to almshouses and indenture, and to city hostels and institutions for homeless children. The free home would take in children, including those too young to work, and treat them the same as would natural parents. The children would remain in the free home until they were grown and would participate in the free home's family economy, usually farming. Out of these beginnings, foster home care and adoption, as currently known, were to develop.

What made this development of foster homes different from the 17th- and 18th-century indenture? Largely the effort to suggest that children be seen as joining the family, taken on even if their work was not needed or if they were too young to work. Eventually, if gradually, the essential protections (which became the core of "child welfare" programs) were to be built in: home study, a professional effort to match children and families, agency supervision of placed children, and the payment of a stipend. For a long time, however, there was suspicion and doubt, and with good reason, since the protections were only partially and poorly implemented in many places. The case could be made (and debated) that the institution was a better alternative. From a broader cultural perspective, one might also note that there were good social, cultural, and religious reasons for a preference for institutions within the Catholic community and a greater possibility of foster homes within the Protestant. In any case, while the debate between the two groups raged, both foster homes and institutions continued to develop. Eventually, all concerned agreed that both foster homes and institutions had their place. After the professionalization of the field of child welfare and considerable improvements in the 1960s and 1970s, two new campaigns began, one advocating deinstitutionalization and the other calling attention to the neglect of many children in foster home care and the failure to return foster children to their own families or to get them adopted. Family protection and preventive services or adoption were now offered as the "better alternative" to foster care, which began what some observers considered to be a decline after legislation in the 1980s, to be mentioned below.

The maternity homes, which were protective of unwed mothers and their children in the sense that they were specialized and not almshouses, were to have their main flowering in the 20th century. By permitting concealment and often, under religious auspices, stressing efforts at moral reform, they provided an interim outlet and transition for some, especially white, middle-class and working-class young women. By channeling most of the children to adoption, they dealt with the long-range issues. But, according to Rothman, as far back as the late 19th century significant numbers of working girls chose boarding homes and lodging houses over the YWCAs designed to protect them, and they avoided use of maternity homes when possible. Some worked and raised their children; others left them in foundling hospitals. They resisted the isolation and "imposed penance" of the homes as they coped with the harsh realities. By the 1960s such institutions were obsolete in a world in which single mothers could keep their children if they wished— or place them—and in which the stigma of out-of-wedlock pregnancy was much less prevalent.

To summarize part of the tradition to the end of the 19th century:

- Family breakup via indenture of mothers and children—along with fathers if they were alive—was a common response to the request for financial aid.
- The condemnation of many "deserving" widows and almost all other single mothers and their children (particularly the unwed and the deserted) to the horrors of the mixed alms-house was common.
- The rescue of children was attempted, successively, through specialized institutions and then foster-home care as an alternative to indenture.
- Finally, there was a tradition of financial help via private charities, at home, for the lucky few who in some way were defined as more deserving or virtuous or able to manage after a modest period.

Widows' Pensions in Suitable Homes

Mothers' or widows' pensions must be understood in the context of the Progressive Era. Child saving was one of the major reform causes of the period.

Particularly in the period between the 1894 depression and World War I, a combination of journalistic muckraking, social work reporting, fictional writing, religious advocacy, and social science began to yield new understanding of the relationships among economy, living conditions in the urban environment, and the personal circumstances of masses of people. More and more observers were to note that "pauperism," by which was meant moral failure, did not really explain extreme economic need, or "poverty," which should be understood as a social problem.[9] Broader reforms and more adequate treatment of disadvantaged people were needed.

In the context of the reforms of the Progressive Era, new initiatives were addressed at children by health, educational, anti-child-labor, child welfare, juvenile court, nursery school, and kindergarten programs. Some people began to ask, If foster-home care is better than institutional care, why not, then, keep children in their own homes? Could campaigns for abolishing child labor or to ensure compulsory education be credible if mothers had to work to support themselves and their family, often then requiring that their children be institutionalized because the mother could not manage their care and work, too? Some reformers went even beyond this and asked whether, just as the country was compensating a large portion of veterans of the Civil War and their widows for war service, could not one conceive of compensating widows who stayed home to care for children for also rendering an important public service?[10] Such assistance would be quite different from poor relief (and, we might add, more like the thinking that later was to create the children's allowances in some European countries).[11]

It is not clear how widespread was the thinking which Leiby and the Pumphreys cite. Most students of the development do agree that a number of forces had joined: new concern for the welfare of children; a recognition that care in institutions and foster homes was probably more costly than care in the child's own home by a widowed mother; and, in the words of Grace Abbott, who earlier was Children's Bureau chief, "public recognition by the states that the contribution of unskilled or semiskilled mothers in their own homes exceeded their earnings outside the home and that it was in the public interest to conserve their child caring functions."[12]

Because the father was incapacitated, dead, or had deserted, the family would need help for an extended period. This would not be assured by prevailing modes of general or emergency relief. To opponents this could mean a return to discredited outdoor relief. However, the dominant view among the reformers was that mothers should be able to stay home to care for their children. The child savers and reformers at the first White House Conference on Children (1909) wrote President Theodore Roosevelt as they concluded their work: "Except in unusual circumstances, the home should not be broken up for reasons of poverty, but only for considerations of inefficiency or immorality."[13]

Although the White House Conference had expressed preference for private over public relief (there still being much concern with potential corruption in public administration as well as doubt over whether it could individualize service), it was to be otherwise. Missouri passed the first Mother's Pension law in 1911, and Illinois followed almost immediately after; 20 states acted almost at once, 40 within 10 years. By 1935, only Alabama, Georgia, and South Carolina had no such laws.[14] These mothers' pension laws—the generic term despite many variations—were, of course, permissive. They often depended on special state or local action and funds and allowed considerable discretion to authorities. Bell states, also, that the aid was conditional. The mothers' pensions came with a "suitable home" requirement: The state would provide enough money to enable mothers to maintain a suitable home, but the mothers had to demonstrate that they were proper and competent custodians.[15] Bell's review of data, admittedly incomplete, shows that only three states explicitly covered unwed mothers; most would in theory help if the father deserted, and half would help if there was a divorce. Administration, however, was tighter than that. By 1931 it could be shown that 82 percent of the coverage was for families of "gilt edge widows," and over 95 percent of recipients were probably white.[16] Unwed mothers and their children simply did not appear.

Abbott reports that the earlier "mothers' aid" proposals favored adequate coverage for unmarried mothers and deserted families, too, but the many fears and objections of opponents led to a retreat. It was "safest" to cover children of widows and of incapacitated fathers. In theory, Abbott states, 10 states covered most categories of children of single mothers. The other states only gradually added categories as the laws were stabilized.[17] Bremner summarizes a 1931 Children's Bureau survey which found that only 55 of 60,119 cases in 38 states on mothers' pension caseloads were families of unwed mothers.[18]

In any case, these permissive laws, perpetuating historical differentiations, limited in their resources, and under constant scrutiny, tended to stay with the "worthy." "Widows' pensions" could be enacted but not yet aid for all single mothers. There was more stress on the children to be aided than on their caretaker mothers, but the mother's category in effect shaped the children's destiny.

In a somewhat broader historical perspective, we may note with Rothman that in one sense some poor women (we would stress, selected, approved poor women) were being permitted to do what middle-class women were doing in the late 19th century: to stay home and make the home a haven and a place for secure child development.[19]

In general, however, aid from mothers' pensions was very inadequate, insecure, and sporadic. Grants were small. Many of the "widows" in fact had to supplement what they received by doing some at-home or outside work.[20]

One might ask, What does this have to do with today's dilemmas about single-parent families? It is part of the story, clearly, but not all of it. Society was gradually arriving at an income-support program for widows and other single mothers, largely as a way to aid children, but was being careful about morality and suitability. What had begun as child saving—the child's own home rather than a foster home or institution—could not yet be achieved because there were larger issues of public administration and policy (how much money would states spend on such programs and how could public agencies be efficient and effective?). Strong traditions also played a role in that only the "worthy" who were not already morally corrupted or who would not be corrupted by the aid could be helped. Such selectivity would take individualization and discretion. Then, too, there was racism (few black homes were deemed "suitable"), as well as strong moral judgments (widows might be "suitable" but what about unmarried mothers?). The few unmarried mothers who were helped were placed in "maternity homes" until their children were born and adopted.

Kammerer, an enlightened analyst writing near the end of the first World War under the sponsorship of the psychiatrist/scholar/ reformer Dr. William Healy, made it clear that the unmarried were regarded as problem "cases" rather than "citizens." The etiology was all or largely "bad" factors: home conditions, environment, companions, sexual trauma or early sexual induction, mental abnormality, physical abnormality, and so forth.[21] Yet this analyst of 500 case records, who built his theories from them inductively (or so seemed to believe), also noted that the cases that get to public and private agencies are, after all, only the "disadvantaged" part of the population. Healy added in a preface that the more affluent have the knowledge and means to avoid "unlawful childbearing" and that as the war ended clearly many nations "encourage such production of offspring because of exigencies." Healy, a pioneering student of delinquency, noted that what makes out-of-wedlock childbearing so difficult is that here one has "the lawbreaker as a constructive agent, giving us as a concrete evidence of her 'misbehavior' nature's highest product, a human being."[22]

Other countries, Kammerer commented, are concerned more with the welfare of illegitimate children as such; there is "an absence of the retributive element . . . and a frank acknowledgment . . . that nothing should interfere with the State's interests with the child who is to be a future citizen."[23] Many feared that helping a child would "remove from the mother a stigma" and thus increase illegitimacy. On the other hand, "few would uphold" a policy favoring "handicapping the child because of the mother's misdeeds."[24] The story of mothers' pensions and early Aid to Dependent Children (ADC) legislation certainly suggests otherwise. These scholars do tell us, however, that there also were other views by this point in the 20th century.

The dominant pattern seemed to be: very modest financial aid for worthy widows, who also had to work; condemnation and little help for "unworthy" single mothers; and maternity homes for hiding and a place for childbirth by the "fallen" whose children soon would be adopted.

ADC, AFDC, Income, and Services

The Social Security Act, enacted in 1935, was preoccupied with unemployment insurance and old age pensions. The public assistance categories—Old Age Assistance, Aid to the Blind, Aid to Dependent Children (ADC)—were incorporated to provide federal financial aid to states that already had their equivalent programs, some better developed than others. Inevitably, then, benefit levels were to vary by states, and there was initially to be much state discretion in administration.

The act itself clearly was intended to differentiate the general relief measures for most of the 7.4 million children on the federal emergency welfare rolls (most of them in two-parent families), about whom the Committee on Economic Security said, "Nothing is wrong with their environment but their parents' lack of money to give them opportunities which are taken for granted in more fortunate homes."[25] Within this group, however, there were some 700,000 children "deprived of a father's support" and receiving help from the state mothers' aid or mothers' pensions laws. The committee interpreted these laws in 45 states as "not primarily aid to mothers but defense measures for children." Nonetheless, "they are designed to release from the wage earning role the person whose natural function is to give her children the physical and affectionate guardianship necessary not alone to keep them from falling into social misfortune, but more affirmatively to rear them into citizens capable of contributing to society."[26]

Since the bulk of mothers' aid costs had been paid by local governments and half of the jurisdictions were not giving any such aid at all, the committee saw great suffering ahead unless the end of the emergency relief era were to be followed by help to localities and states for assistance to fatherless families. Congress, however, was not willing to assign administration of the ADC grant-in-aid program to the U.S. Children's Bureau, the leading agency in child protection. ADC was kept with the other assistance programs under the new Social Security Board, eventually to be supervised by a Bureau of Public Assistance, despite the protests of many social work, child welfare, and voluntary groups.

Quite separately, the committee called for assistance to the states "in providing local services for the protection and care of homeless, neglected, and delinquent children and for child and maternal health services."[27] Here the Children's Bureau's lead was reaffirmed.

The two strains thus clearly were separate in the original act: different titles, different administration, and dramatically different levels of funding. What became known as "child welfare services" continued the policy of a special protective approach to children in difficulty. ADC was to be financial aid for those at home. It helped to support children. The ADC eligible "dependent child" was to be one under age 16, "deprived of parental support or care by reason of the death, continued absence from the home, or physical or mental incapacity of a parent," and who was living with a parent or relative (from an enumerated list) "at his or their own home."[28] In short, almost any category of single parent could be included, if states wished.

The original old age insurance (pension) program was converted by amendments in 1939 to a program of "family protection" that covered wives, widows, and dependent children of retirees and their orphans. ADC, however, did not cover caretakers until 1950. (The record is not clear as to whether or not the lack of a caretaker grant resulted from a drafting error or misunderstanding, as some were to claim. In any case, there was no change for 15 years!) Since widows thus had been assigned to social security early but ADC caretakers were ignored, in effect all single mothers except widows were on their own.

The child protections of ADC allowed very little money, even after the caretaker's inclusion. Despite the philosophy talked of earlier, widows and other eligible single mothers in fact were expected and encouraged to work, as seen in these low benefit levels and (as documented by Bell and others) the discretionary state administrative policies. Local labor market needs were shown to affect aid levels and to shape staff pressures on recipients. It was not until the late 1950s and early 1960s that most racial discrimination was eliminated, despite the Social Security Act requirement of "statewideness."

One thus cannot think of ADC as a program of income protection for most *single mothers and their children* until the 1950 amendments. Even then the evolution was to be slow. For, while the Social Security Act had not specified the "suitable home" premise of "mothers' pensions" or used other screening language with regard to caretakers, the states had been left considerable discretion, and benefit-matching formulas were low. Bell documents the congressional acceptance of state consideration of parent or caretaker "moral character." Professional opinion generally favored such eligibility preconditions.[29] At least 31 state ADC laws had such language, even though federal authorities—according to Burns—wanted "suitability" abandoned as an eligibility standard and urged referral of protective cases to child welfare agencies. As interpreted, in the discussion of the period, a home's unsuitability in this sense was said to be similar to circumstances justifying removal of a child from the home because of neglect, abuse, or exploitation.

While theoretically this latter concept could have minimized case rejections of homes as unsuitable, since not many children were being removed, such logic did not prevail in the early patterns of administration. The states had here a basis for discretion which perpetuated racial discrimination and large-scale rejection of out-of-wedlock children.[30] Homes were refused aid because they were judged unsuitable, but children were not rescued. The federal public administrative structure for the assistance program moved slowly in these areas and with limited leverage. Therefore, not until after World War II did equity pressures, combined with economic and social change, have a major impact.[31] The coverage for blacks improved considerably, as it did for families of unmarried parents. Much administrative abuse remained, however, and ADC was still far from a guaranteed program of financial aid for needy single-mother families.

Despite a series of incidents and episodes in other states, the issue did not come to a head until 1961 with the Louisiana "suitable home" crisis. We rely on the review by Bell. A variety of circumstances in the 1960s had highlighted the problem of welfare fraud, while growing and/or more visible illegitimacy, especially among blacks, and other economic and racial tensions led to increasing efforts to use negative assessments of family morality as a basis for ADC rejections. One state after another was highlighted with regard to the developing controversy. There were anti-"man-in-the-house" and other "suitable home" measures, much debate, and the emergence of a double standard: ADC for the "suitable" and residual general assistance for the others. Intermingled were efforts to deny relief or require people to "work off" their checks.

A series of state restrictive measures and much public controversy prevailed throughout the decade. Louisiana built on these precedents and announced discontinuance of aid to over 6,000 cases, most because the children were illegitimate and some for cohabitation; almost all the discontinued cases were black. We need not repeat Bell's full account of the uproar, debate, slow federal response, and hearings, as well as a decision in which the federal authorities found it difficult to justify interfering with Louisiana. However a new secretary of Health, Education and Welfare, Arthur Fleming, issued a ruling in 1961 which became a watershed: A state could not reject an assistance case as "unsuitable" and then leave the child in the home. And as long as the child remained in the home, assistance had to be continued. Otherwise, states would lose the right to receive ADC matching funds.[32]

The year 1961 was something of a turning point. New developments and initiatives, which still must be dealt with today, saw their beginnings. All the current threads became visible. Early in the 1950s efforts had begun to improve child welfare services. The Social Security Act had recognized "services" as a special independent component for reimbursement as early as 1956, but the record does not show great progress in service upgrading and improvement. The reimbursement remained at the 50 percent level that had prevailed when services had earlier been encompassed under "administration." Several major task forces responded to the public welfare crises in Louisiana and other places in the late 1950s and early 1960s, and they all urged a strengthening of social services: How else could parents be helped to manage and to make their homes suitable—and thus avoid child placement?[33] The 1962 amendments to the Social Security Act raised the federal share of reimbursement for social services to 75 percent. Now, for the first time, there existed a large-scale public capacity to "serve," "treat," and "rehabilitate," single-mother families and others who were receiving public aid. Aid to Dependent Children (ADC) announced its new intent and promise by being renamed Aid to Families with Dependent Children (AFDC) in 1962. In a very different thrust, to decrease family breakup, a temporary measure was passed in 1961 in which states were permitted to include in the ADC program families with an unemployed father. Also in 1962 this provision was standardized into what is now known as AFDC-UP. Earlier, an amendment permitted federal ADC reimbursement on the usual basis for children who had been removed from unsuitable homes by a court and placed in a foster-care home. This was essential to make the Fleming ruling a viable one. By 1967 a more generous formula provided federal support for foster care generally, including institutions, but a court placement was still required.

By the 1960s, in brief, the public response was permitting and protecting financial aid in homes for mothers and children, and the rules of the game were opening the program to a greater diversity of single mothers and their children and to some families with unemployed fathers. Researchers were discovering both the explosion in single parenthood, which had occurred between 1940 and 1960 (especially among young blacks), and the fact that many single mothers were apparently living with their children and performing successfully as parents. The dramatic shifts in the caseload are seen in Tables 2–1 and 2–2. It should be recalled that as late as 1942 some 42 percent of the cases claimed eligibility because of deceased fathers, according to a 16-state survey cited by Burns. By 1961 this number was 7.7 percent (by 1983 it was 1.9). By 1948, 29 percent of the caseload was black. Discrimination by color also had become less prevalent, and the black proportion of the AFDC caseload was 44 percent in 1961 and 45 percent in 1970, stabilizing as seen in Table 2–2. The "out-of-wedlock" part of the load also was growing rapidly in the early 1960s, both because of fertility patterns and because the "social insurance" benefits for widows and orphans had matured and offered relatively good coverage. AFDC also had financial capacity to deliver social services.

In 1960–61 there had been complaints (repeating assertions from the child welfare professionals in the 1950s) that one public welfare staff concerned itself with eligibility for assistance and another with child welfare, and that the two never met in most jurisdictions, despite the obvious need for services for the AFDC caseload. It had been assumed in 1962 that the new, more generous matching formulas, along with the child welfare initiatives of the 1950s, would change all of that. This was not to be. Even the new federal participation in foster care funding in the late 1960s did not make the difference. The policy remained muddled at the operational level. Just when AFDC could be said to be in a position to focus on family strengthening so that children could be reared by their mothers at home and given the funds that the law intended all single-mother families to have, social change entered the picture again (or, more accurately, if we recall the mixed history, old issues were to return). The issue of work reentered the AFDC debate, and it was to be an issue that came to stay.

AFDC and Work

As was mentioned earlier, despite the notion that mothers' pensions and later ADC were intended to permit "suitable" mothers to remain at home to rear their children in the fashion "normal" for the times, the reality of low grants did not actually free them from laundry, seamstress work, taking in borders, housecleaning, and the various other services and agricultural jobs available in their areas at the time. Indeed, in the early years there was even work coercion, without federal authorization.

Nonetheless, the main official and long-term policy thrust was to offer single mothers the opportunity to devote themselves to the care of their children, providing support for mothers as well as

Table 2–1   Father Status, AFDC Families, Selected Years

Status	1961[a] (%)	1967[a] (%)	1969[b] (%)	1971[b] (%)	1973[c] (%)	1975[d] (%)	1979[e] (%)	1983[f] (%)	1984[g] (%)
Deceased	7.7	5.5			4.8	3.7	2.2	1.9	1.9
Incapacitated	18.1	12.0	24.6	23.6	7.6	7.7	5.3	3.4	3.6
Unemployed	5.2	5.1	—	—	3.6	3.7	4.1	9.2	8.6
Total absent from home	66.7	74.4	75.4	76.2	83.0	83.3	86.9	85.5	83.8
Divorced	13.7	12.6	13.7	14.2	17.9	19.4	20.3	38.6	36.2
Legally separated		2.6		2.9	3.9	3.6			
Other separated	8.2	9.6	13.7	12.9	24.6	25.0	24.4	—	—
Deserted	18.6	18.2	15.9	15.2	—	—	—		
Not married to mother	21.3	26.8	27.9	27.7	43.0	31.0	37.8	45.5	46.4
In prison	4.2	3.0	2.6	2.1	—	—	—		
Other	0.6	1.4	1.6	1.2	3.0	4.3	4.4	1.4	1.2
Other Status	2.2	3.0	—	—	—	—		—	—
Deprived of mother support	—	—	—	—	1.0	1.6	1.5	—	—
Total	100.0	100.0	100.0	99.8	100.0	100.0	100.0	100.0	100.0

Note: A blank signifies that the item not reported in that form for the indicated year. Various combinations of divorced and separated given or reported in different surveys. The categories under "total absent from home" are not mutually exclusive.

Sources:

[a]Gilbert Steiner, *The State of Welfare* (Washington, D.C.: The Brookings Institution, 1971), p. 42.

[b]U.S. Department of Health, Education, and Welfare, *Findings of the 1971 AFDC Study,* "Part I. Demographic and Program Characteristics" (Washington, D.C.: National Center for Social Statistics, December 22, 1971), p. 4.

[c]U.S. Department of Health, Education and Welfare, *Findings of the 1973 AFDC Study,* "Part I. Demographic and Program Characteristics" (Washington, D.C., 1973), p. 38.

[d]U.S. Department of Health, Education, and Welfare, *1975 Recipient Characteristics Study,* "Part I. Demographic and Program Characteristics" (Washington, D.C.: Office of Research and Statistics, 1977), p. 31. *Note:* Here report is from perspectives of the children whereas 1961–73 reports refer to families as the unit.

[e]U.S. Department of Health, Education, and Welfare, *1979 Recipient Characteristics Study,* "Part I. Demographic and Program Characteristics" (Washington, D.C.: Office of Research and Statistics, 1984), p. 31. *Note:* Here report is from perspectives of the children whereas 1961–73 reports refer to families as the unit.

[f]"Aid to Families with Dependent Children: Recipient Characteristics and Financial Circumstances of AFDC Recipients" (Washington, D.C.: Office of Policy and Evaluation, 1986). *Note:* Here, too, the count is of children, the sample is smaller than in earlier years, and the error range therefore greater.

[g]Committee on Ways and Means, U.S. House of Representatives, *Background Material and Data on Programs Within the Jurisdiction of the Committee on Ways and Means* (Washington, D.C.: U.S. Government Printing Office, 1987), p. 431.

Table 2–2   AFDC and Race/Ethnicity (Families)

Race/Ethnicity	1971 (%)	1973 (%)	1975 (%)	1978 (%)	1983 (%)	1984 (%)
White, non-Hispanic	32.3	38.0	39.9	40.4	41.2	41.3
Black	43.3	45.8	44.3	43.1	43.3	41.9
Hispanic	16.0	13.4	12.2	13.6	13.0	12.8
Native American	1.2	1.1	1.1	1.4	1.0	1.1
Other	.7	.5	2.0	.4	—	—
Unknown	6.5	1.2	—		—	—
Asian	—	—	.5	1.0	1.5	2.3
Total	100.0	100.0	100.0	99.9	100.0	99.4

Sources: See Table 2–1. For 1971, derived from Table 2 of 1971 *Study*. For 1973, see p. 7 of 1973 *Study*. For 1975, see p. 2 of 1975 *Study*. For 1975 and 1983, see 1983 *Recipient Characteristics*. The Hispanic totals are likely to be the least accurate. The Asiatic breakdown began in 1975.

children. Where there was question about the capacity of the mothers in the early 1960s, the offering of supportive social services finally was made possible. The fallback position, also with federal funding, was the indicated 1967 legislation which made federal funds available to remove a child to a protective institution or foster home.[34] Thus, a principle was enunciated and then buttressed: A home could not be called unsuitable and children left in it. If assistance was denied for unsuitability, it had to be paralleled by child removal for neglect. If there was no intensive service or effort to remove a child, the home could not be deemed unsuitable for AFDC. For the states, the sharing of a low-level, means-tested benefit with the federal government was obviously a more attractive prospect than state assumption of the far greater costs of a much expanded system of foster homes and institutions.

But this was not the only change. At the very time that social supports were being increased, and in a possibly contradictory mode, the work option was also becoming part of the federal program, too. Congress was growing desperate about the growth of AFDC rolls at a time of low unemployment. It seemed impossible to stem the tide of deserted and unwed mothers, many of them black. If not services, then work—or both. Nor was this the viewpoint only of racists or conservatives.[35] Many reformers sympathetic to the poor had noted that large numbers of mothers in two-parent families were in the labor force.

Initially, in 1962, just when social service funding was being increased, states were permitted for the first time to use public assistance funds to set up community work and training programs. No more than 12 states ever participated. In 1965, with full federal funding, as part of the Economic Opportunity Act, the federal government financed another more attractive work and training program for low-income people, including assistance recipients. This program was phased out after the 1967 Social Security Act amendments offered a training and job search program known as WIN and run by the Department of Labor. (A 1972 "WIN II" amendment strengthened the program in various ways and added a strong work registration requirement.) A congressional attempt to freeze the welfare roll totals for deserted and unwed mothers also occurred in 1967. Implementation of this legislation was postponed several times by two presidents and finally repealed in the Nixon era. No one wanted to face the consequences of the burden that such policy would place on the states.[36]

Without tracing the developments of WIN and other related work and training programs in detail, we note that 1967 marked an important transition. Despite some objections to coercive WIN registration (mothers of children under age 6 are exempt), the reality has been that the demand for training and work slots has exceeded the supply, and accomplishments are modest. In one sense, the reactions to attacks on welfare in the Louisiana suitable home rules, and the evidence that discrimination had prevented some eligibles from receiving AFDC assistance, gradually led to better federal administration, increased concern for equity, and an effort to respond to alleged deficits in AFDC homes with more social work services. The notion of "at home" support finally had achieved some buttressing. At the same time, in response to the changing roles of women in society, the growing cost of AFDC, the increase in the numbers of unwed and deserted mothers, and the growth in the general caseload, especially the black caseload component, a work policy for AFDC mothers was adopted and gradually accepted. Registration for work and training became a requirement, although mothers of children age 6 or younger could choose to remain at home.[37]

The work policy was to be both stick and carrot. There was concurrently in 1967 an effort to create a work incentive. Welfare mothers who worked (also fathers in those states covering unemployed parents) could keep the first $30 of their earnings each month and a third of all else that they earned. Some of their work expenses would also be disregarded in computing relief eligibility and setting their grants. The era of conceiving of AFDC as a way to permit single-parent, poor families to live as two-parent middle-class families *once* did—with a child-rearing mother at home—seemed to be over, if it had ever existed. Or was it? The decade of the 1970s was to hear, on the one side, more and more calls for work incentives, work requirements, and "workfare" to pay off welfare benefits. At the same time, the Great Society and the Poverty War, all in the era of much-strengthened civil rights, had generated increasing claims that AFDC should be seen as a right, become more adequate, and eventually be replaced by a negative income tax (or a guaranteed income), if not by a child allowance. Poor single mothers should be able to stay home and rear their children in dignity and adequacy! Applications and processing were to be simplified and objectified.

AFDC "exploded" in this context. The caseload grew from 1.3 million to 2.5 million cases between 1967 and 1970; it continued to grow steadily in the mid-1970s before leveling off. The long debate about the causes of this explosion need not be resolved here. The elements surely include political forces and motives, more eligibles (as benefit levels were raised and demographic and social forces produced the types of families who could be eligible), a markedly reduced stigma effect, more flexible administration, and caseload recruitment by "welfare rights" groups.[38] What is especially interesting for the history here being reviewed is that a decade after the service amendments and increased provision to remove children from unsuitable homes—and concurrently with calls and actions to encourage or even require work and training—there also is a strong assertion of the right to a guaranteed nonwork income, whatever one's family structure (see Table 2–1). In this environment and through federal regulation, public welfare departments separated the administration of eligibility from the delivery of social services to welfare clients less than a decade after the case had been made that they should be brought more closely together. After all, it was argued, some AFDC families are only poor and need money; why coerce them into accepting services? Some other people need services, not money. Services can become a vehicle for arbitrary discretion which undermines the right to financial aid.

As the Johnson administration came to an end and early in the Nixon administration, states separated eligibility determination from services, under federal rules, and many people expected enactment of some form of guaranteed income or negative income tax, perhaps to be administered by the Treasury. Single mothers of all types and their children would obtain income protection objectively determined in accord with their income status, not their family characteristics or alleged moral qualities. The same or a similar program would aid poor two-parent families or single adults. The program would be designed to create work incentives, but not requirements, for mothers of young children.

Such reform was not to succeed in its various Nixon, Ford, and Carter variations, which proposed different guarantee levels, work expectations or incentives, administrative plans, and generosity. Conservative-liberal stalemates were constant, increasing concern for adequacy of work incentives was an important source of blockage, costs were a major problem, and worry about creating presumed incentives for single parenthood (particularly out-of-wedlock parenthood in the black community) was an important factor.[39]

When the Reagan administration's turn came, having been blocked in its efforts to freeze social insurance and services for the aged, generally, it succeeded in the Omnibus Budget Reconciliation Act (OBRA) of 1981 in decreasing the work incentives of 1967 and limiting both the work expense and child care cost allowances. Simultaneously, the Reagan administration began a "workfare" campaign: If people did not get jobs, they should "work off" their welfare checks by doing tasks for public and nonprofit agencies.[40]

The seeming contradiction has never been fully resolved: Why compel work but not encourage it? Clearly, there is skepticism about the incentives created by the work-expense allowances (disregards). Indeed, researchers have found little impact. The cuts in work incentive and disregards also implement a policy against supplementation of earned income: One either makes it without welfare completely or one is completely dependent. In the immediate aftermath of the 1981 legislation, those who were dropped from AFDC continued to work. However, there were gradual impacts. For some years, 14 to 16 percent of AFDC recipients had earned income as well; by 1984 the percentage was to decline to 4.8 percent, only 1.2 percent working full-time—the anti-supplementation policy had worked. Today, the work requirement idea continues to be pushed: Those who do not get work are to feel the pressure and stigma (denied by proponents, of course) of workfare.

Because Congress resisted, the policy direction was to be even less clear than we suggest here. First, in 1984, part of the earnings incentives and expense disregards which had been cut in 1981 were restored. Second, Congress made workfare permissive on the state level but would not make it a national requirement. A significant number of states (see Chapter 5) took up one or another option on a continuum. There were to be education, training, job search, placement, job creation and related demonstration programs, drawing upon both public assistance funds (through waivers of various sorts) and other federal job and training programs (curtailed and redesigned under the Reagan administration and focused on the Jobs Training Partnership Act [JTPA]). When child care is made available, a state may choose to apply its work program requirements to mothers with children under 3 years of age. Thus the policy machine moved, but in circles. What was the policy for single-mother families?

We have yet to add a final component—that of child support—before summing up just where we seem to have arrived.

Child Support

When the issue was widows, it was simple: They either did or did not inherit an estate; they either had or did not have their own resources or the help of relatives; or they might have to work. However, as the caseload changed to include ever-larger numbers of divorced and deserted mothers, the question of actual or potential support by the noncustodial parent became more and more salient. Finally, with the explosion of out-of-wedlock children on the rolls, a sense of morality and outrage developed, and cries for enforced child support began to be heard, even though analysts differed as to how realistic this might be.

Congress began to focus on the issue of child support as far back as 1950 and to add measures periodically in the 1960s, such as notifying law enforcement officials that AFDC children in effect were abandoned or deserted, helping localities locate missing parents, requiring efforts to establish paternity, and allowing social security and tax authorities to release addresses of missing parents. Somehow, little of this worked. There was little pressure from the federal level and hardly any monitoring. Much of it was permission to enforce but not required. Many states doubted that their efforts would pay off, and there was a good deal of inefficient administration. Surveys continued to show that, in many instances, courts never were called upon to award child support in cases of desertion and divorce and that among the awards made, only small percentages were collected. [41]

Gradually, the notion that some single-mother families could be helped by child support won larger constituencies. Those who wanted to cut welfare budgets joined with feminists and others who felt that fathers were evading responsibilities. The 1975 passage of Title IV-D of the Social Security Act marked a turning point in the child support issue. The federal government, although it left enforcement with the states, began to pay three-quarters of the cost of paternity establishment, absent-father location, and child support collection. IRS data could be used. In 1980, service was extended to non-AFDC cases. Finally, in 1984, noting only modest progress in collections to that point, the Congress added "teeth" to the effort: States were required to adopt wage withholding in response to delayed child support payments. States also were required to appoint commissions to set statewide standards for levels of support by noncustodial parents.[42] Implementation is currently under way. Finally, so that low-benefit AFDC families might be helped if missing fathers did contribute (and to offer an incentive to cooperate), the law was revised to allow the first $50 in child support each month to be an income add-on for the family, whereas previously it had merely decreased the welfare grant.

Where Is the Action?

What is the policy? One does not expect complete coherence in the incremental policymaking of a politically complex pluralistic democracy, particularly in a period of considerable social change. As we have seen in Chapter 1, this indeed has been demographically and socially a period of major family change in the United States. We have taken many steps in this country with regard to poor single mothers. Over the years we have developed and revised AFDC, social services, and work programs. We also have affected the income status of other single mothers as well by giving them access to the child support machinery, designed originally for the AFDC caseload. How does it all add up? What is in place? Where are we heading? If, as suggested in Chapter 1, many single parents and their children have problems and some need help, what is the current public posture?

First, we have become more *inclusive with* regard to single-parent families. AFDC is no longer reserved for white, "suitable" widows and their children. Out-of-wedlock children now represent close to half of the AFDC caseload. Minority families represent more than half. However, the reality of minority and out-of-wedlock representation has made the program a more likely target of punitive or parsimonious policy today, just as fears about large minority representation and allegations about incentives for single parenthood in black families in an earlier era inhibited the equity in AFDC. On the other hand, the increased inclusivity has moved beyond the poor. Policy has recognized that many nonwelfare single-parent families also need the help of federally supported child support programs if they are to collect what courts have awarded them. The child support reform effort has broadened the public policy range.

Second, the income support policy for single-parent families remains *inconsistent and ambivalent*. In a major sense there was improvement in the 1960s and 1970s in that the "man-in-the-house" and "suitable home" policies that had led to abuse of discretion and rejection of needy families were finally eliminated. That is why the caseload became more representative of the eligible populations. States were permitted to include families with unemployed fathers (AFDC-UP) but less than half did; and those who did so imposed tough eligibility rules. Similarly, more objective eligibility determination and more uniform budgeting added to within-state equity. However, both budget growth and caseload growth were to reach a plateau in the mid-1970s. As a result of subsequent inflation, fiscal stringencies, and shifting attitudes, we have since witnessed a benefit erosion. Most AFDC recipients are now "supported" well below the poverty level (see Chapter 5). States still have extraordinary differences in the benefit levels under the AFDC program. As a result the United States leads among major industrial countries in single-parent family poverty.[43]

Third, part of the benefit erosion is explained by the *new stress on training and work*, even on coercive "workfare," in some places. "Less eligibility" *à la* the mid-19th century rides high. Yet many defenders of poor families and their children also refuse to reject a work policy, as they might have in the early 1960s. Rather, they want good education, training, placement opportunities, and good jobs for single mothers.[44]

Fourth, if services were the alleged answer to the fear that some AFDC homes were not suitable for children in the 1960s, where do services now fit in? The picture is not at all clear; for example, since the early 1970s there has also been a separate, national focus on child abuse and the creation of legislation, reporting machinery, and demonstration projects with federal financial aid. Then, responding to a campaign about excessive placement of children in foster homes and institutions, Congress also passed legislation in 1980 amending the Social Security Act to create a program of subsidized adoption, a variety of incentives to speed children out of foster care, and to buttress natural families so as to avoid placement in the first place.[45]

Since some of the targets of these new service initiatives are single parents and most are poor, one might have expected that all this would be in some way connected with the AFDC policy thrust, but such has not been the case. For example, there is no device for the easing or increasing of financial aid in response to the family stress that engenders some child placement. There is no pool of new resources to reinforce families or aid them in a transition if they will keep the child at home, while helped by skilled social service supports.

The *fragmentation between child welfare and income maintenance* that concerned all the task forces between 1950 and 1965 continues. We have child welfare placement "prevention" without financial aid, and financial aid with little service. The priority that is given to work apparently makes family protection a secondary goal. This is not the intent, as stated in the preambles to all legislation, but it is the result. There may be social services tied to the work opportunities and to making a work "contract" with AFDC mothers, but these social services are seldom in any way related to the so-called preventive child welfare services or to the response machinery when there is alleged abuse and neglect. In short, these families, like others in need of help, remain fragmented. Different parts of their needs are dealt with by different service mechanisms.

A right to some income, help in getting work or a work requirement, social service protection of the child or supports to a single family, and improved child support machinery: These are the elements. Sometimes they play against one another; at other times they are, or could be, mutually reinforcing. Certainly, the public investment could be better used if Americans were somewhat more in agreement over what our society is trying to do and how.

The many "pushes" and "pulls" have not been lost on those who draft the legislation. The most recent statement in the Social Security Act on the intent of the law contrasts with the 1965 statement of purpose as "enabling each state to furnish financial assistance as far as practicable under the conditions in such state, to needy dependent children . . ."

Now (1985) the stated purposes are

> *encouraging the care of dependent children in their own homes or the homes of relatives by enabling each State to furnish financial assistance and rehabilitation and other services, as far as practicable under the conditions in each State . . . to help maintain family life and to help such parents or relatives to attain capability for the maximum self-support and personal independence consistent with the maintenance of continuing parental care and protection.*[46]

Only legislative drafters can publish such clauses without comment about contradictory pressures and trade-offs.

We have already suggested that one key to policy coherence is to recognize that the families of "mothers alone and their children" encompass several different subgroups and that they may not all require the same thing. We do need a differentiated policy, but not one that is based on punishment or discrimination, or that fails to define the nature of its differentiations. Certainly, as in Chapter 1, we note that a strategy for the poor (Option 1) will not suffice. What of child support for the nonwelfare eligible, of responses to abuse and neglect, of the need for help to mesh work and family life? Nor is the sole answer a specialized program network for single mothers (Option 2). The history has shown that widows and unwed mothers are not alike, that families may need help even if there are fathers at home, and that the demographic concentration (whether in the single-mother or poverty categories) produces vulnerable dependent populations that stimulate stigma and anger as often as they do impulses to help.

Endnotes

1. Irwin Garfinkel and Sara S. McLanahan, *Single Mothers and their Children: A New American Dilemma* (Washington, D.C.: The Urban Institute Press, 1986).
2. Karl de Schweinitz, *England's Road to Social Security* (Philadelphia: University of Pennsylvania Press, 1943).
3. Ralph and Muriel Pumphrey, *The Heritage of American Social Work* (New York: Columbia University Press, 1964); Blanche B. Coll, *Perspectives in Public Welfare* (Washington, D.C.: U.S. Government Printing Office, 1969); James Leiby, *A History of Social Welfare and Social Work* (New York: Columbia University Press, 1978); Samuel Menscher, *Poor Law to Poverty Program* (Pittsburgh: University of Pittsburgh Press, 1967).
4. Karl Polanyi, *The Great Transformation* (Boston: Beacon Press, 1957).
5. Sidney and Beatrice Webb, *English Poor Law History*, Part II, Vol. I (London: Longman's Green & Company, 1929).
6. Webb, *English Poor Law History;* Josephine Brown, *Public Relief, 1925–1939* (New York: Henry Holt, 1940), Chapter I.
7. Norman Longmate, *The Workhouse* (New York: St. Martin's Press, 1974).
8. Henry W. Thurston, *The Dependent Child* (New York: Columbia University Press, 1930); Emma Lundberg, *Unto the Least of These* (New York: Appleton Century, 1947); Walter I. Trattner, *From Poor Law to Welfare State* (New York: The Free Press, 1984).
9. Robert H. Bremner, *From the Depths* (New York: New York University Press, 1956).
10. For more of the context, see Muriel W. Pumphrey and Ralph E. Pumphrey, "The Widows' Pension Movement, 1900–1930: Preventive Child Saving or Social Control?" in *Social Welfare or Social Control?* ed. Walter I. Trattner (Knoxville: University of Tennessee Press, 1983), 53–54; Leiby, *A History of Social Welfare and Social Work*.
11. Sheila B. Kamerman and Alfred J. Kahn, "Explaining the Outcomes: Social Policy and Children in the U.S. and Europe," in *The Changing Well-being of*

Children and the Aged: The United States in a Comparative Context, ed. John L. Palmer, Timothy Smeeding, and Barbara B. Torrey (Washington, D.C.: The Urban Institute Press, 1988).

12. Grace Abbott, *The Child and the State,* Vol. II (Chicago: University of Chicago Press, 1938), 229.

13. Robert H. Bremner, ed., *Children and Youth in America: A Documentary History,* Vol. II (Cambridge, Mass.: Harvard University Press, 1971), 365.

14. Michael B. Katz, *In the Shadow of the Poorhouse* (New York: Basic Books, 1986), 127–129. Also Bremner, *Children and Youth in America,* 369–397. Katz does not list Alabama as lacking a law, but see Bremner adaptation of 1931 Children's Bureau table on p. 393. The New Mexico law also was not operative.

15. Winifred Bell, *Aid to Dependent Children* (New York: Columbia University Press, 1965), 5–6.

16. Ibid., 9–14.

17. Abbott, *The Child and the State,* 234–240.

18. Bremner, *Children and Youth in America,* 395.

19. Sheila Rothman, *Woman's Proper Place* (New York: Basic Books, 1978), 268; Edwin Shorter, *The Making of the Modern Family* (New York: Basic Books, 1975), 264–265; Carl N. Degler, *At Odds: Women and the Family in America from the American Revolution to the Present* (New York: Oxford University Press, 1980), 73–85.

20. Bell, *Aid to Dependent Children,* 16.

21. Percy Gamble Kammerer, *The Unmarried Mother* (Boston: Little, Brown, and Company, 1918).

22. Ibid., ix.

23. Ibid., 282.

24. Ibid.

25. *50th Anniversary Edition, The Report of the Committee on Economic Security of 1935* (Washington, D.C.: National Conference on Social Welfare, 1985), 55.

26. Ibid., 56.

27. Ibid., 26.

28. Title IV, Sec. 408, *Social Security Act.*

29. Bell, *Aid to Dependent Children,* 29.

30. Ibid., 34–35.

31. Ibid., 54–56.

32. Ibid., 147.

33. Elizabeth Wickenden and Winifred Bell, *Public Welfare: Time for a Change* (New York: Columbia University School of Social Work, 1961).

34. For an item-by-item chronology of AFDC amendments, see "Annual Statistical Supplement, 1987," *Social Security Bulletin* (Washington, D.C.: Social Security Administration, 1987), 51–60. For recent program overviews, which cover child welfare as well, see Committee on Ways and Means, U.S. House of Representatives, *Background Material and Data on Programs within the Jurisdiction of the Committee on Ways and Means,* 1987 edition (Washington, D.C.: U.S. Government Printing Office, 1987), 388–451, 613–668.

35. Edward Weaver, "Public Assistance," *Encyclopedia of Social Work,* Vol. 2,

Seventeenth Issue (Washington, D.C.: National Association of Social Workers, 1977), 1132–1135; Gilbert Steiner, *The State of Welfare* (Washington, D.C.: The Brookings Institution, 1971), Chapter 2; Trattner, *From Poor Law to Welfare State*, 306, 321–322; *Background Material*, 391–400. Also, Wickenden and Bell, *Public Welfare*, 26, 32.

36. Steiner, *The State of Welfare*, 329.
37. Weaver, "Public Assistance," 1133–1134.
38. Some of the major viewpoints debated are presented in Frances Fox Piven and Richard A. Cloward, *Regulating the Poor: The Functions of Public Welfare* (New York: Pantheon Books, 1971); Kirsten Gronbjerg, *Mass Society and the Extension of Welfare* (Chicago: University of Chicago Press, 1977); Trattner, *Social Welfare or Social Control;* S. F. Schramn and J. P. Turbett, "The Welfare Explosion: Mass Society Versus Social Control," *Social Service Review*, vol. 57, no. 4 (December 1983): 614–625; Robert Moffitt, "Trends in AFDC Participation Over Time: Evidence on Structural Change," Institute for Research on Poverty, *Special Report*, no. 41 (Madison, Wisconsin, 1986).
39. For the story of aborted welfare "reform" from Lyndon Johnson through Jimmy Carter, see James T. Patterson, *America's Struggle Against Poverty*, rev. ed. (Cambridge, Mass.: Harvard University Press, 1985), Chapter 12; Vincent J. Burke and Vee Burke, *Nixon's Good Deed* (New York: Columbia University Press, 1974); Henry Aaron, *Politics and the Professors* (Washington, D.C.: The Brookings Institution, 1978); Irwin Garfinkel and Felicity Skidmore, "Income Support Policy: Where We've Come From and Where We Should Be Going," DP-490-78 (Madison, Wisconsin: Institute for Research on Poverty, 1978), 32–50; Consulting Group on Welfare Reform, *Report of the 1977 Welfare Reform Study*, Supplement No. 1, "The Secretary's Report to the President" (Washington, D.C.: U.S. Department of Health, Education, and Welfare, 1977).
40. D. Lee Bawden and John L. Palmer, "Challenging the Welfare State," in *The Reagan Record*, ed. John L. Palmer and Isabel V. Sawhill (Cambridge, Mass.: Ballinger, 1984), 188–221; "Work and Welfare," a special issue of *Public Welfare*, vol. 44, no. 1 (Winter 1986); Office of Family Assistance, Social Security Administration, "Deficit Reduction Act of 1984: Provisions Related to the AFDC Program," *Social Security Bulletin*, vol. 47, no. 12 (December 1984): 3–6.
41. U.S. Bureau of the Census, *Child Support and Alimony: 1983* and *Child Support and Alimony: 1985, Current Population Reports*, series P-23, no. 148, no. 152, (Washington, D.C.: U.S. Government Printing Office, 1986, 1987).
42. Irwin Garfinkel, "Child Support," *Encyclopedia of Social Work*, 18th ed., vol. 1, 260–265; *Background Material . . . Ways and Means*, 452–492; Garfinkel and McLanahan, *Single Mothers and Their Children*, 118–119, 135–137; Alfred J. Kahn and Sheila B. Kamerman, eds., *Child Support: From Debt Collection to Social Policy* (Newbury Park, Calif.: Sage Publications, 1988), especially Chapter 2, Lowell Lima and Robert Harris, "The Child Support Enforcement Program in the United States."
43. Committee on Ways and Means, U.S. House of Representatives, *Children in Poverty* (Washington, D.C.: U.S. Government Printing Office, 1985); Timothy

Smeeding, Barbara Boyle Torrey, and Martin Rein, "The Economic Status of the Young and Old in Eight Countries," Paper no. 6, in Palmer, Smeedings, and Torrey, eds., *The Changing Well-being of Children and the Aged.*

44. "Work and Welfare," *Public Welfare;* Julie Kosterlitz, "Reexamining Welfare," *National Journal,* vol. 18, no. 49 (6 December 1986): 2926–2931; Isabel V. Sawhill, "Anti-poverty Strategies for the 1980s," Discussion paper (Washington, D.C.: The Urban Institute, 1986).

45. "The Adoption Assistance and Child Welfare Act of 1980 (P.L. 96–272, June 17, 1980)." See Committee on Ways and Means, *Background Material . . . ,* 556–581, especially 572–573.

46. Joan Carrera, "Aid to Families with Dependent Children," *Encyclopedia of Social Work,* 18th ed., quoting the 1985 *Compilation of Social Security Laws,* 241.

Chapter 3

CLARIFYING THE OPTIONS: INSIGHTS FROM ABROAD

A Fresh Perspective

Why, in a book about single mothers and their children in the United States, do we turn now to the experiences of other countries? The conventional view is that countries cannot "learn," "borrow," or "copy" social policies and programs from one another because political systems, cultures, and most important, values are different. Yet despite this conviction, there is an equally strong popular belief that countries can—and do—learn from one another in technology, organizational management, marketing strategies, and so forth.

We have found from much of our prior work that countries *can* learn from one another—and indeed, already have.[1] There is, after all, a convergence of social realities, especially in the advanced industrialized countries, and an almost uniform search for appropriate social innovations or interventions. Similar social trends and definitions of issues tend to characterize all of the industrialized countries—population aging; declining fertility; earlier retirement, especially among male workers; and increased female labor force participation rates, especially among women with young children. Similar social problems—for example, poverty, alcoholism, delinquency, child abuse, divorce, the tension between work and family life, changing gender roles, and changing family structure—are of concern and addressed in all these countries, to varying degrees. At the same time, concern with the increased burdens of social expenditures for pensions, health care, and so forth, in the face of limited economic resources, is shared in all these countries, too.

The problems, anxieties, and questions related to mothers rearing their children alone are clearly important and difficult. The discussion, indeed the debate in the United States, is intense and emotional across the political spectrum. We would argue that even if there are legitimate doubts about the ability of one country to "borrow" directly from the experiences of another, given the importance of total societal context, culture, and history in these matters, insights clearly can be obtained from the experiences of other countries and from an analysis of how they have addressed the problems they have identified, with what consequences. Simply distancing ourselves from the U.S. debate, albeit briefly, and viewing the phenomenon, the problems, and the attempted interventions as they have developed elsewhere, may allow us to develop a fresh and even unique perspective on the U.S. issues.

In a sense we may regard industrial countries elsewhere as a laboratory in nature, "testing" our options. Have we been correct in the earlier chapters with regard to Options 1 and 2? What about the two alternatives not yet explored: a family-policy strategy which focuses on young children, or an emphasis on support for integration of work and family responsibilities? How do *they* look in action? Obviously, with many variables uncontrolled and many outcomes only estimated, one claims neither full comparability nor certainty; yet the insights do add to our understanding of the American choices.

Mother-Only Families: A Universal Problem for the Industralized World

Our focus here is on western Europe, although any review of demographic patterns would reveal important similarities with eastern Europe as well. More important to many, such non-European countries as Canada and Australia certainly present a similar picture. We generalize here, pointing out that:

- All advanced industrialized countries have experienced a significant increase in the number of female-headed families with children and in the proportion of all families with children these families constitute (see Table 3–1). The amount of time they live as single-parent families varies among the countries.
- All view these families as economically at risk, and often poor or near poor.
- All view them as highly vulnerable to problems of stress, loneliness, and social isolation.
- Many see them as a source of serious social problems or pathology.

Table 3–1   Lone-Parent Families with Children under Age 18[a], Various Years
(Percentages)

Country	Year	Total as Percent of All Families with Children	Female-Headed	Male-Headed
Austria (under age 15)	1984	13	12	1
Britain (under age 16)[b]	1985	14	12	2
Denmark	1984[c]	26	23	3
Finland	1984	15	13	2
F.R. Germany	1985[c]	13	11	2
France	1981[b]	10	8	2
Hungary	1984	20	18	2
Italy	1981	6	5	1
Norway (under age 16)	1982	19	18	1
Sweden[d]	1985	32	29	3
United States	1985	26	23	3
	1970	13	12	1

[a]Or other ages as specified.
[b]To age 19, if in school.
[c]These numbers include some percentages of cohabiting couples but the breakdowns are not precise.
[d]To age 19, if in school. The rates include cohabiting couples. For 1985, 18 percent of families with children were headed by women living alone and 14 percent by cohabiting couples.
Sources: Country census or micro-census reports, reports to 1987 Council of Ministers meeting (see endnote), individual interviews. All percentages rounded.

- All acknowledge that the terms "one-parent families," "lone-mother families," or "mother-only families" suggest a uniform set of characteristics—usually young and poor, and often never married; however, the reality reveals a highly diversified group of women, with not precisely the same characteristics from country to country.
- All identify a changing pattern within the group labeled "mother-only families": a decline in the number and significance of widows; a major increase in the numbers and significance of divorced and separated mothers; some growth, varying across countries, in never-married mothers and in cohabiting but not legally married couples.
- Almost all see a major problem for these families in the failure of noncustodial parents, overwhelmingly fathers, to provide financial support for their children.
- All find that even where these single mothers are in the labor force, earned family income alone may still not be adequate under the living standards as experienced in their country.

- Finally, some are concerned with containing the growth in the numbers of such families while others are not, or at least not as much. Some are concerned with the burden that supporting these families places on public expenditures, while others appear less concerned. All have as their objective for public policy helping these families achieve an adequate standard of living.

The primary questions for us are: What do these countries view as an adequate standard of living for these families? How do they achieve such a standard? And what are the consequences, insofar as they are known, for the families, for the children, and for society?

Although these countries fall on a continuum rather than into clearly separate and discrete patterns, we have chosen to highlight countries that tend to exemplify the four contrasting policy options. (We have stated these more specifically for the U.S. context in the Introduction.) Three involve financial assistance for an at-home role for mothers or a parent, and one involves mothers entering and remaining in the work force:

1. Financial aid for poor families with children, and an assumption that the assisted mothers, whether in one- or two-parent families, will remain at home with their children. Meeting the needs of the poor, generally, helps the single-parent family as well, since these families are disproportionately poor.
2. Special financial aid for single mothers and an assumption that most of them prefer to remain at home with their children and will do so if it is financially viable. In this model, there is a special, categorical single-mother program.
3. Cash benefits for all families with children, in particular those with very young children (under age 3), so that one (or a sole) parent may choose to remain at home in the early years. Single mothers may have special add-ons, but they are largely aided by the overall active family policy.
4. A variety of cash benefits and policy supports for families with children, and particular encouragement for all young mothers to enter and remain in the workforce, earning the income that provides the financial mainstay of the families, as the alternative to being supported at a low standard, at home, by public income transfer payments. Under this pattern, as it has been implemented in Sweden, our illustrative country, family policy measures buttress labor market measures—to create a supportive nexus.

This listing of patterns highlights the current American policy ambivalence. We do none of these fully or comfortably. We neither help mothers enter and remain in the labor force, nor support them adequately if they remain at home with their children. In fact, we are uncomfortable even about making available our inadequate levels of support, as in the first two options.

What is the situation of single-parent families in European countries? What are the policy strategies employed? What happens when these different policy strategies are adopted?

Supporting *Poor* Mothers at Home: Great Britain

A single mother in Britian today may remain at home and receive a means-tested assistance grant until her child or children are 16 years of age. There is no pressure to take training or a job. The tax and welfare system operate so as to create a disincentive for part-time work. Full-time jobs are hard to come by, and mothers of very young children require child care, which is largely unavailable or unaffordable even if available. For a mother who does work at least 24 hours per week, and is a low earner, there are benefits from a Family Credit program that is similar to the U.S. earned income tax credit. There are also child allowances, national health service, and access to public housing. The at-home role for the single mother is the norm.

Britain provided a model for social policy developments from the mid-19th century until the 1960s, which was emulated by all English-speaking countries and often by others as well. The establishment of the British welfare state through the adoption of the Beveridge plan at the end of World War II placed Britain clearly at the forefront of 20th-century developments. U.S. policy debates have often drawn on British proposals and on the British literature. For example, at one time our AFDC programs raised no question if the mother was at home and took no steps to work until children were 16 or 18.

Britain was the first among the European countries to carry out an extensive official study of single-parent families, with special attention focused on mother-only families.[2] The Finer Committee was set up by the government in the early 1970s to study the problems of these families, and a well-publicized report (which looked at trends in several countries) was issued in 1974. Although the report's recommendations have still not been carried out, discussion about the problem and the need for more concerted attention continues, often in the context of that report. The policy goal remains: to assure lone mothers and their children enough income to provide an adequate standard of living even if they are not in the labor force, and *not* to assume that the caretaker should go out to work.

When the Finer Committee report was written in the early 1970s, about 570,000 families were headed by a lone parent, and almost 90 percent of these parents were mothers.[3] A little more than a decade later this number had increased by two-thirds, with an estimated 950,000 such families in Britain in 1983.[4] Currently, about 14 percent of all families with dependent children are headed by a lone parent, overwhelmingly female, with about 1.6 million children or about 12 percent of all children under 18.[5]

Millar and Bradshaw, the directors of a recent study of single-parent families in Britain, state that the "typical" single parent is a divorced woman in her mid-30s who has one or two school-aged children and is not receiving regular financial support from her husband.[6] She is likely to live in public housing and to be supported primarily by public assistance with occasional help from a low-wage, part-time job. If she wants to work full-time, she has a child care problem, and an even worse problem if she has a child under 5; few subsidized child care places are available for pre-schoolers or for school-aged children in after-school programs. The typical mother is likely to be a lone parent for about three to four years, or even longer; her status, as described, is likely to present a wide range of problems—and not just economic—for her and her children.

However, as Millar and Bradshaw point out:

This "typical" lone parent is . . . only one of the very many different types of family all classified under the category "lone parent." People become lone parents in different ways and they therefore experience lone parenthood differently. The young, single woman caring for a baby does not face the same situation as the woman widowed in early middle-age, whose children have either left school or are in their final years of education; nor the woman separated from her husband and caring for several children of both school and pre-school age. Even among those of the same "marital status" there are wide variations: the teenage mother who had never had a paid job and lives with her parents is not in the same position as the professional woman who "chooses" lone parenthood. A woman forced to leave the family home because of domestic violence and take shelter in a woman's refuge faces different problems from the divorced woman receiving regular maintenance payments from her ex-spouse.[7]

Lone mothers in Britain are a diversified group, as we have shown them to be in the United States, but most policy discussion and attention focus on their poverty and assume they are all alike. There is general agreement that most mother-only families are poor. The Finer report found that these families were poor in large part because of the "inconsistent, inefficient, and irrational socio-economic method of meeting the needs of . . . those families categorized as being in need . . . and of the economic impossibility of obtaining, from the income of one worker, sufficient to provide for the needs of two families."[8] A recent reassessment of the economic situation of these families points out that today it has become equally impossible to obtain from the income of one worker enough to support *one* family, in particular when the one worker is female.[9]

At present, almost half the income of lone-mother[10] families (45 percent) is from public income transfers. The major source of income for lone mothers is Income Support (IS), formerly Supplementary Benefit (SB), the means-tested cash benefit that is available to all poor families; more than half these lone mothers received it in 1985.[11] The benefit is indexed and is provided at the same level as that offered the aged and disabled who qualify. In effect, it is similar to Supplemental Security Income (SSI) in the United States. It is set at a higher level than that provided poor husband/wife families or childless individuals or couples. In the most recent reporting year, 28 percent of a sample of low-income, lone mothers received child support payments from absent fathers, and about 60 percent of these women were on SB and therefore received no additional income from the payment. (It is deducted from their benefit.) Family income is supplemented by a universal child benefit, equal to about 5 percent of average wage and provided for each child, and by a special one-parent benefit provided for the first child in a mother-only family. The family has priority access to public housing, and receives medical care through the National Health Service.

These families, as noted, may also qualify for the Family Credit (FC), the income-tested cash benefit that is designed to supplement the incomes of the working poor. With the recent social security reforms, this benefit has become more like a refundable tax credit, something like the Earned Income Tax Credit in the United States. Close to half the beneficiaries (42 percent) are lone parents (who were favored by this program before recent reforms and obtained about one-fifth of their income from child benefits and FIS [Family Income Supplement, an earlier version of FC]).

What are the effects of British policies on mother-only families?

It appears that the situation of these families has worsened, not improved, in recent years. In 1979, the average gross income of one-parent families was equal to about 51 percent of that of a couple with two children. By 1984, this was down to 39.5 percent.[12] The value of child benefits has not kept up with inflation, and the income of two-parent families has gone ahead. The proportion of lone mothers who are supported by IS (SB) has increased substantially, from about 38 percent in 1979 to more than half in 1985.

In Britain, mothers of very young children generally have very low labor force participation rates, and lone mothers are no exception. Lone mothers are less likely to work than married mothers (47 percent versus 53 percent), in part because they are more likely to have younger children. Lone mothers who are in the paid labor force, like married mothers, are likely to work part-time; however, of those who work, more lone mothers are likely to work full-time (almost half) than are working married mothers (one third). Twelve percent of lone mothers, as compard with 6 percent of married mothers with children under age 5, work full-time. Full-time wages for women were 74 percent of male wages in 1983, excluding overtime, but only 66.6 percent if overtime is included.[13] Full-time work would make a financial difference to these women, but the lack of child care services or an adequate subsidy to purchase care is viewed as precluding this option. A part-time job is not financially worthwhile, given the availability of IS. Lone mothers have higher unemployment rates than married mothers.

Under a relative definition of poverty,[14] 36.2 percent of the children in these British families were poor in 1979–80, as compared with 8.1 percent in husband/wife families.[15] (In the United States, using the same measure of poverty, 59.3 percent of the children in mother-only families were poor that same year, as compared with 13.8 percent of those in two-parent families.)

Some view IS policy as a "poverty trap," eliminating part-time work as an economically viable option and creating a dichotomy between what is available for an at-home mother and what is available for the working, low-income mother and her children.

Millar and Bradshaw quote Vic George, writing in 1975, as saying that "social security provision for one-parent families is the most striking example of how very little progress has been made in the past 50 years." They add that the progress over the past 10 years has still left the basic problem untouched.[16] Perhaps the only thing that keeps these families from greater hardship is the availability of a national health service. For the few low-income lone mothers who are working, at least they do not have to be concerned about access to health care.

We do not consider this policy—which in the United States would mean an improved, traditional AFDC program (to include two-parent families and perhaps to ensure a guaranteed minimum benefit scale)—as offering us an important new answer to the single-parent family issue, even though it is far better than what we now have.

Supporting *Single* Mothers at Home: Norway

Norway exemplifies a country that pays special attention to mother-only families. It is generous in providing support for these families and clearly expects most single mothers to remain at home until their children are 10 years old.

Norway is somewhat atypical among the Scandinavian countries in that it is more conservative than the others with regard to women's roles. The Norwegians are proud of their long and early history of support for nonworking mothers. Norway was the first country to cover these women under national health insurance, in 1909. Until very recently in Norway, women did not enter the paid work force. Female labor force participation rates (LFPR) in Norway were much lower than in most of Europe, especially Sweden, until the mid-1970s, when they began to rise rapidly. Between 1974 and 1983 labor force participation rates of women with children under 16 increased from 44 percent to 62 percent—an increase of more than 40 percent in less than a decade. Rates now are comparable to the rates in the United States and Canada but nowhere near as high as in Denmark and Sweden. As in these latter countries, however, most working mothers work part-time. Perhaps because of the more traditional attitude toward women, Norway is the most generous country in Scandinavia with regard to supporting single mothers at home. One result is that lone mothers have far lower labor force participation rates than married mothers; indeed, divorced Norwegian mothers have the lowest labor force participation rates among all mothers in Norway—a pattern that is unique to this country.

In 1980, there were about 756,000 families with children in Norway[17] (see Table 3–2). Of these, about 83 percent were married-couple families, and 17 percent were single-parent families. Among the latter, 85 percent were mother-only families and 15 percent father-only. These numbers are not precise because there is no separate census category for cohabiting couples with children,

Table 3–2   Families with Children by Type of Family (Norway): Numbers and Percentages, for 1960, 1970, and 1980

Year	Total Families with Children	Total Couples with Children	Single Parents with Children		
			Total	Mother-Headed	Father-Headed
1960	677,171	592,838	84,333	57,817	26,516
	(100.0)	(87.5)	(12.5)	(8.5)	(4.0)
1970	712,512	623,567	88,945	74,864	14,081
	(100.0)	(87.5)	(12.5)	(10.5)	(2.0)
1980	755,657	625,206	130,451	110,666	19,785
	(100.0)	(82.7)	(17.3)	(14.7)	(2.6)

Source: Kari Skrede, *Family Policy in Relation to Changes in Family Structure and the Distribution of Income* (Oslo, Norway: Institute of Applied Social Research, 1983).

and this is a growing family type in Norway. Of particular interest, single-parent families had been a relatively stable family type for some decades but then increased by almost 50 percent between 1970 and 1980 (and by 40 percent as a proportion of all families with children).

A special Norwegian family report, published in 1980, highlighted many of the same demographic and social trends occurring throughout the industrialized world: increased divorce, decline in fertility, deferring of marriage, increased rates of cohabitation without marriage, growth in labor force participation rates of women, increased rates of single parenting, and growing economic vulnerability of mother-only families. Although a variety of different recommendations were made in this report, the conservative government was particularly concerned about declining birthrates and about the economic situation of *traditional* husband/wife families with one wage earner. It was not interested in doing anything that would promote or encourage the formation of single-parent families. On the other hand, concern about these families was growing, and a task force was established in the mid-1980s to assess their economic situation.

Single-parent families, overwhelmingly headed by women, are as likely to have low income in Norway as elsewhere. During the 1970s, their economic situation deteriorated more in comparison with two-parent families, as more and more wives entered the labor force, and husband/wife families became two-earner families. Nonetheless, disposable income for mother-only families has been somewhat protected because they receive generous income transfers that significantly supplement family income.

Norwegian family policy includes, as a specific goal, making it possible for lone mothers to choose between staying at home and taking a job. To support this policy of "choice," Norway provides the following "package" of income transfers:

Child Benefit or Child Allowance. All families with children under age 16 are entitled to a child benefit or child allowance. These universal (not means-tested) cash benefits are awarded to families based on the number of children in the family, beginning with the first and ending with the fifth; benefits are adjusted by the age of the child, with the youngest receiving the highest benefit on the assumption that women with very young children need more support so they can remain at home. The benefits are tax free. Single parents also receive a *special supplement* of one child benefit beyond the number of children they actually have (see Table 3–3). The average annual cost of rearing a child, excluding housing, child care, transportation, and vacations, was estimated at about NOK 12,500 per year in 1983.[18] Average female wages are about NOK 100,000 per year; male wages NOK 150,000. These figures provide some basis for assessing the value of these benefits, clearly significant for single parents.

Tax Allowances and Child Care Tax Credits. Tax allowances are granted to taxpayers supporting a child under age 20, and an additional allowance is given to single parents. Furthermore, working families (husband/wife and sole parents) are entitled to a child care tax credit of NOK 9,500 for one child up to age 14 and NOK 12,000 for two or more, against the costs of group (center) care.

Child Care Cash Benefit. Single parents are also entitled to a monthy child care cash benefit of about NOK 450 for care of the first child and NOK 180 for each additional child (about NOK 5300 and NOK 2100 per year, respectively). This benefit is universal (available regardless of family income), tax free, and can be important in helping pay for family day care or even relative care.[19]

Education Benefit. Unmarried, divorced, or separated parents may be entitled to an education benefit, covering the costs of an

Table 3–3   Average Child Benefits in Norway in 1985

Child Benefits	Monthly (NOK)		Annually (NOK)	
	Single Mother	Married Mother	Single Mother	Married Mother
One Child	830	327	9,960	4,524
Two Children	1,397	830	16,764	9,960
Three Children	2,003	1,397	24,036	18,764

Note: Benefits in Norwegian krones. Early in 1988, the krone was worth about US $.155.

educational or training program, if the parent needs training (or schooling) to become employable. Such benefits are available until the youngest child is age 10, or in the case of older children, for one year (or longer in special cases).

Transitional Benefit. The most important source of income for single mothers is the Transitional Benefit, a cash income transfer designed to support lone parents who are temporarily unable to support themselves and their children. The benefit is income-tested and since 1981 has been paid for and delivered through the national social insurance office. (Before that, since 1965, it was provided through local government.) It is available for at least one year or until the woman's youngest child is age 10—sometimes longer, depending on the circumstances. It is available even if the woman is cohabiting, provided that person is not the former (or separated) husband, nor the father of one of her children. More than half the recipients are never-married mothers; the rest are largely divorced, and a small number are separated mothers. Two-thirds of all lone mothers receive this benefit, including 75 percent of unwed mothers and 60 percent of the divorced.

The Transitional Benefit is designed to cover living expenses and is paid when the inability to earn a living is due to (1) the presence of young children under age 10; (2) the need of the divorced or separated parent for a period of transition; (3) the fact that the divorced or separated parent is in the middle of education or training. The benefit is phased out when the mother begins to have earnings; 40 percent of each krone earned over 12,000 is deducted from the benefit in order to maintain at least a modest work incentive.

The rate for a full Transitional Benefit in May 1985 was about NOK 37,000 per year, about 35 percent of an average full-time female wage. The benefit is fixed at the full "basic amount" (the Norwegian reference amount that is fixed arbitrarily and defined as constituting support for one adult). It is indexed twice yearly. Some benefit can be claimed as long as income is below NOK 72,000 a year.

Advanced Maintenance Payments. Advanced maintenance payments are provided by the social insurance agency as a guarantee of child support, similar to the Swedish benefit described later. The assured minimum, available to all lone parents who are not in receipt of child support from the child's father (or who are paid by him at a lower level), is NOK 660 per month (1985) or NOK 7920 per year. Child support payments above this minimum are offset against the Transitional Benefit.

Housing Allowances. Finally, single-parent families may also qualify for income-tested *housing allowances*.

Government income transfers are the major source of income for one-third of all single-parent families. Social assistance, the means-tested cash benefit for the poor (like AFDC or "welfare" in the United States), is relatively unimportant for these families. Only 16 percent use assistance, and they constitute only 20 percent of all social assistance recipients. (These figures are not precise. Since social assistance is largely short term and transitional, families may use assistance more than once in the course of the year— e.g., when school begins, to purchase additional clothing for school-aged children, around holidays or vacations, or when family expenses are unusually high.)

In effect, transfer payments for a single mother with two children under age 10 provide 70 percent of what the average single mother could earn, and are tax free while her salary would be taxable. This is the equivalent of half the median family income for a husband/wife family. In addition, she would be entitled to a housing allowance. Even if she were to take a part-time job, if she is unskilled she is unlikely to come out very much better. Clearly, this is a generous policy. The specifics are illustrated in Table 3–4.

Ninety percent of all single parents in Norway have incomes under NOK 64,500 per year, much less than half the median family income in Norway (NOK 150,000). Moreover, this figure includes lone fathers also; if lone mothers' income only was assessed, the proportion would be even higher. Regardless, this is enough for a mother and two children to live on, albeit modestly; and many do so, even if they complain.

Poverty is clearly not an issue for these Norwegian families. Using the same poverty measure as we did earlier, only 8.6 percent of children in all lone-parent families are below the poverty threshold, as compared with 3.0 percent among husband/wife

Table 3–4 **Social Insurance Benefits for a Sole Mother and Two Children, 1985[a], Norway**

Program	Monthly (NOK)[b]	Yearly (NOK)[b]
Transitional Benefit (income-tested)	3,076	36,912
Child Allowance	1,397	16,764
Maintenance Allowance (guaranteed minimum)	1,320	15,840
Total[c]	5,793	69,516

[a]Tax Free. In addition, an income-tested housing allowance would be available.
[b]Early in 1988, the krone was worth about U.S. $.155.
[c]Average wage for a full time worker was NOK 150,000 for a male and NOK 100,000 for a female.

families. These rates are similar to those in Sweden, and dramatically lower than the poverty rate for children in husband/wife families in the United States, let alone mother-only families. Poverty, Norwegian officials say,

> is not the issue. What is the issue is that the minimum standard of living that everyone expects in Norway is impossible for these families. They may be without a telephone, an absolute necessity if one is to maintain a social connection with others. They are likely to be without a car in a society where almost everyone has a car. They can't send their children to summer camp when all the other children are going. They feel they are constantly having to deprive their children of what other children take for granted. They can't go on vacations or have a vacation home.

Lone mothers in Norway are also alleged to experience serious health problems, to have high blood pressure, and to complain of tension and stress and being tired—exhausted—all the time. Basically, they suffer from the absence of a second adult in the household; they really need a variety of supportive services, some of which a second parent might provide. Home help services could make a difference, but they are not likely to be readily available.

The Norwegians, like those in other countries, note the diversity among lone mothers. There are differences related to marital status. As in other countries, widows are the best off, both with regard to transfer income and to marital status. Divorced mothers are better off than unmarried mothers, but it is unclear whether the difference in their economic situation is a question of age (divorced mothers are older) or status. There are differences between rural and urban single-parent families, with a much higher proportion of families with children in cities being lone-parent families, and with a greater likelihood of divorced mothers in cities, and young unmarried mothers in rural areas. There is a growing group of cohabiting couples who are not consistently classified as either married couples or lone-parent families; at present, a significant percentage of lone-parent families may be cohabiting.

However, the most important difference by far is that between at-home mothers and mothers at work—in the labor force. Employment status is the critical variable in determining the economic situation of these families. The average income of a mother-only family in which the woman is in the labor force is NOK 100,000 per year. The average income for such families in which the woman is at home is NOK 50,000 (plus a housing allowance). One result of a relatively generous tax-free income transfer benefit and service package, compared with a modest, taxable wage, is the creation of a work disincentive. Since many Norwegians believe that women with young children either belong at home or should be able to choose whether they want to work, the results are precisely what were hoped for.

For those who wish to see the economic situation of lone mothers improved, the work disincentive is a concern. The impact of these policies is quite dramatic when female labor force participation rates are assessed. While the labor force participation rates of married women increased dramatically beginning in the early 1970s, the rates for separated, divorced, and unmarried mothers began to decrease at the same time. Labor force participation rates for unmarried mothers declined from 78 to 60 percent, and the rates for divorced and separated mothers decreased from 70 to 48 percent. The Norwegian LFPR for divorced mothers is the lowest among the Nordic countries and the other northern European countries.

In addition to the work disincentive created by transfer payments, several obstacles to women taking jobs are related to childcare issues: (1) the absence of an adequate and affordable supply of child care services, (2) the delayed age at which children enter compulsory school (7 instead of 6), and (3) the short school day until children reach age 10. (Yet, given the low LFPR among these women, of those who work, a far higher proportion than among married mothers work full-time—42 percent as compared with 19 percent work 30 plus hours per week.)

In general, the well-educated mother remains in the work force after having children. The unskilled mother does not. The well-educated mother can usually get a part-time job, if she wants one, and will still have a decent salary; she is likely to see continued labor force attachment as critical for her future career. The unskilled mother sees fewer possibilities and often also no or little economic advantage to remaining at work.

Apart from income, surveys indicate that the biggest difference between married mothers and single mothers has to do with the availability of time: leisure time, personal time, household time, child time. Single and married mothers spend the same amount of time "at work," but married mothers put more time in housework while single mothers are on the job, in paid work; and single working mothers have far less leisure time, with all that means, than married mothers.

In effect, despite what many would view as an adequate standard of living provided by income transfers alone, expectations and aspirations regarding a higher standard of living remain. Norway is a country with a high standard of living and many material comforts. To be without the luxuries everyone else defines as necessities is to be excluded from mainstream society. Those who achieve this higher standard do so by working; but adequate supports for single-parent working families are not yet in place. In effect, some Norwegian policymakers remain convinced that women heading families alone in Norway must choose between adequate income and adequate time. This is especially so for somewhat better educated women.

At-home mothers report that their major problems are economic and health related, while higher-income working women say that their major problem is a shortage of time and help. Women who work full-time have adequate income, especially with the various income supplements available to them. However, they find themselves seriously over-extended as they cope with job and family. Most shops are closed evenings and weekends. Part-time work, which makes it easier to manage time demands, does not provide enough income, especially if it leads to a decline in the Transitional Benefit. "Short" part-time work (less than 20 hours) may help some low-skilled, low-wage women if they remain under or close to the income ceiling for the Transitional Benefit; but if they have young children, the lack of subsidized child care may be an insurmountable barrier. Medical care, as in all of the countries we have discussed, is available to all, but finding child care is often a problem, and when found, good care is expensive. Despite subsidies that cover more than one-third of the costs of care, it is still not affordable to many lone mothers.

Finally, despite all the aid provided, when children become 10, the Transitional Benefit ends. For divorced and separated women with children aged 8 or 9 or older, the Transitional Benefit serves the function it was designed for—to support women in a relatively brief transitional situation, adjusting to single parenthood. It makes possible retraining and education if needed for labor force reentry. For young women with less education, however, it offers a safe and secure way to remain at home, exacerbating still more the problem of labor force entry—or reentry after 8 or 10 years. Many of the small group of lone mothers on social assistance are in this post-transition benefit status, only now confronting the problem of inadequate preparation for work. In contrast, those who are working, although better off economically than the at-home mothers, suffer from an inadequate social infrastructure where child care is concerned. In effect, as a policy designed to support single mothers with young children at home, the policy works; but as a policy designed to support choice, it does not fully satisfy either alternative.

Norway, then, offers the most generous of categorical income support programs for single mothers, and its experience teaches us several relevant things about our second option. First, the policy offers a good income base to single-parent families only because there is a generous base of social benefits for all families with children. Second, the special transition benefits, if available for so long a time, create a major post-transition problem for women in a world in which adequate income requires that they now work. If the goal is to be the offer of a real choice of work or staying at home to care for children, there must be a more adequate social infrastructure. Options 1 and 2 are not enough; the Norwegian approach needs the presence as well of elements from Option 3. Indeed, we see signs of change in Norway.

Supporting *All* Children, Especially the Very Young

France

French family policy is designed to benefit all families with children. The formal objectives of French family policy generally, as enunciated in the IXth national plan of 1985, are to equalize the economic burdens of those with children and those without; to assure a minimum standard of living to families with children; to aid in the care and rearing of very young children; to make child rearing compatible with employment for parents; and to encourage families to have a third child. Helping the parents of very young children (under age 3) is a central component of French family policy, since these are the years when it is particularly difficult for young mothers to work, and the additional financial aid in these early years allows the parents either to purchase care or to excercise the option of remaining home for some time after childbirth. Obviously, this can be especially helpful to the single mother, but it is regarded as transitional help.

Family allowances—the cash benefits provided to all families with children based on the presence and number of children in the family—are the most important family income transfers in France. They are tax free, and the benefit levels, which are adjusted annually, are linked to prices and related on a formula basis to a base amount equal to about one-half the French minimum wage. They are financed largely by employers' contributions of 9 percent on payroll. Certain other allowances, such as the single-parent allowance and the orphan allowance, are financed out of general revenue. Two-thirds of the allowances are universal; one-third are income-tested.

Transfer payments are the most important source of income for single mothers with young children (under age 3) or three dependent children (under age 16). There are few special benefits for them. Nonetheless, since French policy does favor young families, poor families, and large families, lone-mother families may benefit because they tend to be poor and, disproportionately, young.

The family benefit package for all young families that makes it possible for mothers of very young children to remain at home could include:

- The *universal family allowance* mentioned above that is provided for each child beginning with the second, to all families regardless of income.
- An income-tested *family allowance supplement*.
- A *young child allowance* that includes both a universal short-term benefit (lasting 9 months from the beginning of the 5th month of pregnancy through the month in which the child is born and for 3 months after birth), as well as an income-tested longer term benefit (lasting until a child is 3 years old) covering about 80 percent of all families with a child under age 3.
- A *paid maternity leave* covering 16 weeks at the time of childbirth (with full wage replacement).
- A universal, modestly paid, *parenting or "child rearing" leave* available until a child is age 2, for working parents with three or more children, who reduce their working hours by half or more.
- An income-tested *housing allowance*.

Thus, for example, a divorced mother with two children, including one under age 3, or with three school-aged children, could receive cash benefits each month almost equal to what a minimum wage job would provide or what could be earned by working part-time at an average job, if one could be obtained; and these are nonstigmatized benefits. A lone mother might also qualify for the *means-tested single-parent allowance* (worth almost 75 percent of an average female wage), so that even with only two young children she could stay at home for a year, or until her youngest child was 3; but this benefit is stigmatized. Or she could qualify for a minimum child support benefit, which the government would then try to collect from the absent father, and supplement this with earnings from a job. Or she could work, earn a wage, and still obtain all the cash benefits described above as supplements to her earnings. A single mother, with two children aged 2 and 7, working and earning half an average manufacturing wage, could have her income raised by 50 percent through these family allowances.

In theory, French policy is one of offering all mothers of very young children a choice of whether to work or remain at home, and providing a transitional benefit covering modest support for one year for poor single mothers with children over age 3. Once children are 3 years old, parents, including single mothers, are expected to work if they are in financial need. Earnings become critical for mothers with older children.

At 78 percent, labor force participation rates of single mothers are very high in France—far higher than for married mothers. Extensive preschool programs help make this possible for those whose children are 3 and older, as do income transfers that supplement low income. But part-time jobs are few and far between, and neither benefits nor services are sufficient to ease the time and help problems of working single mothers. Moreover, as one study points out, what really makes a difference in the economic situation of these families is whether the mother worked before becoming a single parent and thus will find return to a good job possible as her children get a bit older. If she did work, over time she and her family will be all right; if she did not, the family may be heading for trouble, once it no longer qualifies for the special benefits available to families with very young children, since the general family allowances, while generous comparatively as supplements, are not in themselves enough to support a family.

Hungary

Several other countries also have established a policy of supporting mothers of very young children at home. Hungary, for example, is the country that first developed the concept of an extended, paid, job-protected leave for women with children up to age 3.[20] Although Hungary is obviously not a Western European country, we mention it here because this social and family policy innovation has played a significant (if not necessarily explicit) role in recent policy developments in Europe. Established first as a child-caring or -rearing allowance in 1967, supplementing a paid, wage-related maternity leave for working mothers, this policy has since been adopted throughout much of Eastern Europe (sometimes for a shorter leave) and is now increasingly being adopted in modified form in the Western European countries. Austria, Finland, Germany, and France can all be said to have established some form of this policy—but the development has yet to be discussed extensively.

As modified in recent years, the Hungarian child-rearing grant policy is as follows: Working mothers (85 percent of all non-aged women with children work) are entitled to a 24-week, fully paid, wage-related and job-protected leave at the time of childbirth (4 weeks before birth and 20 after). At the end of that time these women are entitled to an additional job-protected child-rearing leave until their child is 3 years old. The cash benefit covering this leave is equal to about 75 percent of wages (up to the median) until the child is 18 months old and at a lower flat rate until the child is 3. Either parent may use the leave after the child is 1 year old, but in practice, it is used overwhelmingly by women. The rules permit caring for the children of other mothers (child minding or family day care) while one is at home.

The Hungarian policy is not specifically targeted to single parents. But because of the basic expectation regarding work, the modest child allowances provided and the high-level formula for child support that is imposed on men following separation and divorce (and enforced), the child-rearing grant constitutes an interesting illustration of a universal policy benefiting lone mothers. It is primarily of interest because it is a policy of supporting mothers at home while their children are very young, and doing this far more generously for those with a solid prior work history. In effect, Hungarian family policy creates a work incentive for young women; they go to work as soon as they finish school in order to qualify for benefits that can leave mother-only families in almost the same financial situation as husband/wife families. Without work and the related benefits, these families could not manage. (It is unclear what impact recent economic policies in Hungary may have on this pattern.) Part-time work is what is really desired by mothers, according to a recent survey, rather than staying at home or working full-time, but little such work is available.

The French family policy, which helps families with the rearing of all their children, and the Hungarian labor market policy, which in the late 1960s encouraged mothers of infants and toddlers—particularly unskilled workers—to withdraw from work for three years, now appear to be converging. Moreover, this emphasis on helping families with very young children, including making it posssible for mothers of infants to remain at home for child rearing, is now emerging in other countries. Some countries are motivated by overt or latent pronatalist objectives; others are influenced by labor market concerns; but all express concern for child well-being. Since the designs are only being developed and are not yet fully realized and implemented, it is difficult to confirm either

objectives or results. We nonetheless illustrate tendencies with
Austria, Germany, and Finland.

Austria

In Austria, as in Britain, France, and Germany, there is no major
policy attention directed at mother-only families, despite the
economic difficulties these families are acknowledged to have, but
they do benefit for some special measures. As in France, there is
special attention directed in Austria at families with children. All
receive children's allowances worth about 15 percent of average
female wages per child. All lone mothers are guaranteed (advanced) whatever child support the court orders a noncustodial
parent to pay (up to a maximum). And like France, Austria has a
special policy focus on young families.

All working mothers are entitled to a fully paid, wage-related,
job-protected maternity leave (8 weeks before birth and 8 weeks
after). In addition, working mothers are entitled to an additional
10 months of job-protected leave, paid at two rates: (1) a standard,
universal benefit that is indexed; and (2) a special benefit equal to
150 percent of the standard, for single, working mothers. The
benefit is equal to the net wage of a young blue-collar worker.
Almost all women (95 percent) who qualify for what in effect is a
one-year leave take advantage of it. Ninety percent take the full
year; the remaining 10 percent return earlier, sometimes to qualify
for another leave, for a planned second pregnancy. In effect, 60
percent of all women giving birth (almost all who worked while
pregnant) qualify for this benefit.

In addition, there is a targeted, categorical Austrian measure for
lone mothers. At the end of the first year of maternity leave, single
mothers with a prior work history may qualify for an additional
two-year leave, until a child is age 3, paid for through the unemployment insurance system. The benefit level is equal to 80
percent of the unemployment benefit; it is tax free and carries with
it full coverage for health insurance. The benefit is used largely by
never-married, poorly educated, and unskilled young women, who
nonetheless make sure they have enough of a work history to
qualify. When the benefit ends, by far most go to work; indeed
never-married mothers with children over age 3 have the highest
labor force participation rates of all adult women in Austria. Many
also marry when the extended three-year leave ends. In contrast,
divorced women benefit most by the advanced maintenance payment, but they, too, are expected to work, and most do so, because

they must if they are to manage financially. Of lone mothers generally, only about 25 percent receive social assistance.

West Germany

West Germany (more accurately, the Federal Republic of Germany), which has partially phased in its new child-rearing grant (see below), also has the other basic family benefits and social infrastructure characteristic of Western industrialized countries. These include universal children's allowances, which are reduced moderately at higher-income levels, child tax benefits, and health insurance. German women who are in the labor force also are entitled to a 14-week, fully paid, and job-protected maternity leave, 6 weeks before anticipated childbirth and 8 weeks thereafter. Single mothers also may call upon a modest governmental child support benefit if the noncustodial parent ignores a legal obligation to pay. This relatively new, indexed benefit is guaranteed only for three of a child's first six years.

Germany's newest family policy initiative, available to parents without regard to labor force status, is the child-rearing allowance implemented at the start of 1986 but phased in at different times in several of the states. It is considered a major family policy initiative to encourage parenting. This is a 10-month leave paid at a modest flat rate, available to either parent; it is job-protected for working parents and nonincome-tested for the first six months, but income-tested thereafter, however. In effect, an earlier extended maternity leave for working mothers has been replaced now by a longer leave with somewhat lower benefits for all parents, regardless of their work history. The benefit is not sufficient, by itself, to equal a full wage, even for an unskilled female worker, however. For the single mother, at home after childbirth for the full period, it assumes a modest part-time wage, or some child support payment; otherwise, it merely supplements a low social assistance benefit.

Ninety-five percent of all women who gave birth in 1986 used the new child-rearing benefit for the 10 months available to them that year. Of these, 80 percent qualified by income for the full 10-month benefit, half for the full amount, and half for a partial amount. (It is linked to income and phased out as income rises.) Only 4.5 percent of the women who worked before birth worked part-time after childbirth during that year. Most single mothers stayed home but needed social assistance to make it possible. Since the child-rearing grant is not counted as income, the ordinary social assistance benefit that a low-income lone mother might also qualify for would be significantly supplemented in this way. The benefit is clearly popular, but there are complaints about inadequate job protection for those mothers wanting—and expecting—to return to their job at the end of the year. The experience is too new for any evaluation. The intent has been to make the child-rearing grant a two-year federal grant and to encourage a third year financed by the states when financially feasible.

In the 1979–80 comparison of family income transfers in eight countries, we found that single mothers and their children in Germany ranked well behind those in Sweden and France eligible for social assistance but well ahead of those in the United States, Great Britain, Australia, Israel, and Canada. However, because of local discretion and parental responsibility, social assistance coverage rates were not high, and work was often expected or undertaken.[21]

Now, in the context of recent developments, the consensus is that while the totality of German family policy is relatively generous, it is not particularly supportive of single mothers and children. Single mothers must work in order to support their families adequately, and their labor force participation rates, which demonstrate this, are 50 percent higher than those for married women. Yet German working mothers of children under age 10 say that given the short school day they cannot work full-time. They call instead for part-time jobs, but few are available. In addition, many women say that a part-time job is not economically viable. They cannot live on half a wage, and they cannot manage without the benefits that go only with full or near full-time work. Current court awards for child support are said to be predicated on the assumption that women with children under age 10 will be at home; that women with children age 10 and older can be expected to work only part-time; and that only when children are fully grown can a woman be expected to work full-time. There are some critics who say that if a woman is out of the labor force for 10 years (and longer for two children) and works only part-time for another 6 to 8 years, she will not be employable, certainly not at a living wage.

The literal policy in Germany is that single mothers, as all mothers, should have a choice about work or at-home care of their children for several years. Prior to the enactment of the child-rearing allowance, the small three-year child-support guarantee and social assistance were all that was available, and most view this as inadequate. There is a right to assistance under the framework law and a right to remain home to rear a child. Local discretion determines the amount of pressure to work and the usual expectation was part-time work when the child was 3 (since part-day preschool is available for over 75 percent of children).

Now, the child-rearing grant raises the potential support for a year, even for a single mother without a work history. However, the joining of these sources still does not produce the equivalent of the typical full-time wage of an unskilled woman in the work force, and a job would also permit receipt of the income-tested housing allowance.

One sees here a policy in the making, reflecting pushes and pulls from those variously concerned with the labor market, birthrates, public expenditures, and/or family well-being. Longer and/ or more generous benefits would be needed to support the single mother at home. More all-day child care and jobs would be essential for the full-time work option. Part-time jobs with more generous family benefit supplements are essential if part-time work is to be considered an option. The next policy moves are now being debated in Germany.

Finland

Finland's pattern of marriage, divorce, and lone parenting is similar to that of Norway. Although about 30 percent of all children are born out-of-wedlock in Finland, most are born to cohabiting couples who tend to marry soon after childbirth. Finnish female labor force participation rates are the highest in Western Europe, however, and unlike Sweden, most married and single mothers work full-time.[22] In general, what are thought of as the "new family types" in popular discussion are no more new in Finland than in Denmark or Sweden; these patterns have been integrated and stabilized in the 1980s.

Finnish family policy is targeted on *all* families with children. There are some benefits specific to lone mothers, but nothing of significance other than a guaranteed minimum child support benefit. Finnish family policy does, however, provide special attention to families with young children and families with a young head (under 30); these family types tend to overlap, and are viewed as being particularly needy and worthy of support.[23]

The Finnish family policy package includes the following benefits:

- A *universal child allowance* that is tax free, not indexed, and equal to 2,000 FMK per child per year* (about 5 percent of

*Early in 1988 the Finmark was worth about U.S. $.242.

94

average wage but about 10 percent of disposable income for a
lone mother); a *special supplementary allowance* is provided
for children under age 3.

- An *income-tested housing allowance* that is worth about 30
percent of average rent but about 80 percent of rent for very
low income families. (About half of all families with children
qualify for this benefit.)
- A basic *job-protected maternity leave* for working mothers that
lasts for one year, beginning one month before expected birth
and ending when the baby is 11 months old; and a taxable
cash benefit provided at that time, replacing about 80 percent
of wages up to a specified maximum. (Fathers can and do use
some part of the leave and can qualify, therefore, for a portion
of the benefit, too.)
- A *"home-care" or child-rearing allowance*, available after the
one-year maternity/parenting benefit, that is an income-
tested, indexed, taxable, flat-rate cash benefit equal to about
one-third of minimum wage and one-quarter of average female
wage, and is available to working mothers who remain out of
the labor force until their first child is age 2 and their second
(or subsequent children) is age 3. By 1990, the government
expects to make this benefit available to all working parents
until their children are age 3. The objective is to assure
working parents the choice of remaining at home and receiving
a low-level cash benefit or working and obtaining subsidized
child care. Current child-care plans project full coverage for
all children under age 7 whose parents want them in care; the
first priority is children under age 3.
- An *advanced maintenance benefit* that is universal and equal
to 400 FMK per child, monthly, provided to single mothers
when the noncustodial parent fails to pay at least that amount
in child support.

A 1981 study[24] found that the economic situation of lone-parent
families is relatively similar to that of two-parent families. Single
mothers with two children had about 60 percent of the income of
comparable husband/wife families, largely as a consequence of
government income transfers.

Family benefits constitute about 25 percent of the disposable
income of lone-mother families today. These benefits constitute a
significant income supplement to all families with children, and
thus, a strong work incentive for single mothers. Combined with
the wages of full-time work, Finnish one-parent families have a
well-protected standard of living. Surveys have revealed that de-

spite this economic protection, lone parents suffer from time pressures when they work full-time, especially when children are young. It is to address this problem that Finnish family policy is (1) moving toward assuring parents of young children that they can remain at home until the child is age 3, and (2) aiming to shorten the workday for the working parents of young children.

Combining Labor Market and Family Policy to Permit Parenting and Gender Equity: Sweden

In contrast to Britain and France, Sweden's social policy has stressed the importance of full employment and the role of labor market policies in achieving social policy goals. Unlike Britain or the United States, Sweden's policy goals stress reducing inequality and promoting gender equity more than reducing poverty. Like Norway, Sweden provides a special benefit for single parents; however, in Sweden (as in Finland) this benefit is designed only to help maintain the children and not to support the mother and full family at home. Finally, like France, the Swedes pay special attention to families with children, in particular, those with very young children; but much of what is done is designed to support parents in their efforts at balancing work and family life. In effect, Sweden seems to have created generous family policies and parallel labor-market efforts which are mutually supportive and have their own unique consequences.

A job and earnings are viewed as the fundamental source of family income and gender equity in Sweden. Women, like men, are expected to work. There is an "active labor market policy": Government invests heavily in job creation, if necessary, and in training, re-training, education, and relocation. Transfer payments—social benefits—are at best either transitional (and very short term) or supplementary, if and when earnings are low. Social policy is designed to facilitate both employment and parenting.

Labor force participation rates for women with children are very high, among the highest in the industrialized world, regardless of marital status. In 1981, 85 percent of all lone mothers with children under age 17 were in the labor force. The corresponding figure for married women with children this age was 83 percent. Swedish women, generally, tend to work part-time rather than full-time; however, marital status does affect patterns of working hours. Among all working mothers, single mothers are likely to work 11 hours more per week than married mothers. The proportion of married mothers working full-time is 23 percent, while the corresponding figure for lone mothers is 50 percent.

Single-parent families are a common phenomenon in Sweden today.[25] Sweden also has the highest nonmarital cohabitation rate of any country in the industrialized world. More than 30 percent of all families with children, including about 25 percent of all children, were in other than legally married, husband/wife families in 1981. Although many of these families are stable units despite the absence of legal ties holding the couple together, most are "true" single-parent families, usually headed by a woman living alone with her children. Among all families with children in Sweden in 1985 (over 1 million), more than 18 percent were single parents who were not cohabiting; 90 percent of them were female; about 14 percent were single parents who were cohabiting with a partner who was not the biological parent of the child. The remaining 68 percent were husband/wife families having children biologically related to one or both parents.

The number of families in which the parents are married to one another decreased from 83 percent of all families with children in 1971 to 70 percent in 1981. The Swedish marriage rate is now the lowest in the industrialized world; at the same time, Sweden has one of the highest mean ages of first marriage—30 for men and 27 for women in 1983, compared with 25.5 for men and 23.3 for women in the United States in 1985.[26] While the number of families in Sweden headed by married parents decreased by 15 percent during the 1970s, the number of families headed by unmarried or cohabiting parents increased by 77 percent.

Single-parent families, especially those headed by women, are viewed as economically vulnerable in Sweden, as they are in all countries. The Swedish standard of living for families with children assumes two wages. Although the overwhelming proportion of lone mothers work, such families still have only one wage earner. Moreover, women still tend to work in lower-paid jobs, and average wages for women remain only about 75 percent of male wages despite strong efforts to equalize them. Furthermore, since about 90 percent of single parents are mothers, and they carry primary responsibility for their children, many of whom are young, most of these women work part-time. Thus, despite a popular conception of single-mother families in Sweden being well off, recent analyses reveal that these families are still strongly disadvantaged economically. A special Royal Commission, established in the early 1980s to assess the economic and social situation of single-parent families, concluded that indeed they were much worse off financially than married-couple families, and were disadvantaged in many other aspects as well. As surveys point out regularly, time and energy constraints face single mothers as well. Median income for a single mother with one or two children (the typical Swedish family) is about 54 percent of the income of comparable married-couple families. This is a concern in Sweden, yet the percentage is far higher than in almost any other country.

Sweden does not provide a guaranteed minimum income to single parents. Earnings are expected to be the foundation of family income. Yet, clearly, earnings are not always adequate to support the Swedish standard of living. For family income to be adequate when there is only one wage earner in a family, and/or wages are low, Swedish social policy provides a variety of government benefits. None of these are enough to live on if they are the only source of income; all serve instead as a supplement to family income. Social assistance would be needed if earnings were not available. Yet only a small percentage of Swedish lone mothers— 16 percent—use assistance each year; and they constitute only 25 percent of all social assistance recipients. Even among those claiming assistance, use is brief, for about three to four months.

Swedish social policy provides the following major income supplements:

Child or Family Allowance. All Swedish families with children receive a child or family allowance for each child up to the age of 18 and even beyond if the youngster is in school. This benefit, at SEK 4800 per child in 1986, is worth about 5 percent of average wage for each child.* The level is adjusted each year, although it is not indexed, and it is tax free.

Child Support or Maintenance. Lone mothers (parents) receive, in addition, child support or maintenance from the government as an advance payment of the absent father's (parent's) support obligation, when fathers fail to pay or pay irregularly or at a low level.[27] In those cases where the custodial parent is the father, the mother owes support, and the same policy applies. The national government assumes responsibility for collecting from the father through its debt-collection agency. Most private child support is paid through this agency, usually through automatic wage withholding from the noncustodial parent (about 20 percent) or through voluntary payments by the father to the agency. The advanced maintenance payment substitutes for this when necessary or supplements it if needed, basically guaranteeing a minimum amount of support for each child. It also assures the custodial parent (overwhelmingly the mother) of a regular flow of income.

---

*Early in 1988, the Swedish krona was worth U.S. $.165.

The guaranteed child support payment varies by the age of the child, but is equal to between 40 and 60 percent of the Swedish reference wage—the amount defined in theory as adequate to support one adult at a minimum level (which was 21,800 SK in 1987). Payment is conditional on the custodial parent's assisting in efforts to establish paternity. Child support is tax deductible to the payer and tax free to the recipient. Payments are made monthly by check or by transfer to a bank account. The benefit level is indexed at 70 percent of the rise in consumer prices during the previous year. Child allowances are integrated into the advance maintenance payments but are totally separate from social assistance. They are paid out through the social insurance agency. About 83 percent of the potentially collectible debts (the support which is ordered by the court) are repaid; this is equal to about 35 percent of all advanced maintenance payments, since the government guarantee level is higher than typical support awards.[28]

In 1981, advanced maintenance payments were paid for 256,000 children, about 14 percent of all children in Sweden, in both single-parent and reconstituted families (including cohabiting couples in which only one parent is the child's biological parent).

Housing Allowances. Lone parents usually receive housing allowances, also. These are income-tested (not means- or asset-tested) cash benefits that offset some of the costs of housing (rental or owner-occupied). The income ceiling is sufficiently generous so that in 1979 about 50 percent of all families with children received this benefit. In 1983 this figure had declined to 35 percent, in part because the income ceiling was not adjusted to take account of inflation. Nonetheless, 80 percent of single parents received the allowances in 1980. Single-parent families receive a priority for housing allowances in that eligibility is determined on a scale which assumes two earned incomes while these families have only one. Although advanced maintenance payments are not included in computing family income, the income ceiling for single parents to qualify is lower, to take account of their value. About 70 percent of single mothers with one or two children received housing allowances as compared with 15 percent of cohabiting or married couple families; 90 percent of those with three children received them as compared with 50 percent of two-parent families.

Parental Benefits. Finally, working parents are supported by a social infrastructure that includes benefits and services designed to ease the tension between work and family life and to reduce the time crunch these working mothers often face. These benefits are especially important for single working mothers, the vast majority of lone mothers in Sweden. In addition to subsidized health care and child care services, they are entitled to a paid and job-protected one-year parental leave following childbirth, an unpaid but job-protected leave up to 18 months after childbirth, the right to work a six-hour day until their youngest child is eight, five weeks of paid vacation (or more) each year, up to 60 days a year paid sick leave if needed to care for an ill child, time off when a child begins a new child care program or begins preschool or school, and access to high-quality subsidized child care. Children from single-parent families have priority over children from two-parent families for these subsidized child care services. Fees are income-related, and the government is now moving to expand the supply of services once again. Current policy aims at assured child care coverage by 1991 for children aged 18 months and older, for all parents wanting such services for their children, and an extension of the paid parenting leave to 18 months from the current one year.

Assessing the situation of a working single mother with two children earning about half an average wage in 1980 in Sweden, (e.g., working part-time), end-of-year family income after earnings, taxes, and transfers would leave that family about as well off as an average single male worker, with no children, working full-time.[29] This is about twice as well off as a similar family any place in the United States. Gender does not make a significant difference here, either; if she were working full-time, the lone mother would have income almost equal (93 percent) to that of a single male parent. Furthermore, using the same relative definition of poverty we used in assessing the situation of the British, Norwegian, and German families, and the same data source, only 8.3 percent of children in lone-parent families in Sweden are poor, as compared with 4.4 percent in two-parent families (with Norway, the lowest rates among the countries here described).[30]

From the perspective of Swedish policymakers, lone-mother families are economically and socially *disadvantaged; they are not "poor."* From an international perspective, Swedish mother-only families are a lot better off than those in other countries. The U.S. analyst sees many elements in the Swedish option as shared with France: a base of universal benefits and assumptions as to availability of social infrastructure. Given such an approach, the support levels, in U.S. or British terms, are generous. Yet there is a difference: France offers "choice" for the earliest years, then assumes work, even though critics claim that neither adequate support nor sufficient part-time jobs are available; Sweden, noting that women work, tries to attune its policies to that fact from the very beginning (but provides parental benefits for one year and

permits a shorter workday—6 hours—while children are young
(under 8)). The fact of largely part-time work is unintended since
the gender-equity commitments call for similar, but shorter, work-
days for all men and women with young children.

Models and Trends

We have described alternative models of policy response to the
problems of single-parent, mother-only families, using the policies
of several different European countries to demonstrate how these
can be carried out and what the consequences might be. Clearly,
women in mother-only families can be given financial aid and
expected to remain at home; but even when they are supported
generously, if their standard of living is not comparable to that of
two-parent families, they appear—and feel—deprived. Moreover,
if financial support is linked to children's ages—3, 6, 10, 16—the
time comes when aid stops, and women who have been out of the
work force for long periods of time are even worse off when they
try to reenter.

The contrasting position is to assume that women will work—to
obtain basic income and to qualify for benefits contingent on prior
labor force attachment. Once they have children, they will continue to work albeit with a brief interlude when children are born
(one year?), at which time a cash benefit supports a parent at home
on leave from work, at the same level as the wages foregone; and
part-time work is available to permit a phased return. Here the
policy is to invest in the social infrastructure that supports working
parents (single or married), including health care, child care, child-
related leaves for a child's illness, visits to a child's school, employment and training programs, a shorter workday for all, and so
forth.

The relative economic deprivation experienced by mother-only
families can be alleviated—but not eliminated—when women's
wages are closer to male wages and when earned income is
supplemented if low. The income of one-parent families will not
equal that of two-parent, two-earner families because transfers do
not substitute fully for earnings, but the difference can be partially
reduced; at least the incomes of mother-only families can be the
same as those of father-only families, which is not the situation at
present. And where this is done best, the focus is on supplementing family income by providing additional income for children—to
make up for low earnings and/or the limitations of a single wage
for family income.

Despite all this, however, when single mothers work, time pressures that are already severe for working mothers become worse. And even when they work and have the social relationships that go with a job, the constraints on leisure and personal time—and the absence of a second adult and the kin network that usually accompanies this—leave sole mothers more isolated and lonely than married mothers, and may leave children without sufficient time with their mothers or with inadequate care.

The European illustrations suggest that despite these social pressures and the acknowledged diversity of single mothers, the economic situation has taken priority, and the assumption has been that one policy can address all types of single mothers, except perhaps, widows. Widows continue to be treated specially—and better—in many countries, although some, such as Sweden and Denmark, have already moved to treat all single mothers in the same fashion under the law. A shift from family to individual entitlement under social security is probably inevitable. (We will return to this issue in Chapter 5.)

Supporting poor mothers to remain at home—the alternative policy—leaves them badly off everywhere, with all the social and psychological problems inherent in a stigmatized status. Providing help for transitions seems good in principle, but when the transition is extended too long (10 years or longer), the negative consequences of exclusion from the mainstream of society are clear, and the extent of relative deprivation in an affluent society is severe. Only when work is expected and in some sense assured and income is supplemented to reduce the gap between one- and two-earner families is the economic situation improved; families with two parents but low income can benefit from such policy as well. Finally, only when the social infrastructure is extensive and firm do the problems of time poverty and inadequate help get eased. Health care, housing, and child care are all critical aspects.

Clearly the issue for the United States is: Can one devise and implement a policy package that addresses the problems of economic deprivation and the risk of poverty for mother-only families and their children, as well as the need for supportive services? What specific policies and programs are appropriate and supportable on the American scene? What can one derive from the third (France) and fourth (Sweden) policy options? To what extent do specific kinds of single mothers require special, categorical responses as well, on the assumption that a stress on work, income supplementation, parental obligations, and social infrastructure for all families with children is deemed basically attractive and sound? We "test" these possibilities in Chapter 4 with intensive looks at four groups of single mothers frequently discussed in addition to the always visible divorced and widowed women.

Endnotes

1. Sheila B. Kamerman and Alfred J. Kahn, *Child Care, Family Benefits, and Working Parents* (New York: Columbia University Press, 1981): Hugh Heclo, *Modern Social Politics in Britain and Sweden* (New Haven: Yale University Press, 1974).
2. R. M. Finer, *Report of the Committee on One-Parent Families* (London, England: Cmnd 5629, HMSO, 1974). Several of the background studies for this project were published subsequently, including Dennis Marden, *Mothers Alone: Poverty and the Fatherless Family*, published first in London in 1969 by Allen Lane and updated subsequently in 1973; Vic George and Paul Wilding, *Motherless Families* (London: Routledge and Kegan Paul, 1972). In addition, an international study was carried out assessing the situation of these families in other European countries and the policies designed to improve their condition. The findings of this international study are summarized in an appendix to the report, and an article based on the study was published as, Christine Cockburn, "Income Maintenance for One-Parent Families," *International Social Security Review* 1 (1975): 33–60.
3. Jennie Popay, Lesley Rimmer, and Chris Rossiter, *One-Parent Families: Parents, Children and Public Policy* (London: Study Commission on the Family, 1983).
4. Department of Health and Social Security (DHSS), *Low Income Families 1983* (London: HMSO, 1986).
5. Family Policy Studies Centre, London, 1986.
6. Jane Millar and Jonathan Bradshaw, "The Living Standards of Lone-Parent Families," *The Quarterly Journal of Social Affairs* (England) (July 1987). We draw heavily in what follows on this article and related papers by Jane Millar, generously made available to us by Dr. Millar of the University of Bath.
7. Ibid., 1–2.
8. Adela Adam Nevitt, "One Parent Families," *Yearbook of Social Policy, 1974* (London: Routledge and Kegan Paul, 1975).
9. Millar and Bradshaw, "The Living Standards of Lone-Parent Families."
10. The British reserve the term "single mother" for the never-married mother, in U.S. terms.
11. DHHS, Personal Communication, June 1987.
12. Millar and Bradshaw, "The Living Standards of Lone-Parent Families."
13. Jean Martin and Ceridwen Roberts, *Men and Women: A Statistical Digest*, Equal Opportunities Commission (London: HMSO, July 1984).
14. This defines child poverty as adjusted, net after-tax income less than half of the median income, adjusted for family size. Timothy Smeeding, Barbara Boyle Torrey, and Martin Rein, "The Economic Status of the Young and the Old in Eight Countries," in *The Changing Well-being of Children and the Aged: The United States in a Comparative Context*, ed. John L. Palmer,

Timothy Smeeding, and Barbara B. Torrey (Washington, D.C.: The Urban Institute Press, 1988).

15. Ibid.

16. Millar and Bradshaw, "The Living Standards of Lone-Parent Families," 22.

17. Kari Skrede, *Family Policy in Relation to Changes in Family Structure and the Distribution of Income* (Oslo, Norway: Institute of Applied Social Research, 1983).

18. The costs vary from NOK 7,900 for a newborn to NOK 15,250 for a 15-year-old. These data are from a Swedish study which is viewed as valid for Norway also. See K. Strom-Bull, "Economic Security and Family Support in Norway," in *Economic Security and Family Support,* ed. T. Muelders and J. Eekelaar (forthcoming). See also, *Social Insurance in Norway* (Oslo, Norway: The National Insurance Administration, 1986).

19. Strom-Bull, "Economic Security and Family Support in Norway."

20. See Kamerman and Kahn, *Child Care, Family Benefits and Working Parents,* 13–17.

21. Alfred J. Kahn and Sheila B. Kamerman, *Income Transfers for Families with Children* (Philadelphia: Temple University Press, 1983).

22. Central Statistical Office, Finland, *Women and Men at Work* (Helsinki, Finland: 1985).

23. Ministry of Social Affairs and Health, *Social Policy in Finland* (Helsinki, Finland: 1984).

24. Interview, Summer 1987, Ministry of Social Affairs.

25. These data were provided by Soren Kindlund, Swedish Ministry of Health and Social Affairs, and Cecelia Etzler of the Swedish Central Statistical Office, June 1987.

26. David Popenoe, "What Is Happening to the Family in Sweden?" *Social Change in Sweden,* no. 36 (December 1986).

27. For a fuller discussion of the Swedish Advanced Maintenance Program, see Soren Kindlund, "Child Support in Sweden," in Alfred J. Kahn and Sheila B. Kamerman, *Child Support: From Debt Collection to Social Policy* (Newbury Park, Calif.: Sage Publishers, 1988).

28. The advanced maintanance payments were first enacted in 1937 in Sweden in an effort to improve the often difficult condition in which the children of unmarried and divorced mothers had to live when dependent on social assistance. (A similar benefit was first enacted in Denmark at the end of the last century.) Initially, it was means-tested, but this policy was abolished in 1947. The essential character of the present policy was established in the 1964 law, which guaranteed support up to a certain level for each child with an absent parent, regardless of family income and regardless of whether a child support award had been fixed in court.

29. Kahn and Kamerman, *Income Transfers for Families with Children.*

30. Smeeding, Torrey, and Rein, "The Economic Status of the Young and the Old in Eight Countries."

Chapter 4

SINGLE MOTHERS: HAPPENSTANCE AND CHOICE

From time to time the media write about mother-only families, usually one type at a time. They often focus on welfare mothers, especially teenage mothers who live independently and are supported by Aid to Families with Dependent Children (AFDC). At other times they single out the long-time AFDC recipient and her several children. Occasionally, the camera shifts to "human interest" stories about the older "mothers by choice," who may be middle class and professional. When there is special legislative advocacy, the "displaced homemakers" may be featured. Issues of child support generate stories about divorced women and their children. Social security reporting features widows, usually the very elderly.

How is all of this to be sorted out for policy purposes? Which categories need *categorical* attention? What commonalities are usefully addressed? Chapter 4 looks at four major groups, which are hardly mutually exclusive: welfare mothers, teenage parents, somewhat older "mothers by choice," and displaced homemakers. There are policy questions about widows, and these will be mentioned, but the group is clearly identified and the issues well known. The divorced mother and her children have already been discussed in Chapter 1, but we return to them again in subsequent chapters since, in fact, they are the largest single-parent family group, surpassing widows and children, the major concern of earlier years, and far surpassing teenage unmarried mothers with children, who actually constitute a small part of the lone-mother group. Here we merely note the strong body of evidence that more than half of all divorced and separated women are remarried or reconciled within five years. Their economic status is more than

104

restored. However, those who do not remarry or reconcile never recover economically.

After this chapter's review of the evidence for some categorical foci within the single-mother grouping, we turn in the following two chapters to work, income, time, and social supports in an effort to explore an American policy that would include as well elements of the previous chapter's Options 3 and 4, as illustrated by France and Sweden.

Welfare Mothers

The heading "single mothers and children" immediately conjures up the welfare-mother category. There are, indeed, those who see the policy questions on which we are focused as questions for public assistance programs alone. As we write, proposals for "welfare reform" are offered as "the answer."

We find that "welfare reform" (which means different things to different advocates) is certainly critical, but hardly the entire story. Although many single mothers are found on the public assistance rosters, more than half are not.

In the present context, public assistance, or "welfare," means Aid to Families with Dependent Children (AFDC), the large and important means-tested income support program for families of very low income. AFDC is the major cash program for families rearing children deprived of parental support. Except for a very small number of instances (1.5 percent), it is a support program for children living with mothers (or, occasionally, alternative care-takers) in a home without their fathers. A small number of cases in some states also include unemployed fathers. Some cases involve incapacitated fathers.

AFDC is also a "passport" to food stamps and Medicaid, a medical program for the poor. It is a program administered by the states (which define need and benefit levels), but with substantial federal reimbursement and oversight.

Some numbers contribute to the clarification of AFDC's role for single parents. At last report, there were 13.1 million children under age 18 living in mother-only families. There were 7.7 million such families. At approximately the same time the average monthly caseload included 3.75 million families and about 7.2 million children. While over a lifetime many more single-parent families are dependent on AFDC than are counted in the monthly case-load, it can hardly be claimed that all single mothers are "welfare mothers." On the other hand, over half the children under 18 in single-parent families—and their caretakers—are receiving AFDC at a given moment.

Some single mothers are "social security mothers," referring now to the widows rearing some 1.9 million children with benefits in current-payment status early in 1987 as survivors of deceased workers. There might also be said to be a group of "child support" mothers (3 million did receive full or partial payments in 1983, and more were non-AFDC cases than were AFDC recipients) and "alimony mothers" (here the number was only .6 million).

"Welfare reform" could have an important impact yet probably not cover this entire group. Moreover, there are important differentiations within the caseload. Once stereotyping is avoided, however, welfare mothers and public assistance policy do become an important entry point to the single-parent problem. Here, after all, is a statistically large part of the single-parent "problem" as perceived by the public at large. Indeed, it is the combination of the welfare mother and the teenage mother (see the next section) that the public is most concerned about in this field.

Images of the Welfare Mother

Who or what is a "welfare mother"? In a much read and praised sympathetic *New Yorker* series in the mid-1970s, Susan Sheehan told of a Puerto Rican mother of nine children, a woman she called Carmen Santana, who had from her teens lived with a succession of four men, all for extended periods; she had married only the first, at age 14. She had been in New York City from the late 1950s, having come originally for a better-paying job. She was, when visited by Ms. Sheehan in her intensive participant-observer role, living in one of a succession of New York slums in her 10th apartment in 16 years. She had left work and drifted onto the welfare rolls, even though she and her "husband" both had low-paying jobs, at a time when she had her fourth child and could not arrange low-cost, neighborhood, informal child care.[1]

Carmen Santana continuously cheated and lied to the welfare authorities since she found it necessary to hide or misrepresent the income of the man with whom she lived (and income occasionally provided by others), or had to pretend that money was lost or stolen in order to manage with only very limited public welfare funds. She said that her friends and neighbors behaved in the same way. But she and her family lived on what by any measure must be seen as a very low standard, in minimal quarters, with little furniture and few comforts. They were not starving; they lived like many others in their neighborhood, but they certainly did not have great prospects. The children had, or soon developed, all the problems of their neighborhood: serious delinquency, drug addiction, drug peddling, and adolescent pregnancy. They showed no signs of escaping their mother's life-style. A third welfare generation in the family was on the horizon.

Mrs. Santana did no planning ahead and made no effort to take hold of her life. She expressed no need to. From an outside, middle-class perspective she would be described as unable by background, culture, or experience to cope effectively with complex urban living or with the various public bureaucracies. Yet she kept the schools at arm's length most of the time, despite poor attendance by her children, and drew effectively on welfare resources.

Her life was characterized by both anguish and gaiety, deprivation and occasional pleasure, but she did not see herself as suffering. Her daily life was built around personal and household routines, constant TV, family relationships, and friendships—as well as around juggling payments on installment purchases, welfare check cashing, playing the numbers constantly, and dealing with the bureaucracy. She lived in a geographically confined area and seldom if ever saw those parts of the city best known to the outside world. She displayed little ambition and had few goals. She did too little planning ahead to be accused of having babies as a way to increase her welfare budget.

Welfare department staff workers who visited the home over the years described Mrs. Santana and her children as "warm" and "friendly," even though they were aware of the "unconventional" marital and sexual relationships that were present. They were distressed at Mrs. Santana's extraordinarily sloppy housekeeping and household maintenance as well as her casual money management. They realized that Mrs. Santana could neither set an example for nor control or guide her children.

A New York City welfare mother of Puerto Rican background, who remains deeply rooted in Puerto Rican community life, cannot "represent" welfare mothers, although the imagery of Mrs. Santana long dominated discussion of AFDC in the media and elsewhere, evoking diverse responses.

Welfare grants were not indexed to inflation, and their value began to erode in the mid- and late 1970s. Eligibility rules became tighter, and the extra grants for clothing, rent, and furniture that were prominant in the Sheehan story soon became less available, and finally, nonexistent. The AFDC program remained important, and concern about costs, long-term dependency, and possible fraud were widespread in the general society and among public officials. The concept of seeing this program as an unquestioned if inadequate alternative form of at-home support for families with children—perhaps even a "guaranteed income"—eroded (see Chapter 2); new policy approaches were advanced, and administration was tightened.

Ken Auletta was the next to write about welfare mothers in the *New Yorker* (in 1981), and his work, too, was to appear in book form and attract nationwide attention.[2] On this occasion, however, he was telling the story of a group he described as an "underclass." He joined together drug addicts, hustlers, petty criminals, welfare recipients, people unable to hold a job, and participants in the underground economy, and described their experiences before, during, and after enrollment in a pioneering and modestly successful "supported work" training program. Auletta described blacks and whites, as well as Hispanics—in two different parts of the country. His welfare subjects complained that the welfare program was oppressive and controlling and described cheating and misuse of the system. They appreciated the help given, and they identified with taxpayer complaints about people who do not work to support themselves and who can become exploitive and dependent on aid.

To Auletta these diverse types share a relationship to a dysfunctional subculture from which escape is not easy. There is poverty, crime, hustling, a debased daily environment, extraordinary family instability, home violence, lack of exposure to the normal world of work, and frequent dependence on the public welfare system. Central and prevalent is the lack of adequate education or vocational skills. Although Auletta explored a variety of interpretations of the underclass phenomenon, its causes, and its cures, he found no consensus nor adopted any one answer.

What is here immediately relevant are two components of the Auletta analysis that have become part of the current public definition and perspective: (1) the notion of a deeply rooted pattern of alienation and social pathology, from which a person who is so socialized must escape in order to function successfully; and (2) some optimism that for some people in the underclass a combination of training and counseling can and does lead to breakthrough. Auletta reported a series of careful evaluations by the Manpower Demonstration Research Corporation (MDRC), which in a five-year follow-up of an ambitious training/counseling effort reported inconclusive results with ex-offenders, failure with youths who dropped out of school, positive cost-benefit ratios for ex-addicts, and the most promising impact on AFDC mothers. MDRC had concentrated on black and Hispanic women in their late 20s and early 30s who were unmarried and had children age 6 or older.

For the most part they had not completed high school, had limited or no work experience, and were long-time welfare recipients. The program stressed work skills, work habits, and social supports.

Although the successes with these "welfare mothers" were modest by any standard, they met cost-benefit criteria and suggested that a subgroup of welfare mothers could be taught self-confidence and be rescued. The widely publicized reports early in the 1980s helped prepare the way for the new thinking about work and income maintenance which we discuss subsequently. Auletta saw urgent reason for training efforts to tackle behavioral and motivational problems (and for researchers even to explore possible biological and neurological handicaps), while not ignoring that racial discrimination and economic realities often stand in the way of individual success.

Not here relevant is the urgent, probing analysis which should be made of the validity of Auletta's grouping of a diverse group of societal dropouts and failures into what he presents as a coherent analytic category—"the underclass." (Our Chapter 2 history places this classification in a long tradition of the "unhelpable.") Important is the fact that early in the Reagan administration Auletta offered new respectability to the notion of attending to cultural-attitudinal obstacles to success in an environment in which the earlier public debate simply counterposed free-market growth and social programs. He reminded society that there had to be a long-term investment in education, training, and counseling, even in the context of economic growth, that even then only some of the closed-out people would "make it." Nonetheless, some welfare mothers could be good prospects.

More visible than Auletta and Sheehan, and more recent, was the Bill Moyers TV documentary that focused on the young black welfare mother and her environment.[3] With people speaking for themselves, Moyers developed the story of a subsociety of young girls—who soon become women—who drifted into pregnancy and independent living. Theirs is a culture of limited horizons, of young men with few jobs and little opportunity, in which the responsibilities of parenting are hardly understood and precocious sexual activity is all around. Some seem to drift as well into welfare dependence, others to count on it. Some offer clearly articulated rationales, like the young woman who saw men with no prospects all around her. She would not marry: "I don't want no man holding me down." Others make it clear that they didn't want to be pregnant, but once they had conceived, they saw the baby and the apartment as a way of having their "own thing"; but several also tried to remain involved in the social activities of their school-age peers. Many appeared still to be children themselves. Not having gone very far in school and generally without abilities or skills to sell in the labor market, they are adolescents with babies to take care of, then young women with families of one or two children. The boys or young men who fathered the children, or others, often remained in the picture, sometimes also dependent on the welfare check, whether or not living in the home. Several who were interviewed on the Moyers program seemed genuinely interested in and involved with their children. A very few worked and were able to offer some support.

The Moyers analysis and focus, and the related "round table" discussions and interviews, defined the issue as the "black family in trouble." A black social worker, calling upon the adult world to affirm its outrage and to support stronger moral codes, commented, "We are destroying ourselves." Others specified needed policy measures to deal with unemployment, education, housing, and other deprivations in the black community. Developing continuity with the Moynihan warnings of the 1960s and his return to the issue of American family policy in the mid-1980s,[4] the ensuing discussions also looked at the possibility that welfare programs create undesirable opportunities and perverse incentives—and asked whether there were potentially more constructive approaches.[5]

The case stories of Sheehan and Auletta and the dramatic documentary of Moyers have had significant impact on the public at large and on the political community. New demonstration programs also have been effective. Training and work programs are now part of the conventional wisdom. Family policy, generally, and the black family are discussed frequently, and reports and proposals are coming from many quarters. National organizations, particularly in the black community, have undertaken a variety of educational campaigns and social advocacy initiatives over the past five to six years. The analysts in Congress, the executive branch, state government, and research centers also have been influenced by the important new insights systematically developed by a number of research scholars.

The Welfare Mother in Research

In a series of pioneering studies drawing on the University of Michigan's Panel Study of Income Dynamics, Bane and Ellwood have shown that spells of AFDC assistance often *begin* with divorce and separation (45 percent of cases) or birth to a previously childless unmarried woman (30 percent of cases). But there are other causes, including a decline in earnings for a female family head (12 percent of cases).[6] AFDC spells are *ended* by marriage in 35 percent of cases, increased earnings in 21 percent, and the child's leaving the home in 11 percent. The level of income from work, in short, is more important to leavers than to welfare applicants.

In 1984, AFDC eligibility was based on the presence of an incapacitated or unemployed second adult in 12.2 percent of cases. The single mothers in all the other cases were widows (1.9 percent), separated or divorced women (36.2 percent), and not married (46.4 percent).

Additional data reported from periodic federal surveys serve to fill in the incomplete picture drawn by the media and various public figures with dramatic, but not necessarily representative, reporting. For example, the national AFDC caseload is inevitably overrepresentative of minority citizens, but hardly solely minority: non-Hispanic white, 41 percent; black, 42 percent; Hispanic, 13 percent; and Asian, 2.3 percent. The mothers are mostly young (since eligibility requires the presence of young children), mainly in their 20s and 30s (under 20, 3.6 percent; 20–24, 28.6 percent; 25–29, 23.8 percent; 30–39, 27.9 percent; 40 or over, 15.7 percent.)* The "typical" AFDC mother is rearing two children, but in 1984, 44.1 percent actually had one child; 29.6 percent had two; 15.5 percent had three; and 10 percent were caring for four or more children.

A 1979 overview adds a picture of the mothers' education, but there were no reports for 47.8 percent of all AFDC mothers. Where there were data, over 5 percent had less than an 8th grade education, and 4.4 percent had completed only the 8th grade. In addition, 20.8 percent dropped out after one to three years of high school. Only 20.5 percent were high school graduates, and 2.7 percent had some college.

As surveyed in 1984, 21.6 percent of AFDC mothers had children under age 3; 21 percent had children age 3–5; 31.9 percent, age 6–11; and 25.5 percent, over age 12. Few AFDC mothers were in the labor force. Only 1.2 percent worked full-time, and 3.6 percent part-time, in contrast to the 1979 picture of 8.7 percent working full-time and 5.4 percent, part-time. (In Chapter 2 we discussed the 1981 program changes apparently implicated in this decline.) In 1984, 87.8 percent of AFDC mothers reported no income other than what AFDC provided.

The policy debate has been enriched in recent years by the

*Where a mother is absent, the age is that of the caretaker.

important research of Mary Jo Bane, David Ellwood, Greg Duncan, and others who have added a "stock and flow" analysis of AFDC cases to the descriptive picture. We have already referred to their findings about entrances and exits. Of great interest is their further finding that, whereas a majority of AFDC users are involved in relatively short-term episodes (half of the cases are open under two years), each new cohort leaves behind a subgroup, so that at any given moment the majority of users are in the midst of long (over eight years) welfare episodes. Moreover, there are significant numbers who are "recidivists" to AFDC or other assistance programs. These cases generate the heavy program costs. Put another way by Ellwood: Chronic recipients are only one-quarter of those who need to turn to AFDC, but they constitute a majority of those on the rolls and account for 60 percent of the costs.

More specifically, of those on the caseload at a given moment, 15 percent are in a one-to-two year spell, 36 percent are getting aid for three to seven years, and 49 percent for over eight years. However, to consider a family's total time on welfare, including possible multiple "spells," of a new cohort just coming on the rolls, 30 percent eventually will be on for one to two years, 40 percent for three to seven years, and 30 percent for eight or more years[7] (see Table 4–1).

Who are the long-term chronic users? Disproportionately, they are the teenage mothers and others who seek aid when young; they are uneducated; they are the never-married; and they are black. Indeed, if one looks at the young starters, the "short-spell" cases appear less important.[8] Earlier Congressional Budget Office analyses also found that the longer term cases often began with adolescent mothers.[9]

What does this suggest about the single-mother exploration? Only that the "welfare mother" designation is misleading if believed per se to provide a reliable, uniform picture of a group or if applied to all single mothers. "Welfare reform" is not a full response to the policy challenge of single mothers. On the other hand, significant numbers of single mothers do depend on public assistance, and they constitute almost the entire AFDC caseload. AFDC and its reform therefore cannot be ignored in any proposed intervention strategy, but one should not ignore the distinction recipients make between transition aid and long-term support. Also, as we have seen, the teenage mother often becomes a long-term welfare mother. However, we shall add—in the next section—that these teenagers also face some special problems and require some appropriately shaped interventions. A universal pro-

Table 4–1 Distribution of Length of AFDC Spells and Total Time on Welfare

	Length of Individual Spell					Total Time on Welfare (includes multiple spells)	
	Persons Beginning a Spell				Persons on AFDC at a Point in Time	Persons Beginning First AFDC Spell	Persons on AFDC at a Point in Time
			AFDC Case Records				
Data Source:	PSID	NLS	1965 Cohort	1975 Cohort	PSID	PSID	PSID
Duration							
1–2 yrs	48%	61%	59%	69%	15%	30%	7%
3–7 yrs	35	27	25	24	36	40	28
8 or more yrs	17	12	16	7	49	30	65

Notes: PSID = Panel Study of Income Dynamics
 NLS = National Longitudinal Survey

Sources: Weinberg, "The Economic Effects of Welfare," summarizing Ellwood, O'Neill, Michigan PSID reseach (Duncan), as well as AFDC record studies done within the Department of Health and Human Services. Full citation in Endnote 6.

gram attuned to income, work, or both, will need to consider teenagers separately, and even then such a program may not be sufficient.

Teenage Parents: A Problem of Adolescents or of Single-Parent Families?

Adolescent pregnancy and parenting has emerged as a major item on the social problem agenda in the United States only since the mid-1970s. Earlier, while the problem was hardly small, most adolescents who became pregnant out of wedlock got married; and those who did not marry had their babies but gave them up for adoption. There was concern about unwed mothers in earlier years, but not with unwed teenage mothers. The public costs of early, unmarried parenthood were modest, and the private costs were not measured. Unwed mothers were severely stigmatized in most of society, and relatively few women attempted a sustained life-style as unwed mothers.

The Phenomenon

In the 1970s, certain changes occurred that led to a very different picture and a very different expression of public concern. First, unmarried girls were more likely to be sexually active, and girls became sexually active at younger ages. In 1971, little more than a quarter of never-married women aged 15–19 reported they had engaged in sex. By the end of the decade, the proportion was 45 percent, and by the mid-1980s, more than half of young women this age were likely to be sexually active.

Second, the pregnancy rate for teenagers has continued to rise, and there is some evidence to suggest that if it were not for increased contraceptive use, both the number and rate of adolescent pregnancies would be substantially higher.

Third, despite this increase in pregnancy rates, the number and rate of out-of-wedlock births has declined since 1970, largely because of the increased rate of abortion. About 30 percent of all abortions performed in the United States are to adolescents; and about 40 percent of all teenage pregnancies are ended by abortion.

Fourth, the largest increase in fertility since 1970 has been for unmarried women, especially teenagers. More specifically, out-of-wedlock births to girls under 18 constituted more than half of all births to teenagers in the early 1980s compared with only about one third in 1970. Moreover, rates for very young teenagers, those under 15, also increased. Nonetheless, out-of-wedlock births to teenagers have decreased as a proportion of all out-of-wedlock births, from about half in 1970 to less than one-third in the mid-1980s.

Fifth, in contrast to 1970 and earlier, only a tiny minority give up their children for adoption. Fewer marry upon discovery of a pregnancy. About 95 percent of all unmarried births, including those to teenagers, result in single-parent, mother-only families.

To understand the implications of these developments, all this must be placed in the context of the cohort of adolescents. In the mid-1980s (1984), out of a cohort of about 9.2 million adolescent girls aged 15–19, there were an estimated 1.0 million pregnancies annually. Of these, almost half were voluntarily terminated. Of the approximately 470,000 births, about half (260,000) were to unwed adolescents. Thus, unmarried teenage parents constitute less than 3 percent of the whole cohort.

These teenage mothers are disproportionately black. Blacks constitute 14 percent of adolescents but account for about 45 percent of adolescent births. In 1984, 89 percent of births to black women under 20 were out of wedlock in contrast to 42 percent for white women. At the same time, however, out-of-wedlock births to white teenagers have increased dramatically since 1970s (by 62 percent), while the rates for black teenagers have decreased by 10 percent.

Thus, in contrast to earlier years when most teenage pregnancies were among 18- and 19-year-olds who often were married before or after the pregnancy, and if not, gave up their babies for adoption, most pregnant teenagers today keep their children if they have them and do not marry the fathers of their children. Almost half the pregnancies are terminated by abortion; but those that result in births lead to the formation of single-parent families (or subfamilies), usually poor.

The Problem

Adolescent pregnancy is defined as a social problem largely because of the high rate of out-of-wedlock births occurring to very young girls, the subsequent high rates of welfare dependency among women who begin their families as teenagers, the high proportion of public assistance expenditure that is spent for women who had their first child as teenagers, the generally unsatisfactory life histories reported for many, and the high probability that the children of these women will repeat their behavior.

About half of the AFDC caseload at any point in time is made up of households in which the female head had her first child as a teenager. Of all mothers under age 20, one-third receive AFDC payments in any one year. Among teenagers not married when their first child is born, three-quarters receive AFDC within four years.[10] The cost of AFDC, Medicaid, and Food Stamps in 1985 for women who had been teenage mothers is estimated at more than $16 billion.[11] Although Furstenberg[12] found that over time teenage mothers coped much better than expected, their children often end up repeating the earlier behavior of their mothers, becoming teenage parents themselves or having other problems.

There is extensive research indicating that those teenagers who become single mothers are more likely than is typical in the population to have experienced difficult pregnancies;[13] their babies are likely to be at great risk physically and developmentally; their marriages, when they occur, are more likely to result in divorce; they are more likely to experience unemployment and poverty and to end up on welfare; and they are more likely to have daughters who themselves will grow up to be teenage parents.

The burden of public expenditure may be what is driving public concern with adolescent parenting, but clearly the private costs—the poor life prospects for these mothers and their children—are substantial, also, and merit concern.

Theories about why teenage pregnancy and parenting have increased so significantly in our time abound, but no evidence unequivocally supports any of these theories. Some researchers are convinced that the behavior relates to the decline in the traditional family and traditional values, and to the increased permissiveness of society generally.[14] However, we note that other countries in which life-styles are even less traditional than those in the United States have lower rates of adolescent pregnancy. These differences have been ascribed to knowledge about, availability, and use of contraceptives.[15]

As we noted in the previous chapter, other analysts have concluded that out-of-wedlock childbirth by teens and by women generally is the direct result of the availability of AFDC and related benefits. Many researchers respond by pointing out that real welfare benefits (adjusted for inflation) have been declining since the mid-1970s, the same period that births to unmarried women were increasing. In addition, studies of the relationship between welfare benefit levels and births to unmarried women[16] show almost no correlations. If anything, the birthrates are lower in high benefit states.

Again, not specific to teens, some observers link the out-of-wedlock marriage parenting phenomenon to other aspects of social and cultural change, including changing patterns of adult sexual behavior, marriage, gender roles, and the context of adolescence in general. Here, too, the United States is not unique, yet the rates of teenage parenting particularly are far more extensive in this country. Observers cite sexual "permissiveness" and the challenge and glamorization of sex on TV and the other media and contrast all of this with the "official" and "public" call to adolescent abstinence. Can one wonder, they ask, at the high rate of adolescent sexual activity? Other countries in which adolescents are equally active sexually do not experience the same rate of adolescent fertility; again, the differences are ascribed to the greater "normalization" of contraception through easier, assured access to instruction and supplies.[17] The United States abortion rates and out-of-wedlock childbearing are both exceptionally high—an international anomaly.

Still others who have joined the discussion ascribe the patterns to a pervasive poverty problem among families with children, including the problems of limited education, high rates of youth unemployment, and a decline in the availability of marriageable employed, self-supporting minority males. Finally, there are those who would characterize all of this as part of the overall problem of adolescence in a society in transition; they see a cluster of problems as needing coherent attention, including high school dropouts, youth unemployment, and teenage substance abuse as well as teenage pregnancy. But here, some would say, the key question is why some youths experiment and then reject this behavior while others continue with it and are caught up and trapped by it.

Obviously, some of these views are not mutually inconsistent, but several do lead to different assumptions about appropriate levels for intervention. Social change has undoubtedly led to different attitudes and values regarding sexual behavior; adolescents are having a different life experience now; the reward systems do appear to be skewed; and the chronic problems of poverty, discrimination, and limited expectations do have an impact on adolescent aspirations.

There are those who define the most urgent problem as the need to attenuate the negative prospects for teenage mothers. Others insist that reducing the number of births to teenagers is the problem needing attention. Still others stress that preventing pregnancy should be the goal, and the fundamental issue is how to reduce all adolescent sexuality.

Our question here is, Can universal or broad social policies and programs for single-mother families or for families generally address the problems and needs of teenage mothers or should there also be special policies and programs for these very different young families?

The research and debate are extensive. Our review of both the knowledge available and the value trade-offs implied leads us to concur strongly with the recommendations of the recent National Academy of Science (NAS) report[18] urging that the priority for attention for this group should be on prevention. Indeed we find (Chapter 7) that adolescent childbearing is the type of single parenthood most clearly requiring prevention. However, when the teenager does nonetheless become a parent, young parenthood must become the major concern. Once a child is born and the teenager keeps the baby, then the focus must be on addressing this new family effectively as one subgroup of single-mother families. In other words, special programs may be appropriate to deal with the problems of adolescent sexuality and teenage pregnancy in the context of programs serving adolescents generally, but when that adolescent becomes a parent, the program emphasis must, inevitably, shift.

Seeking Effective Interventions

Among the various interventive strategies that have been introduced to address the problems of teen parenting, one involves encouraging the teenager to relinquish her baby for adoption. A second concentrates on helping the young mother to become a self-sufficient, responsible, and nurturing parent.

Despite the substantial proportion of teenage pregnancies and births that are unintended, teenagers who have babies have been keeping them in growing numbers in recent years, rather than relinquishing them for adoption. By 1970, 86 percent of 15–19-year-old mothers apparently kept and reared their children themselves.[19] This figure represents a major departure from the past. The availability of adoption services per se does not appear to have any effect on the rate of adolescents giving up their baby for adoption, either. About 96 percent of all unwed mothers, including teenagers, now keep their children. Whether more extensive counseling of pregnant teenagers would lead to a more realistic assessment of their—and their children's—futures, and thus to greater willingness to give their children up, is unclear. A number of groups (often motivated by opposition to abortion) are reviving both the maternity home as a facility and supportive social services to encourage such outcomes.

The NAS points out in its report that no matter how intensive the prevention efforts, childbearing among school-age adolescents will never be entirely eliminated and many (if not most) of those teenagers who do become parents will keep their babies. These young mothers are at particular risk of health problems, poverty, unemployment, and long-term economic dependence; their children are similarly at risk of physical, social, and cognitive problems and deficiencies. Teenage mothers may constitute a small proportion of the overall adolescent population and an even smaller proportion of single mothers generally, but their problems and needs, which are extensively documented, entail high public costs. They and their children also pay a high personal price.

For these very young mothers to become self-sufficient, and to become responsible and caring parents, certain "building blocks" are essential. There is widespread consensus that these include education, nutrition, health care, employment and training, child care, parenting, and income support. The alternative is another pregnancy and dependence on public welfare programs.

Some of these components already are addressed by public programs, yet their availability and efficacy are limited. Sometimes what is needed may be a reassessment of what is now provided, and just how. Sometimes the problem may be a matter of more needed funding, or more outreach and advocacy. Often the resources are just not available at all—or in a given place—even though the need for such resources has been identified. The following are some of the important programs not sufficiently available or adequately implemented.

Title IX. Title IX of the 1972 Education Amendments requires schools to serve pregnant teens and teen mothers. As a consequence, such girls now are more likely to remain in school even after their babies are born than they were earlier. The special school programs that have been established are very uneven, however. There is no consistent program pattern and no rigorous evaluations have been carried out to see what curriculum is especially successful. Indeed, it is not even clear whether available special programs in fact are the appropriate vehicle for educating these young women. Yet completing high school is absolutely essential if a young mother is to become economically independent.

WIC (The Women, Infants and Children Nutrition Program). WIC, a special federal program for nutritionally deprived babies and their mothers, has had important positive impacts on the low birth weight of teenagers' babies. Outreach efforts to serve more of those who are eligible and advocacy to assure the adequacy of these programs could be helpful.

Promoting Good Health. Promoting healthy birth outcomes and the physical well-being of young mothers and their babies is the first step. Early and regular prenatal care, appropriate medical care during delivery, and well-baby care are all essential, since teenage mothers and their babies are at special risk of developing health problems. School-based health clinics are particularly important for the teenage mother who remains in school. Alternatives are needed, however, for the teenager who is not in school. Adolescent health care generally has had limited public funding in this country. In many other countries (Canada, Australia, western and northern Europe) health and medical care has been far more available to adolescents.

Child Care. Several studies have demonstrated the importance of child care if these girls are to finish school, training, and learning how to be a mother. Many of these young mothers continue to live with their own families and draw on grandmothers or other relatives for child care; but many others do not live with their families, or have mothers who may have jobs themselves. Many of the special programs for teen parents have not provided adequate child care; and many schools with special programs for teen mothers believe that child care should not be their responsibility. Public financing for child care remains very limited.

Parental and Family Support Services. The importance of parental and family support services for young mothers has also been demonstrated. Such programs combine parenting education, monitoring, emotional backup in crises, and offering of role models. They appear under many auspices and in competing forms. Public and private backers of these programs properly stress the desirability of diversity, yet there is need for more analysis and for accumulation and evaluation of experience so as to maximize the impact of this important community resource element.

Public Assistance. Finally, of course, there is the basic issue of *income—and public assistance.* The primary income transfer program providing benefits for some young mothers is Aid to Families with Dependent Children (AFDC), or "welfare." This is the program that has recently been criticized as creating an incentive for teenagers to have babies.[20] There is no evidence that the levels of welfare benefits and acceptance rates instigate either sexual activity or pregnancy.[21] However, as we have suggested in Chapter 1, the potential availability of AFDC could in some instances be associated with whether or not a girl who is pregnant decides to abort, marry, or have a baby; AFDC may also affect the living arrangements which are made. Abortion rates are higher in states with *low* AFDC benefits; and girls in states with AFDC-UP (the

AFDC program available to two-parent families—not just mother-only families—that exists in about half the states) are *less* likely to have an out-of-wedlock birth.

Analyses of AFDC caseloads yield some hypotheses about useful program targeting. It has been noted that while the median length of time on AFDC has declined by almost 50 percent since 1965, from 18 months then to 10 months in 1980, the probability of remaining on welfare beyond two years is more than 90 percent for a woman with only eight years of schooling, who is black, lives in the South, has five children, has no work experience, was never married, and who grew up in a single-parent family.[22] Of all these variables, schooling, work experience, and number of children seem to be the most readily addressed for program impact. Since work is affected by reduced schooling, schooling and subsequent fertility seem to be especially important to address.

Illustrating Program Strategies

Two programs may serve to illustrate the major alternative strategies directed at helping teenage mothers become self-sufficient. One is a multi-service center; the second is a comprehensive service program. A third strategy involves a special focus on the young fathers, although these other programs may incorporate such elements, too.

The Door. The Door has long been known both nationally and internationally as a model program serving adolescents. It is a multi-service, community-based center for adolescents between the ages of 12 and 20 in New York City. It was first established in 1972, under voluntary auspices, to serve multi-problem youth. Funding is provided from a combination of public and private (including corporate) resources.

The program takes a holistic approach, offering services related to physical, mental and reproductive health, education, employment and vocational information and referral, and personal development. Extensive creative and recreational activities are available. A learning center, youth leadership program, drug and alcohol abuse treatment program, young parents and child health services, and psychiatric treatment are all part of the cluster of services provided at the Door. Outreach programs are provided in local junior and senior high schools, also. Although the program has been effective in increasing the use of contraceptives by sexually active teenagers, there are no data on the impact of this program on teens who are already parents.

Project Redirection (PR). PR was a national demonstration

program, funded by the Ford Foundation between 1980 and 1983
in five locations, and evaluated by the Manpower Demonstration
Research Corporation (MDRC). It has since been replicated in
seven additional sites by several foundations as well as local funding
sources.[23] The project was launched as an attack on adolescent
motherhood. The approach was to link teenage mothers and
pregnant teens "with a variety of services aimed at helping them
to complete schooling, acquire employment skills, and ultimately,
attain personal and economic self-sufficiency."[24] The target population consisted of young women under the age of 17 who were
receiving AFDC either as independent recipients or as members
of eligible families. The specific objectives were continuation of
education, delay of subsequent pregnancies, acquisition of employability and job skills, improved maternal and child health, acquisition of life management skills, and eventual reduction in welfare
dependency.

The following were the major interventive strategies of Project
Redirection.

- An Individual Participant Plan (IPP) combined a social worker
  case assessment of the teenager and her needs, with planning
  in a team conference, and reshaping and completion of the
  plan in interaction with a program component called the
  Community Woman.
- A peer support program combined instruction with mutual
  aid.
- A Community Woman component, the most innovative aspect
  of the program, attempted to provide these young girls with
  support, control, and more appropriate adult role models.

The various services that would be needed by the teenagers
were expected to be available within the community. Social worker
staff were expected to link these services together as needed, and
to "broker" them for their young clients. Where needed services
were not available, the concept was that the program could develop
and provide them.

The programs were implemented, and by and large the girls did
participate. There was no clear-cut "model," in that the programs
operated differently at the different sites. The final impact analysis,
however, suggests its limitations. As the MDRC final report states:
"The underlying question to which an answer was sought was
whether these teens' lives were improved after enrolling in the
program relative to what their lives would have been like had
Project Redirection never existed. The question that many readers
may well be asking is whether teen parent programs in general are

a worthwhile social investment. *Unfortunately, neither question can be answered unambiguously.*"[25]

There were some modest impacts on those most deprived at the onset—those who were school dropouts, those who lived in AFDC households, and those who had a pregnancy after enrollment. Overall, the results were not overly encouraging. Only one-fourth had earned diplomas, nearly one-half had second and third children. There is some feeling that the expectations from a two-year program were too high and that there was need to continue the program—and the services to these youngsters—longer.

A recent evaluation of comprehensive service programs directed at adolescent pregnancy and parenting suggests an important caution regarding these programs:[26]

> *No program . . . offered an all-inclusive range of services. The program that had the best child care facilities, for example, was unable to offer vocational education, while the program that did the best at vocational training served almost exclusively already-delivered mothers . . . but had no day care center. None of the programs initiated services prior to pregnancy. Few followed the participants more than briefly after delivery, although that is when the most severe crisis for young mothers generally begins. Even the very best programs reached only a limited proportion of those potentially in need of services. . . . The programmatic reality, in other words, fell far short of the ideal conveyed by the term comprehensive. . . .*
>
> *The many existing programs that provide supportive services to pregnant and parenting teenagers do help. That they are able to serve only a part of the population in need, and to accomplish only some of their goals, reflects, we believe, on the dearth of resources available to them and on their hostile environment. Were programs able to extend their services well beyond delivery—that is, to view pregnancy not as a short-term crisis, but as a transition to a new phase of a girl's life, a phase when she will need more support than ever—they might have greater success at achieving long-term goals. And were prevention to be given a higher priority, the help of service programs would be less necessary.*

Programs for Teenage Fathers. A much neglected focus thus far has been on the males who father children with teenage girls. There is evidence from several studies of more actual and potential involvement than generally believed. The National Urban League and Bank Street College have programs with this orientation, and several other programs have recently been established to concentrate on teenage fathers. None has received any systematic evaluation as yet. One promising strategy studied by Esther Wattenberg involves the formal establishment of paternity and helping girls get assurance of future child support when the fathers will have or do obtain a regular job.[27]

Present Limitations of Comprehensive Program. To sum up on the program side, there are no validated exemplary models. Most so-called comprehensive programs identify the need for educational services to allow young mothers to complete schooling, health services for mother and child, job training and employment services, parent education and training services to help these girls learn how to parent, and child care services so that mothers can finish schooling, enter training, take jobs—all of which are supposed to give them and their children better opportunities for development. Increasingly, even housing is being mentioned.

The comprehensive services programs note that while these services are essential, most are dependent on linkage mechanisms (especially case management) to assure access and service coordination for the young mother. But, and this is the core point, comprehensive programs can be effective—and linkage mechanisms work—*only* if service programs in fact are in place in a community. At a time of federal cutbacks in social programs, resources that have always been limited are now even more so. When the services do not exist or are in short supply, they cannot be provided. When that happens, one or another problem occurs: the program is not implemented or it is implemented inadequately. The girls drop out or become pregnant once again. Ultimately, these young single mothers are faced with the whole cluster of problems related to their poverty and exacerbated by their youth, immaturity, and limited personal resources. Adolescent parenting is not a short-term problem that can be "cured" with a brief "treatment"; it is a long-term, if not permanent, condition, and at best any intervention must be designed with a long-term perspective.

In brief, while a consensus exists for *comprehensive* strategies, comprehensiveness probably means access to a far richer structure of community programs and benefits than now prevails. Such programs and benefits, as developed, we shall argue, probably need to respond not only to adolescents but also to all single mothers in some respects and, as we have already suggested in the previous chapter, to all families with children. They must be part of larger social policy. The special programs for schoolgirls and schoolboys who have babies will still be needed, however, and their program focus as well as their quality need continuing attention—that is, we need a universal (not income-tested) general public response to families with young children, a response to single mothers, and a response to teen mothers. It will be useful to consider these distinctions further as we proceed.

Public and Private (Personal) Costs

Thus far our focus has been on modifying the behavior of adolescents to make them more effective adults and parents and to improve their life prospects. One might predict—although one would at the moment be hard-pressed to prove—that success along these lines would increase family stability, improve socialization and development of children, and maximize the likelihood that the parents of *their* children would be self-supporting. For those skeptical about such outcomes or concerned with immediate public costs, research suggests that the greatest impact on public expenditures (AFDC, food stamps, Medicaid) for teenage pregnancy and parenting would result from reducing teenage fertility. Eliminating all births to unmarried women under 18 would lead to an estimated savings of 17 percent in these programs. Reducing teenage fertility by 50 percent would lead to a 14 percent saving. Reducing subsequent childbearing would result in an 11 percent saving. In contrast, reducing school dropouts has a disturbingly low payoff—only 2 percent savings on public expenditures according to Sandra Hofferth, a leading expert in the field.

There is some evidence that teenage parents are beginning to exercise greater control over their fertility. It is reported that teen mothers have resorted to sterilization in unprecedented numbers once they reach their early and mid-teen years. This conclusion is in the context of the tremendous increase in the use of sterilization as a contraceptive measure generally. If this is a new trend, it could be very important, because the previous pattern was for teen mothers to have more children, closer together. More than 80 percent of the difference in poverty status between teen mothers and other mothers is accounted for by larger family size. Each year a birth is delayed, family income rises about $500—another reason for attempting to delay sexual activity, or to avoid or postpone pregnancy.

Sterilization, however, is and must remain a voluntary measure. Historically, sterilization has been a measure associated with efforts to eliminate groups that were described as "inferior" so as to justify the maltreatment. One need merely recall campaigns to sterilize the retarded and some black welfare mothers in the South as late as the 1960s.[28]

A simpler, more immediate, and rational way to achieve lower birthrates is to do what most other advanced, industrialized countries do—that is, improve sex education and ensure the availability of contraceptives to teenagers after properly educating them as to their use. The special review by a National Academy of Science–National Research Council has made the case.[29] The European contrasts are instructive. The strategy could decrease both unwanted fertility and abortion. The adoption of such a strategy need not stand in the way of religious groups, parents, and others in the society who wish to promote the case for voluntary abstinence and other behavior consonant with their fundamental values.

Teen parenting is the problem of poor single mothers generally, exacerbated by youth, immaturity, and lack of familial and personal resources. A foundation of good social policy is essential if any age or problem-specific intervention is to be effective. As we shall note in a later chapter, teenage mothers could be required to complete high school as a condition of receiving their AFDC grant; they could be required to live with their own parents, unless circumstances suggest that would be inadvisable. We have suggested that they could be provided with case managers to help them "broker" existing service resources. But ultimately, if an adequate social infrastructure does not exist to assure them access to health care, child care, parent and family life education, training programs, jobs, and so forth, then, we are convinced, only limited success will result from the miscellany of special programs, no matter how dedicated their staffs and supporters.

Single Mothers by Choice

In the mid-1980s a "new" type of single mother family caught the fancy of the media: "Single mothers by choice." The unwed mothers, in this case, are not the immature and/or impulsive adolescents just discussed—some of whom are victims while others may have exercised "choice" of sorts, but rather mature and responsible single women in their 30s (see Table 4–2). They are not high school dropouts—unskilled, untrained, and unemployed—dependent on their families or on public assistance for economic support. Instead, they are largely middle class, well-educated working women, more often white than black or Hispanic, and frequently professionals or executives. "Choice" in this case refers to women who decide after extensive deliberation, and for a variety of reasons, to bear children despite the absence of a husband. By far, the baby they have usually is their first child; often it becomes their only child.

Merritt and Steiner begin their book about these older single

Table 4–2   Nonmarital Births by Age of Mother (30 +) and Race, for 1970,
1980, 1984

		Age of Mother		
Year	Race	30–34	35–39	40–44
Rate per 1,000 unmarried women in specified group				
1970	All	27.0	13.3	3.6
	White	14.2	4.4	
	Black + others	69.9	21.6	
1980	All	21.1	9.7	2.6
	White	13.6	6.8	1.8
	Black	48.2	19.6	5.6
1984	All	23.2	10.9	2.5
	White	16.1	8.0	1.9
	Black	45.0	20.3	4.5
Rate Per 1,000 Live Births, Unmarried Women Aged 30–34				
1980	All	74.5	93.7	120.5
	White	44.8	62.5	84.7
	Black	291.5	280.8	293.0
1984	All	90.0	106.8	137.8
	White	56.3	74.7	104.0
	Black	344.8	329.2	329.2

Percent Having Nonmarital Births

Women Aged 30 +	*1970*	*1975*	*1984*
Total	4.8	5.8	9.5
White	2.4	3.0	6.2
Black	19.2	24.0	34.1

Source: Data supplied by Martin O'Connell, Chief, Fertility Statistics Branch, U.S. Bureau
of the Census.

mothers, *And Baby Makes Two*, by describing a new and significant
social phenomenon, stating that in 1978 more than 40,000 babies
were born to single women in their 30s.[30] In fact, by 1980 the
numbers of single women age 30 and older, having out-of-wedlock
births, had increased to 59,000, and by 1984 to more than 84,000!
More than half of these nonmarital births were to white women,
but the rate is much higher for blacks, nonetheless. In 1984 more
than 11 percent of women in their 30s, including 45,000 (8 percent)
white women and 35,000 (34 percent) blacks, had their children
out of wedlock.

Every year during the 1980s more and more single women in or
approaching their 30s begin to consider a future without a husband
and with their "biological time clock" ticking away. Economically—and often psychologically—independent in a way their
mothers never were, a growing number are unwilling to relinquish
the idea of having and rearing children, even if it means doing so

outside of marriage. They decide to "go it alone," and have a baby, their first, on their own. How numerically significant or permanent this phenomenon will eventually turn out to be remains to be seen.

Why are these women having children alone? Do these families constitute a distinctive type of single-parent family? Should these families be considered a "social problem"? Should they be a target for social policy? We address some of these questions in what follows.

Why the Choice?

The Marriage Squeeze. In 1986, the report of a modest study analyzing census data and projecting marital and fertility patterns captured the attention of the media—newspapers, magazines, and television. The authors became instant celebrities when several news services picked up the story and made it their cover story.[31] Subsequently, a census bureau demographer debated their findings, insisting that their estimates were incorrect; the debate still continues.

The major research finding about which there is consensus is the declining probability of marriage for never-married women aged 30 and older; the debate is only over whether the specific projected very low probability of marriage for such women is accurate or too low. Resolving the debate is not our issue. Our concern is with the response by American women to a projected future that many clearly already have sensed, and some have feared.

Later Marriage. Deferring marriage in order to complete an education and, perhaps, become established in a career has been a new, much discussed trend for women over the past decade. Throughout the 1980s, the median age at first marriage for women, now almost 24, has been higher than ever before recorded, and it is still rising. By 1985, the proportion of women in their early 20s who had not yet married was larger than ever recorded (59 percent of those 20–24), while the proportion of never-married women in their late 20s and early 30s was at a level near the previous high recorded around the turn of the century. The proportion of women aged 25–29 who had never married almost tripled between 1970 and 1986, from 10.5 to 28.1 percent, while the proportion among those aged 30–34 rose by 130 percent, from 6.2 to 14.2 percent.

Increased Infertility and Childlessness. Closely linked to this delay in marrying is an apparent increase in fertility problems of married couples, and an increase in childlessness, generally.[32]

Thus, although the percentage of women aged 18–44 who are childless has remained about 37 to 38 percent since 1980, age-specific rates have begun to suggest a significant change. Between 1976 and 1985, childlessness increased from 31 to 42 percent for the cohort aged 25–29 and from 16 to 26 percent for those aged 30–34. In effect, marriage rates are declining for never-married women over age 30; age at first marriage is getting later; problems of infertility are rising; and childlessness is increasing, especially for women in the age groups over 25.

Changing Social Attitudes. In the 1970s, the articles on the subject of single parenting as a deliberate choice were relatively few in number and still reflected the stigma that was long attached to unwed motherhood. Thus, for example, there were such articles as "In Trouble: The Story of an Unmarried Woman's Decision to Keep her Child,"[33] and "Confessions of a Single Mother."[34] In the 1980s, the titles changed; for example,

- "Parents without Partners—By Their Own Choice."[35]
- "One Hand to Hold."[36]
- "Why I Became a Single Mother."[37]
- "Mommy Only: The Rise of the Middle Class Unwed Mother."[38]
- "A Report on the Rigors and Rewards of Unmarried Mothers."[39]
- "Having Babies without Husbands."[40]
- "The New Choice: Single Motherhood after 30."[41]

Surveys carried out by two major women's magazines in late 1985[42] reported extraordinarily high rates of support for "going it alone" as a single mother from among their readership of well-educated female professionals and executives. Seventy percent of the respondents to one survey said they would consider having a child alone (Exhibit 4–1), while 40 percent of the nonmarried women respondents in a second survey said they were currently considering doing so. Most said that if they decided to parent alone, they would turn to the man with whom they were currently involved, but 13 to 27 percent, depending on the survey, said they would use artificial insemination. Moreover, one-fifth of all married respondents to the *Working Woman* survey had given birth out of wedlock, already. Interestingly, although most of the women received no financial support whatsoever from the biological father, more said they received some support from the fathers than do divorced and separated women generally, but the financial support is very modest at best.

What does all this mean? Why does it matter? One thing that

1. Do you approve of single women choosing to have children?

77 percent say yes

"If a woman is emotionally and financially secure and is realistic about being a single mother, it can be a wonderfully satisfying experience. The chance of that child growing up with stability and confidence is greater than for most children, if only because that child is so wanted. Two parents do not necessarily make a perfect household."

22 percent say no

"Children have enough difficulty growing up in today's complex world. Deliberately giving a child only one parent from the outset is simply selfish and irresponsible."

1 percent don't know

2. Do you approve of single women adopting children?

82 percent say yes

"I think that adoption should be a choice open to single women, since many older children are available. I don't feel that this would harm the child any more than living in an orphanage would, and it would give a single woman the chance to have a family without being tied down with an infant."

16 percent say no

"There are far more couples wanting to adopt than there are children available. These couples should be higher on adoption waiting lists than single people."

2 percent don't know

3. Is a single woman's support group of friends and relatives an acceptable substitute for the traditional nuclear family?

71 percent say yes

"My baby son is five days old. I'm single and living with my parents until I finish college. My family is very supportive and, although they aren't equal to a father's role, they are a great substitute."

29 percent say no

"My sister had a baby as a single woman. She was, as are most new mothers, unprepared for the strains of motherhood. Unlike many married mothers, however, she had no husband to turn to, and her 'supportive' friends eventually grew disenchanted with helping out. She is now wading through the tangle of day-care options and is exhausted and resentful. She often feels trapped."

4. Do you think raising a child without a father is psychologically damaging to a child?

62 percent say no

"I am the single mother of a thirteen-month-old son. He is loved by many people and has a lot of male role models. His father has chosen to live out of state and out of our lives. He would only have been a negative influence on my son. I hope I will marry some day, but only for love, not 'respectability.' My son is the best part of my life."

24 percent say yes

"I think children need a father and a mother in the home to honestly feel secure. Children are not pets."

"I am single and have a child and think it has a very negative emotional impact on him because I am raising him on my own."

14 percent don't know

5. Would you consider having a child alone?

70 percent say yes

"I am twenty-nine and single and I've made a conscious decision to have a child within the next three years, even if I am single. I feel strongly that although I haven't yet met the man I want to live with, I should not be denied the joys of having a child."

30 percent say no

"Women should have a choice. My choice would be marriage and then parenthood."

6. If yes, by what method?

69 percent say impregnation by a lover

31 percent say adoption

27 percent say artificial insemination

27 percent say impregnation by a friend

7. What income do you think is required for a single woman to have a baby?

44 percent say $20,000 to $30,000

"I don't think a single woman should conceive a child knowing that she can't support it and that she will have to rely on the state or the father for financial support."

30 percent say $30,000 or higher

"I think a single woman needs an income of at least $50,000 to raise a baby well. One needs high-quality child care plus household help to give the mother time to spend with her child. Also, it's unfair to bring a child into the world without planning to put her through college."

22 percent say $10,000 to $20,000

"I believe it is extremely difficult to raise a child on less than $10,000 a year, but that is not to say that poor women should not be allowed to have children."

1 percent say $5,000 to $10,000

1 percent say they'd seek public assistance

2 percent did not reply

Exhibit 4–1 Glamour Magazine Survey, "Having a Child Alone."

When asked if they approved of single women choosing to have children, 77 percent of the respondents answered affirmatively. An even higher 82 percent approved of adoption by single women, and a full 70 percent would consider having a child alone. Of those who would consider single motherhood, more than two-thirds said they would want to become pregnant by a lover, and slightly less than one-third would choose to adopt. (Source: Courtesy *Glamour*. Copyright © 1986 by The Conde Nast Publications, Inc.)

seems to be happening is that some unmarried women are looking ahead at about age 30 and deciding that they are unlikely to find the husband they want. Of these, some decide they want to have a child, nonetheless, and some even may find themselves questioning whether a husband is essential for child rearing, given the high probability of divorce. Some of these women then decide to go ahead and have a baby, either with a man with whom they are currently involved, or with a male friend, whom they like but with whom they have no current sexual involvement; some elect artificial insemination.

In 1984, childbearing by unmarried women reached the highest levels since 1940 when national statistics were first collected on the subject. More than one out of every five births was to an unmarried mother, but this total goes beyond the circumstances we are describing. The rapid rise in the number of births to unmarried women during a period when total births have increased only slightly reflects large increases in two measures that determine the number of out-of-wedlock births: the number of unmarried women of childbearing age; and the birthrate for unmarried women. Between 1980 and 1984, the number of unmarried women increased by 9 percent and the birth rate by 5 percent; at the same time, the total number of women in the childbearing age increased by only 6 percent, and the overall fertility rate declined by 4 percent. The growth in the population of unmarried women outpaced that of all women because of the growing tendency to delay marriage as well as the increasing number of divorces. For example, in 1974, about one in seven women aged 30–34 was unmarried, while in 1984 the proportion had increased to one in four.

The increased number of unmarried women at relatively older ages, along with the rising rates of nonmarital childbearing among these women, has led to a considerable increase in the total number of births. Of particular interest, unmarried post-teenage women account for all of the increase in the number of nonmarital births since 1980. These women also account for a growing percentage of all out-of-wedlock births—65 percent in 1984 as compared with 59 percent in 1980.[43] Unmarried women in their 20s may constitute the majority of women having out-of-wedlock babies (54 percent), and those under 20, the next largest group (35 percent); nonetheless, women age 30 and over constitute a significant percentage (11 percent) of all nonmarried births in 1984, and the rate of growth since 1980 (22 percent, up from 9 percent) may well be the most significant new development.

Anecdotal Insights

Thus far, there is no systematic research on who these women are, why they make their choices, and with what consequences. Books,[44] like the articles listed above, are either journalistic accounts of individual cases or small, unsystematic samples. Yet they provide a preliminary picture of the kinds of women who make this choice. As Merritt and Steiner say in their 1985 article, "To become a parent under any circumstances is to undertake an enormous commitment. Raising a child consumes extraordinary amounts of time, love, patience, and money. And once you've become a parent, there's no turning back. So what are the factors that lead a woman to make this big decision?"[45]

Jane L. could be described as a representative case. In her mid-30s and successful in her career, she felt that the time had come to switch her attention to home and family. She wanted a child and was afraid that if she waited until she got married it would be too late. The fact that there was no man around with whom she wanted to start a family didn't deter her. She began to talk to the single parents she knew, and to go to meetings where they would be in order to get a feel for the life-style. She found it acceptable but continued to worry about the potential stigma attached to an out-of-wedlock pregnancy and childbirth. She was concerned about the consequences for her career, her relationships with her family and friends, and with the effects on a child. She explored adoption but decided she wanted her own child if she could have it. On her 39th birthday she faced the fact that either she was to go ahead and have a baby or it would be too late; everyone else and everything else would adjust. She rationalized her decision where the child was concerned by convincing herself that if she were married, the odds were high that there could be a divorce, and by having a child alone she was sparing it the painful experience of living through a divorce. Once having decided to go ahead with her decision, she was spared the difficulties many other women have in becoming pregnant. She spoke with a man whom she had known for some years and liked as a friend, but not as a husband or as a lover. He agreed to be the biological father, and indeed continues to see his daughter despite Jane's insistence that he has no ongoing obligations.

In the summer of 1987, the media reported a public controversy following the announcement of Liz Walker, an evening news anchor for WBZ-TV in Boston, that she was unmarried and deliberately pregnant because she was in her 30s and had decided it was time to start a family.[46] Declining to state whether the preg-

nancy was planned, Ms. Walker said that it was a purely personal
matter but that she had made the announcement before the
pregnancy became visible and questions were raised. She commented: "I'm 36. I finished my education. I've been working for
the last 15 years. I've had to work hard to get where I am." Walker,
who is black, was castigated by some reporters and columnists as
being among those who "thumb their noses at the old social and
moral conventions." However, the director of the Big Sister, where
Ms. Walker serves on the advisory board, refused to repudiate her
as a role model for young girls. He said: "Our agency deals with
girls and women and the choices that women make with as much
awareness as possible of the options and the consequences. . . .
She has made a difficult choice." Officials at Liz Walker's TV
station offered full support and shrugged off the criticism. The
mail was 90:10 in her favor.

A few months later, a Jewish family weekly addressed to the
middle class devoted three pages to a series of case stories, all
telling sympathetically of women who had "begun to feel the
pressure of the biological clock and saw no marriage partner in
sight," therefore being "forced into unilateral action."[47] The
women described were all independent, educated, and in good
economic circumstances. Some were artificially inseminated, others unintentionally pregnant by men they would not or could not
marry. The paper noted that these mothers could face family and
community problems, but that the children were not illegitimate
under Jewish law unless the union was forbidden (a married woman
with a man other than her husband, for example). But social
acceptability was seen as not yet forthcoming. If the numbers were
to continue growing, community religious institutions and other
organizations would need to develop an "understanding" about
"this new type of Jewish family."

Strategies for Support

Single Mothers by Choice (SMC) is a national group founded in
New York City in 1981 to provide information and support for
single mothers and single women considering motherhood. The
information provided includes lists of fertility specialists and adoption resources, and names of sperm banks and of supportive
physicians. Both information and support are provided through
workshops held several times each year for women considering
single parenthood. Support groups for pregnant single women and
those with new babies are a major part of the organization's
ongoing activities.

A single mother by choice is defined by this group as "a woman who decided to have or adopt a child, knowing she would be her child's sole parent, at least at the outset." The organization's brochure states: "Although we believe that single motherhood is a viable option, we are not an advocacy group and feel that the choice to become a parent is a most individual one."

The membership is described as, typically, career women in their 30s and 40s, "up against their biological clocks," facing the fact that they can no longer wait for marriage before starting families. Some became pregnant accidentally and discovered they were delighted at the prospect of having a baby. Some intentionally conceived with a man. Others went to a doctor for artificial insemination or found a child to adopt. Most say they would have preferred to have brought a child into a good marriage. However, as many point out, while women have a lifetime to marry, nature is not so generous in allotting childbearing years. According to SMC, single motherhood is ideally for the woman who feels she has much to give to a child and has adequate emotional and financial resources to support herself and her child.

Jane Mattes, the director of SMC, is herself a single mother and a trained and practicing psychotherapist. She started the organization when her son was 6 months old, thinking that it would be helpful to know a group of women who were having the same experience. She announced the formation of such a group and eight gathered at the first meeting. A few were pregnant, a few had babies, and a few were thinking of getting pregnant.

The original and continuing purpose of SMC is that of emotional and social support for its members. Single mothers tend to be very independent, self-reliant women, according to Mattes. Nonetheless, she stresses that the most important thing for many single mothers to learn is that they must be prepared to get help and support because it is impossible to manage alone, all the time. And that is what the organization provides—access to a support system for those who do not have their own supportive family and network nearby. A secondary purpose of the organization is to provide a common group experience for the children.

The New York group has a membership of about 400, and the national organization, about 1,000. However, local organizations spin off from the New York organization once they get started, and there is no expectation of continued membership in the New York group. A Los Angeles group which was started earlier has primarily a lesbian membership. There are local organizations in every state, Canada, and even some European countries now.

Group members are "thirtyish," well educated, and professional. About 20 percent are therapists; the others are academics, teachers, lawyers, executives. Average income is described as "upper-middle class," with a few women earning over $100,000. Half of the women had been previously married and divorced.

Over the more than six years of the organization's life, there have been significant changes in how this new family form is viewed. Dealing with stigma, which was a major concern initially, is no longer included on the agenda of discussion items; women no longer see this as a problem. Similarly, family support has also become easier; few women report serious problems with their families any more, certainly not beyond the first announcement about being pregnant and deciding to have the baby. The one ongoing concern reported is the absence of a "backup" person in an emergency, and the fear of a "crisis" when the mother is sick or the child is sick. SMC deliberately set out to provide a way for women to develop an informal support network that continues after formal membership ends; and most women tend to drift away from the organization within a few years after they become new mothers. The organizational role seems to be most effective during the decision-making process and pregnancy, as well as right after childbirth.

The decision-making process is often a very long one. Many of the members are described as "working on the decision for as long as ten years." They are described as "deliberate, not impulsive." Many have bought houses, changed careers, and put money away in preparation for parenthood. Women who have not been motivated to do this kind of planning are often helped to realize that becoming a single mother may not be the right choice for them.

Personal Choice or Social Problem?

Clearly, a small but growing group of women are deciding to have a child on their own, making the decision in a relatively considered and deliberate fashion, and managing successfully, albeit often with difficulty. Most view this as a personal and individual choice, made not as a political statement but because this is the only way they can have a child. Others in society may view this as a selfish decision, but these women would respond that to some extent all decisions about becoming a parent are selfish. Most acknowledge that theirs is not a route for many and that it is not a decision to be made casually. Most acknowledge that the choice is not "single parenting *or* marriage and parenting"; if that were the choice, for most there would be no issue. Rather it is "parenting alone or not at all." As Renvoize states: "It will be 20 years or more before we can properly evaluate the wisdom of the women who have decided that they do not need a man in their lives to allow them to 'fulfil their lives' and have a child."[48] In reading their stories and hearing individuals speak, one concludes that none find their decision easy but most seem to have no doubt they would do it again if offered the chance. They have the problems of all single mothers, and note that both the economic and emotional responsibility of parenting alone is often a heavy burden, but most consider themselves as better off than many other families in the general population.

Many people will continue to regard parenting alone by choice as a rejection of accepted morality. There also are those who claim that it is not proper deliberately to create one-parent families and to expose children to the experience. Separation and divorce are perhaps unavoidable or even desirable, but why this, which is avoidable? We are not certain that children are victimized if mature, well-established women decide to undertake single parenting, hardly a rare phenomenon. We see these women as basically independent and self-sufficient in their parenting, and as responsible, caring, and nurturing mothers. The problems they describe are not problems of inadequate parenting but rather of inadequate help. The help they seek—child care, help when a child is ill, more sensitivity to parenting at the workplace, occasional personal help and support—are the concerns of any working mother, exacerbated only because these are single parents raising children alone. Whether this type of single-parent family will continue—and grow—remains to be seen; those who choose their life-style make the choice in full knowledge that it will not be easy. They appear very much attuned to the well-being of their wanted children. Society could, nonetheless, help by including them among the families for whom institutions seek to be more responsive. They do not require anti-poverty programs or special categorical aid but would be positively affected by elements of Options 3 and 4—as adapted to the United States.

Displaced Homemakers (DHs)

The term, "displaced homemakers" was invented in the 1970s and conjures up both a status and a cause. Its leaders favor the intertwining. The advantages of the "discovery" and efforts to organize and respond to "displaced homemakers" (DH) are apparent and substantial. Nonetheless, the long-time usefulness of the category may not be as clear.

In 1977, testifying before a hearing of a subcommittee of the

Select Committee on Aging, then California representative Yvonne Brathwaite Burke stated:

> *First, the displaced homemaker should be defined. A displaced homemaker is usually a women between 35 and 64. She is the person who falls between the cracks of our income security program. She has spent her life working in her home, raising her children. She may be from any economic background. She may be a person who has never had a job or she may be a professional woman who has decided to stay home to take care of her children. She is financially dependent upon a breadwinner and suddenly, either as a result of divorce or widowhood, she loses her means of support. She is then unemployed and often has no financial resources to fall back on. . . .*
>
> *To a great extent the displaced homemaker is a phenomenon of a modern society. In the past, if a woman became divorced or widowed, her family would take her in. Today strained finances and the lack of large homes make it very difficult to take another person into a household, so what at one time was a family problem, is now becoming a societal problem. . . .*
>
> *The displaced homemaker cannot turn to the usual sources of financial assistance. She does not have unemployment compensation. She is usually not eligible for social security, unless she has been married for over 20 years before she is divorced.* Unless she is disabled or has young children, she is not eligible for a Federal welfare assistance program. In fact, she may not even have health insurance because she loses her husband's rights to health insurance. . . .*[49]

The initiators of the "movement," Tish Sommers and Laurie Shields, began as part of the NOW (National Organization of Women) Task Force on Older Women. Working in the mid-1970s on California's legislation to fund a pilot center for job training, referral, and job creation for the 40–64 age group in Alameda County, they were attracted to the DH name suggested by one of their leaders. The intended imagery was of refugees, "displaced persons." "Displaced," they were reminded, means "forcibly exiled and that's precisely what these women are."[50]

The Shields' volume, with an "epilogue" by Sommers, tells the story of an effort by feminist activists who were "older women" to advocate on behalf of themselves—and the successful campaign to turn their achievements into service programs that could be funded, largely by government. Consciousness-raising moved on to social action, successful legislative lobbying to careers (and the creation of new leadership) in the centers, and related programs.

---

*Note: This is now 10 years.

One might add two items of relevant context: First, women were streaming into the labor market in the 1970s despite obstacles, discrimination, and personal handicaps. The DH movement was a special effort at creating help for one important subgroup. And second, this was the era of militant feminism in a time that many interest-group movements were being organized by disadvantaged groups. The DH banner attracted women whose personal experiences testified to the unfairness of many current institutional arrangements.

On the consciousness-raising side, the major writing is rich in moving anecdotes of depressed and despondent widows, deserted and divorced women, or wives of disabled spouses who saw ahead a tunnel with no light, until their encounters with the "cause"— especially during the brief period between the first California law in 1975 and the inclusion of DH as an eligible CETA (Comprehensive Employment Training Act) category in 1978. By then, more than half the states had passed some laws, largely to finance "centers" or placement programs or to implement federally funded efforts.

These widows and divorced women, long deemed too old to reenter the labor market and lacking access to Aid to Families with Dependent Children (they had no young children) or alimony (those covered by court awards are a minority), faced major economic risks. Some had social insurance as widows—and many did not. They often could not collect on ex-spouse pensions. Major medical problems could precipitate a personal crisis. In the first stage a small group rallied. Consciousness-raising and sharing created morale. Achievements in California and Maryland engendered confidence. By 1978 they had enough backers and endorsers to achieve a significant yet modest victory: the recognition of the DH as one of a number of categories of disadvantaged workers who could partake in CETA. They did not win the special, separate program they had hoped for. Nor could they get the federal law to define the DH as "over 35/40 years of age" (they feared that the limited program would be swamped by young welfare mothers and wanted a section designated for older women).

Yet it was an important victory. This "older" women's lobby gained visibility and a sense of some power. They were part of the second wave of social activism, joining ethnic, social, and various types of handicapped advocates in seeking both legislative recognition and some type of specialized services. Their achievements did not match the civil rights campaigns of the 1950s and 1960s, or the welfare rights effort of the late 1960s and early 1970s, but they built upon these and were significant. On the basis of their modest victories of the late 1970s, sometimes in coalition and at other times alone, the DH groups have continued and, in fact, have grown substantially in the years of lean Reagan administration social budgets.

Who Are DHs? What Is the Program?

In contrast to our discussion of teenage motherhood, we cannot summarize sophisticated literature reviews, research, searches for "causes," and prevention. Indeed, such activity could be in some ways questionable.

Early in the campaigns, when asked for numbers, advocates estimated 3 to 6 million DHs (presumably drawing upon data on divorce, widowhood, alimony, and single parenthood). Later, with a charge to allocate its funds among its regions, the Department of Labor called upon a special census panel study, *Survey of Income and Education,* to look at marital status, labor force participation, and income. An estimated 4 million DHs were identified, of whom 3 million were between ages 40 and 64.[51] This group, of course, is not much smaller than the total of single parents on the AFDC rolls, but the latter achieve their eligibility for aid because they are rearing young children. In mid-1987, the Displaced Homemakers Network issued a new analysis, based on tabulation from the 1980 census. Now a claim was made of 11.5 million displaced homemakers, but this included women who were both younger and older than those usually cited. Those in the "prime working years, 35–64" were said to be 32 percent of the group, or about 3.7 million, not really changing the picture. About 43 percent of those were widowed, and most of the others were separated and divorced.[52]

Since the concept was invented for advocacy purposes, it should not be pressed into precision. The DHs, as described in newsletters, testimony, and the writings of the leadership, are (in our phrasing) widows; divorced, separated, and deserted women; the wives of handicapped spouses; and not young (the ages 35–64 are usually mentioned). They have devoted years to rearing children, homemaking, helping their spouses in careers and business—without time, opportunity, need, or apparent intent to obtain a specific career, job-related training, or education. Then, following the trauma of the event that leaves them on their own, they face financial and resource crises and are personally "lost." DH programs and activity seek to foster their self-confidence, purpose, and direction and to lead them in the direction of solutions to their respective financial problems.

In some ways these are subcategories without boundaries: not *all* widows, divorced, and separated women, not *all* former home-makers, and so forth are displaced homemakers. It would take a well-focused special data collection effort to get an exact count—depending as it does on some self-evaluation and self-identifica-tion. For present purposes, California's legislative language ex-presses the perspective and analysis of those who self-identify as DHs and work in the field: A DH is an individual

> . . . *over 35 years of age; [who] has worked without pay as a homemaker for his or her family, is not gainfully employed, has had or would have difficulty finding employment, has depended on the income of a family member and has lost that income, or has depended on government assistance as the parent of dependent children but who is no longer eligible. . . .*[53]

The activity has yielded program resources. The NOW task force on older women created an Alliance for Displaced Homemakers to lobby for state and federal action. Success was followed by the establishment of the present leadership group, the Displaced Homemakers Network, which has both individual and organiza-tional members. By now, various federal and state job placement and training programs, state women's programs, and various other offshoots from state departments of labor, human services, educa-tion, and equal opportunity have created a large national network of programs.[54] At the heart of it all are what are called "displaced homemaker programs." The 1987 network *Program Directory* lists 900 such programs. These are not all "buildings" or free-standing programs. Many are specialized services or service units or schools and junior colleges, YWCAs, various federally funded work and training programs, and community action agencies. Some are free-standing and also have social service and foundation program funds or affiliations. Others are part of the outreach of state commissions on the status of women.

There is no systematic data collection, and available overviews are anecdotal, since the DH is not per se the target of any one specialized federal program. States and localities have channeled, assigned, and garnered funds from various federal programs, and there has been a modest amount of state money for these pro-grams, too: adult education, career counseling, job training, voca-tional education, the Older Americans Act. This is the core. To this are added various special projects that cover consciousness-raising, re-socialization, personal counseling, and the rest. The environ-ment of many of these programs features advocacy related to the programs on which they depend. They are, in fact, a provider lobby, created by the funding—as are many such social service lobbies in fields in which public programs are implemented through the nonprofit sector.

The ten regions into which the network is organized are represented on the board and constitute an important, well-knit group, both for advocacy and for sharing of program experience. Indeed, the major current activity as we write is the creation, with funding by the Women's Bureau of the U.S. Department of Labor, of a "resource bank." The national network has contacted all 900 programs and requested that they complete forms describing their "areas of expertise." The purpose is to "assist local program operators in obtaining information on practically any program issues from other local programs. . . ."

This, then, is the spirit of the endeavor, not a standardized program centrally funded; rather, grass roots, diversified, consciousness-raising, and much education and counseling—and a broker role between women seeking to enter or reenter the labor force and the various education, training, counseling, and supportive programs that can aid them. It is not *one* specific program, not one professional group, not one benefits system, or one specific type of aid. The resources come from state programs that have been created as a result of advocacy on behalf of these "older" women workers and from federal programs that have gradually over the past decade come to include them under "projects for special populations" (the language in the Joint Training Partnership Act). The heart of it all is work/training/referral/placement brokerage and counseling pitched to a particular group and guided by an ideology that believes participants have much unrecognized experience and ability upon which to build successfully.

As a service activity, the centers in the network do not and cannot be expected to have the full range of concerns or policy interests of the feminists or those concerned with *older* women—the ones who created the movement. Much of the initial solidarity came from such issues as recognizing all homemaking as work, albeit unpaid, and insisting that it be credited for social security, fringe benefits coverage, and work experience. There was and is as well much enthusiasm for social security reform, the better to protect divorced women and young widows. There has been and is much concern over the underestimation of the labor force potential of women in their late 40s and 50s who need to begin paid work or to return to it. The importance of opening nontraditional work to women was stressed at one point (although less as the traditional manufacturing fields began to cut back even on male work forces). Fundamental to the group have been attacks on "ageism" and "sexism." Finally, there has been commitment to job creation and recognition that it might be difficult otherwise to demand training and entry opportunities for older women. There was special interest in paraprofessional and professional service careers relevant to the social service and medical care infrastructure for low-income people generally. The inability to achieve much along these lines was the major disappointment of the late 1970s. The issue has been raised again, but in a less hopeful environment.

From the beginning, the DH network has sought to attract both "feminist activists" and "just housewives." The activists are by now part of a larger national and state lobby on gender issues that range from affirmative action and comparable worth to adequacy of funding for employment and educational programs. Many types of organizations take part. Depending on the year and the time, they speak out on pension reform, social security, medical care coverage, and tax policy. It is difficult to separate the specific accomplishments of any one group (and this applies as well to the DHs) from the total impact of the "movement." The Displaced Homemakers Network's periodic newsletter, *Network News*, and its recent conference announcements suggest close relationships with Wider Opportunities for Women (WOW), The Women's Equity Action League (WEAL), and various other advocacy groups for older women.

In her "epilogue" to the Shields volume, Sommers, the "wise woman" of the "movement," comments that it took an apt and catchy name to create a new category of the disadvantaged and to have it recognized for public policy purposes (especially job training and placement). Nonetheless, writing in 1981, she does not exaggerate the accomplishment, noting that "too many of the proliferating programs . . . will use the new popular label to continue business as usual (p. 191)."[55] She comes back to the need to change the public perceptions of middle-aged and older women—and to address in a more basic way the public policies that leave so many without resources and care: social security, pensions, health care.

The Future

One notes in the books, newsletters, and testimony some tension as to the identification of the group in focus. Some are clearly concerned with older women, programs for the aged, ageism. Others define the problem as for the "middle-aged," women 35–45 and in their 50s, women who were homemakers and who need support and service to become self-supporting and to make a new life for themselves. Since the centers and agencies have a broad mission, despite differing emphases, the issue of the group really in focus is not discussed, but it does affect their futures, for we are dealing, we believe, with the problems of a transitional generation in a form appropriate to them.

The labor force participation statistics tell us that soon we will no longer have a full age cohort of women, stranded by divorce and widowhood, who have never been related to the labor market. Now, many mothers continue to work as their children grow up. Others are out for a while and, then, back in. The reasonably educated and the well-educated may need a period of skills updating, reorientation, and placement help, but women are far better represented than they were in the professions, management, and better-paid jobs generally, whatever the major problems yet unresolved. They may need transition funds. Some may need counseling to help them and their children deal with the trauma of divorce-separation-injury or disability of spouse-widowhood. But the needs will be common, understood, and encompassed, one would hope, by the societal institutions created to deal with such matters. The situations are too common to await self-organization and advocacy for the creation of service responses.

At the same time, there has been a significant start on pension reform which protects spousal rights, modest health insurance reform which offers access to group rates during the transition, and active debate—but no action—about social security "earnings sharing" as the way to help the divorced woman who by agreement between the couple has stayed away from a job to rear children at home. The issues raised and the problems to be solved are not limited to DH and probably should not be: The solutions to the benefits policy issues require a broad field of vision and complex balancing.

Although the DH label may eventually become obsolete, there is evidence that for the present, certainly—and we do not know how far into the future—it is for many women a socially acceptable *entry* into a service system which they need. Since service access is a complex thing to arrange and implement, one would want to see this brokerage and support system sustained. Similarly, some programs must be adapted to population subgroups: thus, the Wellesley Women's Center and the American Vocational Association worked on adapting vocational education programs. However, the system obviously must feed into educational, vocational, training, and even counseling programs, which are best not limited to specific "categories" of women. The point of the DH label is to provide support for reintegration, resettlement, and "normalization," so to speak. As long as people so identify, the network needs support, but its goal should be mainstreaming. With regard even to the present group, Shields comments that "the vast majority of displaced homemakers do not remain 'victimized' if given an assist and the opportunity to take responsibility for the rest of their lives."[56]

Similarly, the important social policy issues require attention and advocacy. As public policy begins to move, it is urgent that it be assessed from the perspective of the unique circumstances and needs of many subgroups. Thus, as long as there are DHs in the sense of the 1970s and 1980s, an advocacy presence with this preoccupation remains a valuable component of the policy community.

In short, the DH movement has created a helpful service and policy category which differentiates and features a subgroup of single women—some, but not most, mothers of minor children. The self-identification as DH does not apply to some and, with labor force trends continuing, is likely to become less important. Others fit the DH definition but are probably seen and dealt with as welfare mothers. Still others are adolescent mothers. Some prefer to ask for help through minority organizations. Some join organizations of women entrepreneurs or managers. As one looks at these several different groups, some of their shared needs show much overlap: work, training, interim and transitional income support, social services, and more. Yet in some instances—and for a time here—the identification with a specific category like DH fulfills a valuable social function as long as it does not lead to combat on behalf of one single-mother "interest group" as opposed to another. For the policymaker this poses a complex challenge: creating adequate shared institutions, particularistic entry and advocacy opportunities, equity whatever one's choice, and a sense of direction which suits the needs of the groups affected and the society at large.

Specifying a U.S. Approach

As have the earlier chapters, our examination of these four groups of single mothers suggests that we need more than a program for poor families or a monolithic "single-mother" categorical program in response to the family changes that are occurring. On the other hand, it is also clear that no other country has a fully realized package that contains all the answers. A full strategy requires elements of general family policy, including attention to all families with children and responsiveness to working parents per se, and concern for the poor—plus some special things for *some* single mothers. Chapters 5 and 6 explore these specifics.

Endnotes

1. Susan Sheehan, "A Welfare Mother," *The New Yorker* (1975), published as *A Welfare Mother* (New York: New American Library, Mentor Books, 1976).
2. Ken Auletta, "The Underclass," *The New Yorker* (Nov. 16, 23, 30, 1981). Also published as *The Underclass* (New York: Random House, 1982).
3. Bill Moyers, "The Vanishing Black Family," CBS-TV, January 25, 1980.
4. Daniel Patrick Moynihan, *The Negro Family: The Case for National Action* (Washington, D.C.: U.S. Government Printing Office, 1965); and *Family and Nation* (Cambridge: Harvard University Press, 1986).
5. Charles Murray, *Losing Ground* (New York: Basic Books, 1984); Lawrence M. Mead, *Beyond Entitlement* (New York: The Free Press, 1986); "Welfare and Work," a special issue of the journal *Public Welfare* (American Public Welfare Association), vol. 44, no. 1 (Winter 1986); Robert Reischauer, "Prospects for Welfare Reform," *Public Welfare*, vol. 44, no. 4 (Fall 1986): 4–11; Isabel V. Sawhill, "Anti-Poverty Strategies for the 1980s," Discussion Paper, Changing Domestic Priorities (Washington, D.C.: The Urban Institute, 1986); Task Force on Poverty and Welfare, *A New Social Contract*. Submitted to Governor Mario M. Cuomo, December 1986 (Albany); Bruce Babbitt and Arthur Fleming, *Ladder Out of Poverty* (Washington, D.C.: Project on the Welfare of Families, 1986); *The New Consensus on Family and Welfare* (Washington, D.C.: American Enterprise Institute, 1987).
6. Mary Jo Bane and David T. Ellwood, "The Dynamics of Dependence: The Routes to Self-Sufficiency" (Cambridge, Mass.: Urban Systems Research and Engineering, Inc., 1983); Greg J. Duncan, *Years of Poverty, Years of Plenty* (Ann Arbor, Mich.: Institute for Social Research, 1984); David T. Ellwood, "Working Off Welfare: Prospects and Policies for Self-Sufficiency for Female Family Heads," Discussion Paper #803-86, Institute for Research on Poverty, University of Wisconsin, 1986; David T. Ellwood and Mary Jo Bane, "The Impact of AFDC on Family Structure and Living Arrangements," in *Research in Labor Economics*, Vol. 7, ed. Ron G. Ehrenberg (Greenwich, Conn.: JAI Press, 1985), 137–207; June O'Neill et al., *Analysis of Time on Welfare* (Washington, D.C.: The Urban Institute, 1984). For a general overview, see Daniel H. Weinberg, "The Economic Effects of Welfare," Technical Analysis Paper No. 35, Office of Income Security Policy, U.S. Department of Health and Human Services (Washington, D.C.: 1986). These studies also are summarized in the following congressional source book, which also provides documentation for our AFDC program overview: Committee on Ways and Means, U.S. House of Representatives, *Background Material and Data on Programs within the Jurisdiction of the Committee on Ways and Means, 1987 Edition* (Washington, D.C.: U.S. Government Printing Office, 1987).

7. A number of studies are summarized in *Work in America: Implications for Families,* Hearings, Select Committee on Children, Youth, and Families, House of Representatives, April 17, 1986, testimony by Kevin K. Hopkins, esp. tables on pp. 105 and 109. (Washington, D.C.: U.S. Government Printing Office, 1986.)

8. Charles Murray and Deborah Laren, *According to Age: Longitudinal Profiles of AFDC Recipients and the Poor by Age Group* (Washington, D.C.: American Enterprise Institute, 1986).

9. Committee on Ways and Means, *Background Material and Data . . .* , 618.

10. Kristin A. Moore and Martha R. Burt, *Private Crisis, Public Cost* (Washington, D.C.: The Urban Institute Press, 1982). Also, Kristin A. Moore, "Facts at a Glance" (Washington, D.C.: Child Trends, 1986 and 1987).

11. Martha R. Burt with Frank Levy, "Estimates of Public Costs for Teenage Childbearing: A Review of Recent Studies and Estimates of 1985 Public Costs," in *Risking the Future: Adolescent Sexuality, Pregnancy and Childbearing,* Vol. II, *Working Papers and Statistical Appendixes,* ed. Sandra L. Hofferth and Cheryl D. Hayes (Washington, D.C.: National Academy Press, 1987).

12. Frank F. Furstenberg, Jr., Jeanne Brooks-Gunn, and S. Philip Morgan, *Adolescent Mothers in Later Life* (New York: Cambridge University Press, 1987).

13. See the several chapters by Sandra L. Hofferth, in Hofferth and Hayes, eds., *Risking the Future,* Vol. II.

14. George Gilder, *Wealth and Poverty* (New York: Bantam Books, 1980); Murray, *Losing Ground.*

15. Elise F. Jones et al., *Teenage Pregnancy in Industrialized Societies* (New Haven: Yale University Press, 1986).

16. Sandra L. Hofferth, "The Effects of Programs and Policies on Adolescent Pregnancy and Childbearing," in Hofferth and Hayes, Vol. II, *Working Papers and Statistical Appendixes.*

17. Jones et al., *Teenage Pregnancy in Industrialized Societies.*

18. Cheryl D. Hayes, *Risking the Future,* Vol. I (Washington, D.C.: National Academy Press, 1986).

19. Ibid.

20. Murray, *Losing Ground.* See also Murray, "No, Welfare Isn't Really the Problem," *The Public Interest,* no. 84 (Summer 1986): 3–11.

21. Hofferth, "The Effects of Programs and Policies . . . ," 257–60.

22. Martha R. Burt and Freya L. Sonnenstein, "Exploring Possible Demonstration Projects Aimed at Affecting the Welfare Dependency of Families Initially Created by a Birth to a Teenager" (Washington, D.C.: The Urban Institute, 1984), processed; June A. O'Neill et al., *An Analysis of Time on Welfare* (Washington, D.C.: The Urban Institute Press, 1984).

23. Alfred J. Kahn and Sheila B. Kamerman, "Personal Social Service and Income Transfer Experiments: The Research and Action Connections," in *Children, Youth and Families,* ed. Robert N. Rapoport (New York: Cambridge University Press, 1985); see also several evaluation reports published by Manpower Demonstration Research Corporation, New York, between 1981 and 1985.

24. A Branch and J. Quint, *Project Redirection: Interim Report on Project*

Implementation (New York: Manpower Demonstration Research Corporation, 1981).

25. D. Polit, J. Kahn, and D. Stevens, *Project Redirection: Impact Analysis* (New York: Manpower Demonstration Research Corporation, 1985). As we go to press, we are told that *later* follow-up shows greater impact. Reports are not yet published.

26. Sylvia B. Perlman and Richard A. Weatherley, "Limits of the Comprehensive Services Model: The Case of Adolescent Pregnancy Programs," *Journal of Policy Analysis and Management*, vol. 5, no. 2 (Winter 1986): 326–39; see also Richard A. Weatherley et al., "Comprehensive Programs for Pregnant Teenagers and Teenage Parents: How Successful Have They Been?" *Family Planning Perspectives*, no. 1 and no. 2 (March/April 1986): 18/73–78.

27. Esther Wattenberg, "Paternity Adjudication and Child Support Obligations of Teenage Parents" (Minneapolis, Minn.: Center for Urban and Regional Affairs, 1984), processed. On factors related to living with one's child, see William Marsiglio, "Adolescent Fathers in the United States: Their Initial Living Arrangements, Marital Experience and Educational Outcomes," *Family Planning Perspectives*, vol. 19, no. 16 (November–December 1987): 240–51.

28. Daniel J. Keveles, *In the Name of Eugenics* (New York: Alfred A. Knopf, 1985).

29. Hayes, ed., *Risking the Future*, Vol. I, 1986.

30. Sharyne Merritt and Linda Steiner, *And Baby Makes Two* (New York: Franklin Watts, 1984).

31. David E. Bloom and Neil G. Bennett, as reported in "Demographers Converge on Chicago," *Population Today*, vol. 15, no. 6 (June 1987). A less gloomy scenario is outlined by E. Moorman of the U.S. Bureau of the Census in *Population Today*, September and October (1986) and June (1987).

32. U.S. Bureau of the Census, "Marital Status and Living Arrangements: 1985"; "Marital Status and Living Arrangements: 1986"; "Fertility of American Women: June 1986"; *Current Population Reports*, series P-20, Nos. 410, 418, and 406 (Washington, D.C.: Government Printing Office, 1986; 1987; 1987).

33. J. Harriman, "In Trouble: The Story of an Unmarried Woman's Decision to Keep Her Child," *Atlantic*, May 1970, 94–98.

34. S. Griffin, "Confessions of a Single Mother," *Ramparts*, April 1973, 41–44.

35. P. A. Avery, "Parents without Partners—By Their Own Choice," *U.S. News and World Report*, 20 June, 1983, 50.

36. Patricia Hope, "One Hand to Hold," *Ladies' Home Journal*, October 1983, 62.

37. S. Walker, "Why I Became a Single Mother," *Ladies' Home Journal*, March 1985, 22.

38. P. Morrisoe, "Mommy Only: The Rise of the Middle Class Unwed Mother," *New York*, 6 June 1983, 22–29.

39. M. Boess, "A Report on the Rigors and Rewards of Unmarried Mothers," *Glamour*, March 1982, 176.

40. Merritt and Steiner, "Having Babies without Husbands," *New World*, May 1985, 88–92.

41. Stephanie Stokes Olliver, "The New Choice: Single Motherhood after 30," *Essence*, October 1983, 131–33.
42. "This Is What You Thought," *Glamour*, January 1986, 15–18. Molly McKaughan and Julie Kagan, "The Motherhood Plunge," *Working Women*, February 1986, 69–71.
43. U.S. DHHS, *Advance Report of Final Natality Statistics, 1984:* vol. 35, no. 4, Supplement, 18 July 1986.
44. Merritt and Steiner, "Having Babies without Husbands"; Jean Renvoize, *Going Solo: Single Mothers by Choice* (New York: Methuen, 1985).
45. Merritt and Steiner, "Having Babies without Husbands," 89.
46. "Pregnant, Unmarried and Much in the Public Eye," *New York Times*, July 12, 1987, A-27.
47. Ruth Mason, "Where's Poppa? Bringing Up Baby, Sans Daddy," *Jewish World*, 12–18 June 1987, 10–12.
48. Renvoize, *Going Solo*, 33–34.
49. U.S. House of Representatives, Subcommittee on Retirement, Income and Employment, and Select Committee on Aging, *Alternatives to Retirement: Employment Problems of Older Women*, Hearings, 14 July 1977, 164–65.
50. Laurie Shields, *Displaced Homemakers: Organizing for a New Life* (New York: McGraw-Hill, 1981), 35.
51. Ibid., x.
52. Displaced Homemakers Network, *A Status Report on Displaced Homemakers and Single Parents in the United States* (Washington, D.C.: 1987).
53. California Senate Bill, 825, quoted in Shields, *Displaced Homemakers*, 224.
54. Office of Technology Assessment, Congress of the United States, *Displaced Homemakers: Programs and Policy* (Washington, D.C.: U.S. Government Printing Office, 1985).
55. Shields, *Displaced Homemakers*, 191.
56. Ibid., 24.

Chapter 5

INCOME: WORK, CHILD SUPPORT, AND PUBLIC TRANSFERS

We have looked at the single-mother phenomenon—at numbers, trends, types, and societal concern. We have stressed the need to avoid stereotyping and instead to make distinctions; we have also found reasons for action and for a public response. And we have looked historically at a pattern of U.S. policy which is not yet attuned to current developments.

The previous chapters suggest that the diversity in types of single mothers argues for doing nothing at all in some instances, and for establishing special, categorical policies in others. Yet the very diversity also tends to turn attention from the fact that there are important commonalities spanning many of the elements of the single-mother phenomenon, which society defines as problems and for which those in the status would appreciate help. Yes, there must be categorical specifics, especially with regard to teenage mothers (as seen in Chapter 4). But the commonalities require major attention, resources, policy, and program energy.

Inevitably, we begin with the questions of how single mothers and their children are to be assured income, whether from work, private transfers, or public programs. Eventually, other issues will come to the fore, but services, social supports, and guidance are empty gestures unless there is attention to food, shelter, clothing, medical care, and all the rest. Nor can there be a coherent approach to any of the resource questions without some resolution of the fundamental policy issue: Are we to assume work or emphasize support for an "at-home" role for single mothers? And if there are to be differentiations, what are we to assume and about whom?

There are alternatives and they have consequences. In the absence of articulated choices, public policy will drift and accomplish little.

An Approach

The history of public aid for single mothers and their children has been a history of formal and informal priority for work. When the husband left a sufficient estate or the children were old enough to help the mother on the family farm or in the family business, there was no crisis. Or, often, relatives might help. Otherwise, widows initially had no systematic source of aid. Later, mothers' pensions protected poor widows so that their children might be kept out of foster homes and institutions, but these women were often not given sufficient aid and therefore needed to seek out opportunities to supplement the meager benefits provided. With limited work opportunities, many became seamstresses, laundresses, or did other work. Early ADC programs in the states set benefits very low so that work was essential—particularly before parents-care-takers were added to the budgets in 1950. Then, as soon as significant numbers of unwed and deserted mothers and blacks began to apply and had their rights to welfare protected in the mid-1950s and the 1960s, work-training opportunities, incentives, and eventually requirements were added to the picture. These latter topics continue to dominate the policy debate with regard to poor single mothers.

In recent decades, many mothers have become single without necessarily facing financial crises because they were themselves adequate earners. Divorced women also may combine their own earnings with alimony and property settlements. Legally established child support payments by the noncustodial spouse may supplement income. Widows (and their minor children) collect basic monthly payments under the social security system, often supplemented by private pensions and life insurance. However, as already seen, large numbers of single mothers are in desperate economic circumstances among most of the subgroups we have mentioned. The questions of the public policy posture and the forms and level of economic aid for single mothers require major attention.

Some in the United States would adopt each of the foreign "models" we have summarized as general policy approaches or specifically to aid the many single mothers who are poor: The poor should be given more help. Single mothers who are poor should be given enough financial support to avoid working away from home while rearing their children. The society should guarantee some material support for all children, enabling all mothers to remain at home—at least while their children are very young (under age 3). In addition to providing some help for all families rearing children, parents—including married and single mothers—should be given special aid, income supplements, training and opportunity to enter, reenter, or remain in the labor market and support their families. Each of these patterns has its variations.

Policies imply resources, however, and cash benefit programs for low-income two-parent families or single mothers are paid for—among others—by people of modest means, not very far above them in the income distribution. While some of the public negativism about AFDC may be derived from racism and exaggerated estimates of the black and Hispanic proportions in the caseloads, a significant component of public resentment also is derived from the view that young, healthy, and—to some—"immoral" women are asking for public support paid for in part by hard-working taxpayers of moderate means, who do not themselves see or choose the alternative of remaining out of the labor force. In a world in which the majority of women and of mothers—even of young children—are in the labor force, can one make a case for the poor single mother as exception?

State task forces, a series of resolutions by governors at their recent conferences, congressional hearings, and the reports of "policy analysts" have been converging on the notion that public policy with reference to low-income single mothers and their children should assume work and maximum self-support. (Obviously, they are not concerned with those who do not turn to public aid.) While there are different views of what this means and how it should be implemented, it is a view which suits the ethic and conforms to societal realities. Indeed, as we have seen, if one separates the rhetoric of the 1909 White House Conference on Children or the ADC discussion of 1935 from what actually was implemented, this acknowledgment of the centrality of work in public policy for single mothers is not even new. What may be new is the resolve to recognize the reality and to make it the explicit framework for policy. We also may be observing new determination to implement such policy in a fashion which truly benefits mothers and children, rather than punishes them.

Thought of in this way, a pro-work policy is both inevitable and just. It must, of course, depend on the continued capacity of the economy to create jobs. Some of the European policy compromises described in Chapter 3 grew out of high unemployment.

There was a brief moment in the 19th century when middle-class families who could afford to do so made it possible, even necessary, for mothers to remain at home and not participate in paid employment outside the home. Home became a woman's "proper place," and women of education and means developed it as part of their own "special place" in society. "Staying at home" also offered an example which set the pattern of aspiration for the less affluent.[1] The development was a departure from a long, historic pattern. It resulted from major changes in the urban-industrial economy. Women had played central roles in agriculture and domestic production economies throughout history, and low-income women, especially immigrant women, had taken on the factory jobs of the new industrialization as well as the low-pay service and domestic jobs. In theory, these were jobs for young women before marriage, but the reality often required otherwise.

The culture and ethic supported the notion of home as woman's "proper place," even if the model worked well only for the home with a middle-class income. Even this began to change with the large influx of women into the labor force during World War II and the continuation of higher female labor force participation rates afterward, despite the many departures to relinquish jobs to men. Then came the economic expansion of the 1960s and the unprecedented entry of women into paid work. During the 1970s and 1980s, massive numbers of mothers of young children, in particular married mothers, remained at work or joined an expanding labor force. Women have constituted the major component of labor force growth in the 1980s as in the prior two decades.

The at-home mother who cultivated domestic arts and child rearing, while serving as a charity volunteer, typified the middle class of 1895 and 1920.[2] The working mother, managing job and family life and ever-concerned with child care, is the norm today. Table 5–1 reports the labor force participation rates for mothers in 1987.

In recent years, the labor force participation rate of married mothers of very young children has begun to surpass that for single mothers. The rate for white single mothers has reversed a long-term trend and become higher than that for blacks.

In general, divorced single mothers are far more likely to be in the labor force (80 percent and most employed full-time in 1986) than the widowed (57 percent), separated (65 percent), and the never married (54 percent). These differences are somewhat connected to educational and ethnic differentiations as well.

There is yet another argument for a work presumption. All analyses of the circumstances of single mothers yield the same results: Work is far more successful than transfer payments in

Table 5-1   Mother's Labor Force Participation Rates by Marital Status and Children's Ages, 1977–87

	Age of Youngest Child				
Year and Family Status of Mothers	*1 Year or Younger*	*2 Years*	*3 Years*	*4 Years*	*5 Years*
1977					
Total mothers	31.6	42.3	45.9	48.8	50.6
Wives	31.4	40.9	44.1	47.0	48.5
Women maintaining families	33.1	52.8	56.0	56.8	60.8
1982					
Total mothers	43.3	52.0	56.4	56.0	57.4
Wives	43.1	51.3	55.2	54.6	53.7
Women maintaining families	44.3	55.9	61.7	60.7	71.3
1987					
Total mothers	51.9	58.5	60.4	62.4	63.1
Wives	52.6	59.0	59.0	61.7	62.5
Women maintaining families	47.5	56.2	66.1	65.4	64.9

Source: Bureau of Labor Statistics, U.S. Department of Labor.

keeping these families out of poverty. For example, the most recent official poverty rate for married couples (with children under age 18) who had only one earner was 16.3 percent in 1985 (the most recent report), whereas the mother's work, even if part-time, reduced the poverty rate to 5.0 percent. The dramatic difference held in the instance of parents with children under age 6, as well. When mothers in two-parent families with children under age 6 worked full-time, the poverty rate fell to 3.9 percent (see Table 5–2).

In the instance of the single mother, the differentiation was even more striking. In female-headed households with children under 18, the total poverty rate was 47 percent; however, it was 88.3 percent for mothers who did not work outside the home at all, and 28.4 percent if they did. In female-headed families with children under age 6, the poverty rate was 93.9 percent for nonworkers and 30.1 percent for full-time workers. Work clearly is important, and two salaries are most desirable.

Overall, public assistance programs are an insignificant source of income for married-couple families and of very modest importance, compared with work income, even for the total group of female-headed families.[3] In fact, AFDC plus social security benefits reduced child poverty only by 4.0 percentage points in 1985, and food stamps, which should be added, only a little more.[4] Yet,

Table 5–2 Poverty and Mothers' Employment Status, By Family Type and Children's Ages (1984)

Family Type and Children's Ages	Percentage Below Poverty
Married Couples, Children under 18	
Total	9.2
Mother worked last year[a]	5.0
Mother did not work	16.3
Married Couples, Children under 6	
Total	9.5
Mother worked last year[a]	5.5
Mother did not work	17.6
Mother worked full-time	3.9
Female-headed Household, Children under 18	
Total	47.0
Mother worked last year[b]	28.4
Mother did not work	88.3
Female-headed Household, Children under 6	
Total	60.9
Mother worked last year[b]	40.9
Mother did not work	93.9
Mother worked full-time	30.1

[a]Two-adult families in which *both* worked. The mother may have worked full-time or part-time. If the husband did not work, the poverty rate was 26.3 percent—for married couples with children.
[b]Full-time or part-time work.
Source: U.S. Bureau of the Census, "Characteristics of the Population Below the Poverty Level: 1985," *Current Population Reports,* series P-60, no. 158 (Washington, D.C.: U.S. Government Printing Office, 1987), tables 21 and 23.

poor female-headed families depend on cash welfare for half their incomes and earn another third. Non-poor single parent families depend on earnings for 78 percent.[5]

Put differently, almost everywhere in the United States, the AFDC-plus-food stamp income is below the poverty line. The one major advantage of receiving welfare over income from a low-paying job is that welfare serves as an entry card to Medicaid, the source of medical care for oneself and one's children. If the health-coverage problem were otherwise solved, larger proportions of single mothers might see themselves as better off at work. Others, even if unskilled and untrained, could immediately become better off if low-wage income could be supplemented in some of the other ways mentioned later in the chapter.

The evidence tends, then, to favor a pro-work option. It fits the current ethic and the current American pattern for those not "welfare-poor." It is the most promising way of improving economic circumstances; that is why so many married and single mothers in fact do work. And in a society where the work ethic remains strong, a job is the vehicle for developing self-regard, public respect, and remaining in the mainstream. Working women as a group earn less than men, and single mothers who are uneducated and untrained even less than that. If their work could be upgraded, their relative advantages over those who rely on transfers alone could be further enhanced.

Would the work option be bad for children? Given the already high labor force participation rates of married mothers of the very young, the question perhaps becomes somewhat academic. The labor market refuses to await the outcomes of child development research, and parents exercise their preferences. In the present instances, one would want to know specifically the impact of the mother's work in a one-parent family. Thus far the research is in some ways too general in that it fails to distinguish type of work, type of family, parental background factors, child age and sex variables, and so forth.[6]

All things considered, there is widespread agreement that the employment of the mother outside the home is not contraindicated by available studies. A case could be made that children might pay a price—perhaps boys more than girls—and may also have the benefits of better living standards and better role models—perhaps girls more than boys. But one must also put on the scales the long-term economic advantages for the family of the mother's work and the potential contributions to her own self-respect and development. We shall suggest that some societal supports for such families could increase these positive outcomes.

Here we add a caveat. Consideration should be given to the very young child's age. Elsewhere we discuss, separately, infants under 1 and youngsters under 3. To the extent that work, whether by fathers or mothers of very young children, is eventually found to have some undesired effects on family life, the challenge faced would be to reconcile these two domains[7] and not to further institutionalize the burden for the single mother or for all female workers alone.

If it is understood and agreed that the preference is for work, even work on the part of most mothers of young children who do not have other sources of support, an economic security program may be developed and specified. The fuller context of such an approach should be outlined before we examine work and economic assistance strategies in further detail.

The Broader Policy Context

There are those who ask, Why provide special help for single mothers? If women have babies, it is the choice they have made for themselves. If women prefer to be on their own, whatever the reason, why interfere?

We are not promoting or supporting an era of increased social control. Public policy is an issue only to the extent that people call upon the public to finance their choices or leave their children in damaging situations. Then it is appropriate to ask whether society's interests do not also enter into the choices—and whether the case for a policy that assumes and expects work is not strong. We shall leave for a later point the issue of what is to be done in the instance of those unable or unwilling to conform to the generally accepted norms of child protection.

The main thrust of policy, then, would be to cut the personal and societal costs of the single-parent status through an effort at "mainstreaming," which would include an expectation of work in a society in which most women and most mothers work. This is a nonwelfare strategy. Central to the policy would be the notion of least possible intervention. Most people manage most of the time in a society in which public policy concerns itself with creating infrastructure and context, protections, rights, opportunities, support available to all people or all people of specific status (young children, unemployed workers, etc). Special, individualized attention is sometimes needed but is not the point of departure. This is not a laissez-faire regime: Modern societies do not thrive with minimalist governments on the model of the 19th century. However, societies which continue to value pluralism and individualism favor universal, general, and unobtrusive provision as the starting point.

The economic security policy for the single mother, then, would build from the completely private and self-reliant to the individualized and case-supportive public aid. The remainder of the chapter discusses the specifics. Here we introduce the component principles:

1. *Maximum self-support is preferred for single mothers, as for others.* Single mothers should be encouraged in their own efforts, to remain in and related to the labor force and to improve their situations. Law, policy, and provision will be needed to support this perspective. New York's Senator Daniel Patrick Moynihan has said, "It should be thought normal and natural that mothers work and bring home income." Gov. Bill Clinton of Arkansas, at the

time chairman of the National Governors Association, said in presenting the association's 1987 "welfare reform" report: "What we want to do is to turn what is now primarily a payments system with a minor work component into a system that is first and foremost a jobs program, supported by an income assistance component." It is recognized that age, education, labor force history, and access to such other help as widow entitlements under social security and other social insurance make this principle more applicable to some single mothers than to others.

2. *Private transfers have priority over public transfers.* In more general language, child support by the noncustodial parent obviously should be pursued and should take precedence over or be integrated with public income maintenance efforts.

3. *Public aid in obtaining needed education, work training, and job search help should have priority over long-term financial assistance for single mothers.* Stipends to cover living expenses and training costs make more sense (and should be more generous) than long-term support in a dependent status. Adolescent mothers who want help should be expected to complete basic schooling while aided financially—so as to prepare for self-support.

4. *In the absence of one's independent success in the labor force or in getting and holding work after support for education-training-job search, provision of guaranteed public work which enables one to earn a basic support grant is to be preferred over public assistance entitlements which do not expect or require any work at all.*

5. *Transitional financial aid and services should be available* to help absorb the crises after separation and divorce, where necessary, or to aid after childbirth—and to allow time as needed for personal planning, counseling, and entry into work, training, or educational activities, or to permit time for processing of social insurance, pension, child support, benefits, or assistance applications.

6. Since the labor market does not connect salary levels to family needs, *there should be a policy of income supplementation, whether for one- or for two-parent families,* so that working families may manage and be encouraged to continue in maximum self-support. A number of measures will be involved.

7. *Special policies and provisions need to be in place to deal with those unwilling or unable to meet the expectations here reviewed.*

There is one more principle, reserved for elaboration in the next chapter: *The workplace itself should be encouraged and aided to be supportive of the efforts of working adults, whether in one- or two-parent families, to manage simultaneously the responsibilities of both job and family life.*

The sections which follow explore the ways in which these principles might be operationalized.

Women in the Labor Market

The status of women in the labor market generally shapes the context of any policy that proposes work as central to the well-being of single mothers and their children. Only if women have equal access to jobs and are fairly paid can one urge and expect single mothers to pursue this course.

First, many questions face our economy and are of concern to everyone—not just women: Economic growth, trade balance, international competition, and numerous elements of fiscal and monetary policy and regional economic development are issues debated in many forums. The country's economic well-being is a major determinant of the feasibility of anything we might propose for single mothers. During downturns, options are far more limited, and new policy initiatives are less likely—or their implementation becomes constricted and self-defeating.

Second, a growing economy with a tight labor market opens new opportunities for all women, but efforts begun in recent decades nonetheless must continue in schools and in all social institutions to widen the range of occupational aspirations and preparation of young women. Such a course will require the continued support of affirmative action, antidiscrimination, and pay-equity legislation and enforcement machinery.

Women are in the labor market and in a greater range of jobs than ever before. More and more working single mothers will, then, be on a decent footing as a starting point. They will have salaries and, increasingly, fringe benefits. Their financial and fringe benefit protections will be a good foundation for family well-being, as single mothers become less concentrated, as a group, in the low-paying, unsuitable jobs to which many have been relegated in the past. This does not mean, as we shall suggest below, that some attention will not need to be given to the problems of the one-earner family in a two-earner economy.

Private Support, First

Obviously, fully adequate child support and alimony payments would relieve the mother in the female-headed household from pressure to work unless she preferred to do so and would decrease the applications for public assistance. Of equal importance, such payments would reflect and reinforce norms of personal responsibility and equity. At the very least, fathers able to do so should support their children; and the relationships of noncustodial parents with children could in general—but with some obvious exceptions—be strengthened and child development enhanced if developed in the context of on-going shared responsibility of custodial and noncustodial parents.

On premises such as these, one could readily develop a program of child support adjudication and collection not at all limited to the welfare poor. In the American context, however, only the desire to curtail AFDC or collect funds for reimbursement to welfare authorities could create the impetus for governmental action. Subsequently, the machinery became more generally available. By now, child support enforcement is a popular issue in government and the media; the story is well known, the issues are identified, and the accomplishments are significant but not to be exaggerated.

As noted in Chapter 2, the modern turning point in federal action regarding child support accountability occurred in 1975. Since then, the child support program components have been increased and strengthened to include, with federal aid and pressure, legal establishment of paternity, absent-father location, and child support collection. Tax and social security records are now used; there is wage and tax refund withholding and asset attachment in the face of nonpayments; and state commissions are specifying statewide standards for child support levels, while examining such other important questions as custody and interstate cooperation. A $50 monthly disregard ensures some financial advantage to AFDC families if the father does contribute— whereas previously his payment was seen only as partial repayment of the welfare grant.

Federal aid, incentives, publicity, and requirements have won widespread approval. The laws have been strengthened in many states, and the administrative machinery improved everywhere. These measures are of some help to the non-AFDC divorced families. The results are not yet sufficient to justify the claims of likely major impact on AFDC rolls. Some collections were made in 1985 in almost 680,000 out of 3.7 million AFDC cases, but fewer than 37,000 cases could be closed as a result. Furthermore, the collection amounted to only 7.3 percent of the sums paid out. The collections "paid off" in an economic cost-benefit sense ($1.16 was collected per $1.00 spent, for AFDC cases) and thus were worth the expenditures, although the 3.34 to 1.00 ratio for the country as a whole depended on the inclusion of non-AFDC cases as well. For these cases, $1.98 was collected per $1.00 spent.

There is general consensus that the machinery and laws that are still being developed are essential and reflect improvements, especially for the nonwelfare poor. Support is also widespread for an experiment in Wisconsin, based on federal waivers, and for similar initiatives beginning elsewhere, that would benefit poor single mothers in particular, as well as all other single mothers. These experiments involve (1) a clear payment standard (in Wisconsin, 17 percent of the noncustodial parent's income per child per year, up to 34 percent for five or more children); (2) automatic income withholding from the noncustodial parent following the award; and (3) a minimum support level, assured by the state, if the parent's contribution cannot meet that level.

There has been considerable feeling over the past decade that AFDC programs have made it easy for men to desert or divorce their families, or to start families without prior marriage—and then to walk away without any assumption of child support obligations. The public has been outraged to learn the facts, as we have summarized them in Chapter 1, even though the picture has improved slightly in the last several years.[8] The research literature reflects a debate as to exactly how far child support collection could take us toward decreasing the need for AFDC or its alternatives.[9] The issues are the income capacity of the noncustodial parent and concern about the economic well-being of a possible "new" family. There is no controversy, however, about the need to ensure fair contributions by noncustodial parents, whatever their incomes and capacities—or the need to legally fix the potential future obligations, even of teenage fathers, who indeed have traditionally "walked away" from all obligations.

A full child support program must deal with many other elements about which there is both research uncertainty and value debate: the noncustodial parent's obligations to "first" and current families; proposals to use support payment or nonpayment as the basis for rights to or constraints upon visitation; attempts by noncustodial parents to specify how child support funds are to be spent; and the financial responsibilities of the custodial parents.[10]

We think that special attention should now also be directed to the issue of advance or guaranteed child support or maintenance as a possible future U.S. program. It is part of the Wisconsin experiment. As documented in our earlier research and in our report on an international working party on the subject which we organized, a number of western European countries have established programs which include public support guarantees. Depending upon the policy thrust, a few of these are means-tested and welfare-related; others are income-tested and targeted, but not stigmatized; several are not income-tested at all. Some are time-limited and clearly meant to cover the period when a child is very young, but most continue through adolescence. Also, the benefit levels vary, and, thus, can be more or less valuable. Nonetheless, the notion of government child support "insurance" or "backup," preferably as a universal and nonwelfare program, is attractive. It obviously is not the same thing as the support for a child that a court may order to be paid by fathers with more adequate financial capacity. However, if available as an entitlement and not means-tested or income-tested, such a guaranteed advance payment of support for a child can become an important part of an income maintenance package for a custodial parent. As shown in Chapter 3 and elaborated on below, it is a supplementation vehicle which could combine with a modest wage and other nonstigmatized help and constitute one element, but only one element, in an income package above the poverty line. Most single-parent families cannot expect child support to solve their economic problems fully, whether from payment by noncustodial parents or future parental guarantees. It is an important component, not a full answer.

Facilitating the Transition to Work

Significant numbers of single mothers who are rearing children are not in the labor force. According to the latest statistical reports, at least 3 million single mothers are supported by AFDC, with very few working even part-time. Indeed, Reagan administration policies have discouraged part-time or low-pay work, and only those who obtain adequate full-time jobs seem now to be leaving the welfare rolls. In addition, some single mothers in the low-income categories avoid AFDC but are in need of help in gaining access to work.

A full summary of recent publicly initiated or proposed work programs and experiments on behalf of "welfare" mothers, food-stamp recipients, and others would fill a volume, with supplements added monthly. The issue has been central to the "welfare reform" and "single-parent family-poverty" discussion for the past several years. As we write, there is literally an avalanche of studies, research reviews, task force reports, conference resolutions, volumes reporting relevant congressional hearings, and newspaper stories and editorials, as well as integrated summaries of what is going on.[11] By the time these pages are in print, new contributions will have been made in all these categories. We fully expect that there also would have been some new legislative enactments, but that current policy ambivalence and inconsistency, as well as limited commitment to adequate implementation or sufficient funding, will still be problems to be addressed.

The discussion of needed measures might well begin with the category popularly known as the "displaced homemaker," as described in Chapter 4. Despite overlap, one does not deal here with the historical baggage and moral ambivalence associated with "welfare mothers." The "displaced homemaker" is a recent widow, the spouse of a handicapped worker, or a divorced or deserted woman who earlier removed herself from the labor force—or remained out of it—to rear children and create a home life supportive of the husband's career and her children's development. Now, cut off from financial support and without job connections, or often skills, she needs to find her way. The topics in the policy discussion encompass child support, social security, pension rights—and work. It is of interest that unless and until the "displaced homemaker" becomes a "welfare mother," the response tends to be supportive and sympathetic (although not yet sufficient or generous). There are special placement programs in state employment offices, access to higher education for launching careers, referral to vocational rehabilitation programs, and "privileged" attention in all public work programs that are not predicated on welfare status. None of this is unusual, and many see it as insufficient. At best it offers a model for employment and related programs for all single mothers who need and want to work and have not already developed a foothold in the labor market through the usual education and application streams.

In the mid-1980s, some states began to focus on the more "difficult" circumstances of AFDC mothers by developing new demonstrations and programs under such rubrics and mnemonics as "supported work" (in several cities), GAIN (in California), ET (in Massachusetts), MOST (in Michigan), and WEET (in Maine). They drew upon "work incentive" (WIN), "community work experience" (CWEP), and various waiver and demonstration authorizations enacted in 1981 and 1982 to explore, test, or demonstrate new approaches—or to join the national initiative sufficiently to meet public pressure without overcommitting to an uncertain strategy. After all, WIN funding in 1986 was far below that for the 1970s!

While ever newer programs may have bypassed some of this by now, a 1987 survey via mail questionnaires and visits by the staff of the Human Resources Division of the General Accounting Office (GAO) seems to suggest the state of the action and the then-identified possibilities. Earlier, the Manpower Research Development Corporation (MRDC) reported—three years into a five-year evaluation process—on an 11-state demonstration of state work/welfare initiatives. These and similar reports offer reality touchstones for whatever one projects in this field.[12]

The GAO reviewed 61 of these new initiatives and waiver programs in 38 states in 1985 through a combination of mail questionnaires and visits. They found, as reported earlier by the U.S. Committee on Ways and Means, that although most states are active in some way in the fields here discussed, most special, intensive programs are not statewide and are available to limited numbers of mothers on the AFDC rolls.[13] The specific GAO conclusions should be held as the starting point for future initiatives:

> *In 1985, the work programs reached a minority of adult AFDC recipients, an estimated 22 percent in states with WIN Demonstrations operating a full year. Most women with children under 6, the largest group of adult recipients, were not required to participate. Some programs also excluded people with minimal work histories or severe educational deficiencies who would require more expensive support or education and training service. . . .*[14]

The legislative authorization operative in early 1987 tells us something about the state of the action. By the mid-1970s, earlier federal employment programs had been replaced by the Comprehensive Employment and Training Act (CETA). This block grant in support of state employment efforts had been somewhat supportive of entry of women into the labor force and also had opened the way for some into public employment. It was of very limited help to AFDC recipients. CETA was abolished in 1982 in favor of a much smaller, less costly, and more privatized and targeted Job Training and Partnership Act (JTPA). JTPA remains the major employment program in the country. It focuses on the unemployed, although it may be of considerable use to some women in the job-market. Inevitably, however, it favors those most qualified and ready to work and is unlikely to have much impact on AFDC.

It is within this context that we have turned to the work programs with a public-assistance connection, and where the issue of a work requirement arises. WIN, as noted in Chapter 2, now requires registration by all "welfare" mothers of children over age 6 (except for cases of illness or "incapacitation," for those aged 16–17 who are attending school, or for women who are pregnant and in the third trimester). While registration may seem onerous, it has meant very little in the past, since the opportunities opened by the registration requirements have not in most places met the demand from welfare recipients who volunteered to participate. In the period 1981–1986, totals in the range 870,000 to 1.15 million registered annually, but only 200,000 to 310,000 were placed in jobs, and another 130,000 to 700,000 left the rolls because they found work. All of this was in the context of over 3 million adults on the AFDC rolls—but most (60 percent of mothers) caring for children under age 6. These numbers reflect the AFDC turnover story as told in Chapter 4: a year or two of aid for those who recover financially from a status transition (divorce, separation, widowhood) or job loss, and long-term dependency for a subgroup of those who come on the rolls and stay, and at any one time constitute the majority of recipients.

The legislation that created the WIN *demonstrations* (as an alternative option for the states) did not change the eligibility criteria; for those who were not excluded or for volunteers, the states or localities were offered new incentives and flexibility to provide job training, job search help, work experience, and the right to divert welfare funds for these purposes. WIN also offered the opportunity to contract with JTPA, private placement agencies, and state employment offices. WIN had traditionally been a partnership between the state welfare and labor departments but currently comes under state welfare authority—for purposes of WIN demonstrations—unless a choice is made to subcontract.

Among the related and somewhat overlapping programs is Job Search. A state may require eight weeks of participation at the time of initial AFDC application and, again, eight weeks each year. Job Search follows the WIN exclusion criteria. By contrast, the Community Work Experience Program (CWEP), optional for the localities, may include a requirement for participation of mothers whose children are 3 years old. These are the "workfare" programs: Recipients perform some sort of community work at the minimum wage to "work off" their benefits. More than half the states use this option but in limited numbers of communities.

The final components among the new initiatives elaborating on the WIN and the welfare titles of the Social Security Act are "Work Supplementation" and "Grant Diversion," two similar programs. Building on earlier legislation which was too restrictive for the states to use, this 1984 program allows welfare recipients to be placed in jobs offered by private and nonprofit employers. The states may allow recipients the income disregard incentive available to employed adults on AFDC; the AFDC grant may—for a limited period—be diverted to supplement or pay wages in a number of ways. Limited programs had been developed in 16 states at the time of the last report.

What did the GAO conclude about these WIN Demonstration, CWEP, Job Search, and Work Supplementation efforts? First, as we have already noted, there is a societal consensus emerging about the desirability of linking current welfare reform with work-related programs. Second, "such programs establish an obligation for participation in return for benefits, an opportunity for participants to obtain needed skills, or both" (p.15). Only a minority of recipients have been exposed to such offerings as yet, despite the media attention. Under the legislation, as we have noted, WIN and Job Search may be required for mothers of children over 6 years of age, CWEP for mothers of children over 3. GAO found that only 14 of 50 programs with registration requirements in fact applied them to mothers of children under 6. With federal permission, a state can lower the age cut-off, even for WIN Demonstration and Job Search; thus far, because program participation opportunities are still rationed, the takers are few. Finally, although the press talks frequently about workfare, few of these programs really are that—so that the term "work programs" is more appropriate.

In the most rigorous evaluation available to date, the MRDC has examined a range of strategies involving one or more of the above-described program elements, in several combinations, and with different philosophies. Overall, the interim conclusion (after three years) was "that a number of quite different program approaches will lead to increases in employment, but that the gains will be relatively modest and in some cases will translate into smaller welfare savings." Programs seem to have larger effects for the "harder-to-employ" groups. More recent results are consistently positive but improvements remain modest.[15]

The GAO, in identifying the long-term AFDC core, which uses up the bulk of the budget and constitutes almost 60 percent of recipients at any one time, notes that most were high school dropouts, black, entered the AFDC system when very young, had little or no prior work experience, and had never been married before their AFDC application.[16]

Thus, the analysis yields insights as important as the general conclusions: It appears possible to impose "obligations," but this usually means an obligation to take part in a work experience, not (merely) to "work off" a check. However, these model programs do little to enhance work skills. It may be that the "job search" component is most important. Of some interest, too, is the fact that these particular types of efforts are most effective (despite modest success rates) with the hard core; others come and go and make it on their own.

All of this is quite modest, but it combines with earlier work by MRDC on so-called supported work programs (as mentioned in Chapter 4), which suggested that of the several "hard core" case types in what is popularly being called the "underclass," AFDC mothers are worthy of concentration and program investment. Work programs do help some of them. None of what has gone before suggests that all the design answers are in. But the studies, testimonials, and observations all suggest that the core approach taken is right and that a developmental process must continue.

Exhibit 5–1, reproduced from the GAO report, is a most useful summation of program components potentially useful to some single mothers. An effective program would be one that was able to channel different women as they became ready for the job market, based on their need of skills or education, or preparation other than job skills. A California commission, describing the GAIN program, suggests that a differentiating strategy can be mounted administratively and can even place these options into a sequence that stresses lower-cost services needed by most applicants (job search) before higher-cost services essential for only the most difficult cases (supported work).[17]

Overall then, states and localities may develop case-by-case strategies composed of:

- Educational support for the mother, with child care and stipends as well, to complete the equivalent of high school, or (on the basis of careful assessment) junior college—as an investment in self-support. This policy is standard in Sweden and part of ET in Massachusetts.
- Strong counseling, job search, vocational guidance, mutual support (job clubs), and job placement services.
- Flexible federal rules to permit AFDC funds to be utilized for the above purposes and to partially subsidize or supplement private industry, nonprofit, or public job placements for limited times and under closely monitored rules to avoid exploitation and misuse.

The current welfare environment will need to be redefined so that all new arrivals are seen—*not* as new members of a caseload for ongoing support entitlement—but rather as people to be helped temporarily with funds concentrated on job-career-worklife preparation and the early work period. New terms, titles, and procedures will be required. The minority not considered suitable

Exhibit 5–1

---

1. Activities assuming clients are ready for the job market

- Individual job search—Client looks for employment, sometimes with requirement of reporting to program staff the number of employers contacted
- Group job search—Groups of participants receive training in job search techniques and, under an instructor's supervision, identify and contact potential employers
- Direct placement assistance—Job developer in program or at Employment Service tries to match client to jobs and refer him/her directly to employer

2. Activities assuming clients need preparation other than skills

- CWEP work experience—Experience or training provided through work in public or private non-profit agency in return for AFDC benefits, hours determined by dividing AFDC grant by minimum wage
- WIN work experience—Work in public or private nonprofit agency to develop basic work habits and practice skills; state sets hours, but assignment limited to 13 weeks

3. Activities assuming clients need skills or education

- OJT—Training placement, often subsidized, in which clients are hired by employers and engage in productive work while being trained
- Supported work—Subsidized work experience or training where work standards are gradually increased to those of an unsubsidized job; support provided by counselors and peers
- Vocational skills training—Occupationally oriented skills training usually provided through classroom instruction.
- Remedial/basic education—Instruction to raise basic reading and math skills or to prepare for a GED examination.
- Post-high school education—Program in a college or technical institution leading to a degree or certificate.

Source: United States General Accounting Office, *Work and Welfare: Current AFDC Work Programs and Implications for Federal Policy* (Washington, D.C., 1987).

for the "workstream" should be elsewhere, in another long-term program, helped adequately, and not expected to participate in employment-related efforts.

The fact that the available work programs seem to do most for the hard core is relevant here. Those who can manage alone need brief, transitional help. The others will not achieve spectacular success rates or accomplishments levels, but if they can be launched on the path of maximum self-support, their lives and the lives of their children can be changed significantly. Society needs to continue to share some responsibilities, as we shall suggest, since the modest work successes, in many instances, will not ensure adequate incomes or medical care.

Because the programs have evolved over time, via patchwork legislation and in the midst of controvesy about policy, the GAO report contains considerable evidence of the need for an affirmation of direction, division of responsibilities, and consistent federal funding strategies. The GAO has recommended that Congress "develop a coherent, streamlined federal work policy that would preserve some of the more desirable features of the programs begun in the past five years" (p. 5).

The details need not be pursued here. Our specifics would be obsolete before they got to press, since this is now a very active arena. Many states are experimenting with their own variations. However, both the GAO and the MRDC overviews, as well as an early 1987 report from the Congressional Budget Office, all indicate that the country is inching toward the work program that is needed and the necessity of a stronger affirmation of direction, as well as more adequate administrative and financial support. Many more mothers need access to such programs. Public policy both grows out of changed expectations and affirms new community norms. The families involved would benefit from clearer affirmations, more expectations, and more apparent opportunities and support. One should resist the tendencies that are currently visible in the media and at congressional hearings to gloss over problems, ignore costs, and promise too much; nevertheless, these new programs are heading in a sound direction. *Along with the other policy components to be discussed,* they can be an important part of a new beginning for low-income single mothers.

The temptation exists to create special programs for welfare recipients only (therefore, preferably, administering them out of the public assistance offices). The record gives pause. The best programs—in the sense of results achieved and level of opportunity opened up—are the ones targeted to the population at large. Indeed, with limited places, the current major federal effort, the Job Training and Partnership Act (JTPA), tends to select the most qualified, most-likely-to-succeed applicants. There is not much room for welfare mothers. On the other hand, the modest, documented successes with AFDC mothers are with the programs designed for them; this unresolved issue of broad targeting or welfare-specific programming contributes to policy uncertainty. Most special programs for welfare mothers historically have not had notable success.

There is also another consideration. If programs that become desirable—such as some of the educational and training offerings, stipends, and child care priorities in several states—are to be reserved for welfare recipients or for single mothers, they could be said to create perverse incentives (whether or not they actually operate as such) or to unfairly discriminate. A new reform for single mothers would avoid some of this only if it were part of a broader offering—universalism rather than excessive categorization.

The argument over welfare categorization versus broad-based programs is a strange one because one cannot be sure about client and community response. We favor a universal, general program because it is likely to be better and less stigmatized—and thus to lead to better opportunities for disadvantaged single mothers, including welfare recipients. We also prefer programs with general access because good, successful, attractive programs that are reserved for single mothers alone can create resentment and community problems.

All this said, we also acknowledge that this philosophy will not necessarily be easy to realize. Ours is a society that finds it easiest to mobilize for categorical initiatives responsive to specific problems. Society may be willing to act with regard to single-mother families or welfare reform before it develops training/educational/ work opportunities for a larger group in the population. And some of what we propose—the "community work" programs described in the next section—clearly are backup offerings for welfare clients per se. The compromise answer? General or universal strategies supplemented with some categorical single-mother programs that are determined to be essential.

We discuss child care in Chapter 6. This section, however, should not be concluded without acknowledging that child care is the obvious prerequisite of any work strategy, whether addressed to women who find and maintain their own jobs or to those who need job search, training, educational, and placement help. According to the GAO report cited earlier, with one or two exceptions, all work programs understand the need to offer child care, and child care was identified as the crucial support service. However, work programs that were studied tended to use services or funding outside of the work programs and differed as to whether the lack of resources was in fact a serious obstacle.[18] While there is much evidence that states and localities are making progress in the child care field, a satisfactory financing, delivery, and supply situation has yet to be achieved.[19]

Public Work as a Last Resort? Should Work Be Required?

Two questions arise: If, after all the training, educating, counseling, referring, and searching, the poor single-mothers involved still have no work, should a public work alternative be ensured? And, should participation in the public work alternative be required?

We do not assume that welfare recipients who complete training and job search programs will not find work. We are in the midst of a growing economy in which many people are finding jobs. Further, unless the economy experiences a major slowdown or mass immigration completely nullifies demographic trends, there actually could be shortages of workers in the 1990s as the "baby-bust" birthrate is reflected in the size of the cohorts ready for jobs. In addition, work programs in California and in other states have reported that "contrary to expectations . . . the unemployment rate is not a particularly sensitive measure of opportunities available to AFDC recipients." Targeted training has successfully produced jobs for AFDC recipients in high unemployment and low unemployment counties, rural and urban.[20]

Once it is agreed that an individual who cannot successfully find a job that fully meets his or her full aspirations must take the best that can be offered or found, there is much higher placement success than has been traditional in this field. In short, one posits both obligations and the best available opportunities, but the obligations are not forgotten.

We emphasize here a somewhat controversial shift from the philosophies of earlier decades. Physically healthy people are expected to take work they can get and not to hold out for long periods for work that would meet their aspiration levels but that they cannot find. The rationale is that one can be as selective as one likes *if it is at one's own expense*, but that when there is a request for public support, the public has the right to hold to a work obligation. Obviously, jobs should meet labor law standards and pay the minimum wage. California has exceeded these minimums, as should most labor markets, at least until the minimum wage catches up with the inflation during which it has been eroded.

In some places, despite such a policy, there will be no jobs in the market or at least no jobs for some of the unskilled and uneducated women on the welfare rolls. One must then wonder if it is good public policy to create work.

New practices in many places turn welfare "grant" monies either into subsidies for nonprofit or private jobs or into direct salaries for community work in nonprofit or public programs. Opponents complain about "slave labor" and "coercion." Proponents note that there is an enormous reservoir of work to be done in schools, parks, libraries, hospitals, public offices, public spaces, transportation facilities, in the homes of the handicapped or frail, and in recreational centers and child care programs. While not the choice of those in need of a job—perhaps not even skill-enhancing, often monotonous, and probably below the aspirations of the people involved—these jobs accomplish needed community work and thus are inherently dignified. The argument, then, is that the community has a right to expect that the work be done in return for community help and support. Opponents may stress the coercion, and proponents may range in their rationale from the desire to create a welfare disincentive to conviction that it is good for morale, dignity, and mainstreaming because it respects the dignity of those who want help in that it also expects reciprocity. How is this debate to be viewed?

So-called "workfare" programs have expected AFDC recipients (also food stamps and, in some places, general assistance recipients) to "work off" their welfare grants. In some places, their hourly rate is the minimum wage. In the California GAIN program, the wage is the (much higher) hourly average of the jobs to which AFDC recipients have successfully been referred. In some instances, the emphasis is on "working off" the grant; in others there is obvious concern with offering a useful work experience that will enhance self-esteem and employability.

Given the long history of punitive workfare legislation from the 1950s and the public assertions of some anti-welfare advocates, those who are concerned with the future well-being of the affected single mothers and their children have hesitated to align themselves with what could be perceived as a punitive policy. Nonetheless, public sentiment has been shifting, and there is—despite ongoing disagreements—a remarkable convergence of liberal and conservative thinking in favor of some type of work-participation requirement. Once there is consensus that job search, registration, education, training, assessment, and related activities are reasonable "social contractual" obligations of healthy, employable women who ask for public aid, it would appear reasonable as well to expect those who do not make it in the marketplace to take some publicly provided work and to use it to show their seriousness of purpose— and, preferably, to enhance their employability. If the work requires little skill and does little to enhance existing skills—but is all that the public can offer—it can nevertheless be viewed as a way of establishing regularity, reliability, and ability to manage peer and supervisor relationships—and a claim on public aid.

While recognizing the possibilities of abuse and misuse of a work requirement, we support its use and note the evidence that good training, education, and work programs find most of their offerings swamped and most of their potential eligibles flocking to take advantage of the opportunities.

Employability: What Age Child?

As we have noted, the AFDC tradition from the time of the original 1967 WIN legislation has been to define mothers caring for children under age 6 as out of the labor market. Earlier, of course, widows' pensions had similarly protected all mothers of school-age children. Those who defended the traditional AFDC program constantly reiterated that few of the parents aided were "employable," by virtue of child-rearing obligations.

The new female labor force participation patterns have changed all this. In 1970, 43 percent of all children aged 6–17 had mothers in the labor force; for those under 6, the rate was 28 percent. By 1987 the rate for children in the 6–17 range was 64 percent, and for those under 6 it was 53 percent. We already have noted as well that by 1987 half of all women with infants under 1 year of age were in the work force, and 62 percent of mothers of preschoolers (age 3–5). Even the full-time to part-time work ratios for women with children under age 3 are on the order of 3:1. For single mothers with children in the under-6 category, participation had reached 56 percent by 1987; it was 48 percent for single mothers with children under 1 (see Table 5–1).

The 1971 WIN amendments mandating work program registration if the youngest child was over age 6 represented a watershed, which in fact constituted catching up with social realities. Coercion was limited because available opportunities were grasped by volunteers. WIN and Job Search retain the age-6 cut-off, but CWEP has moved the requirement to mothers of children age 3. We cited the GAO report that, as yet, few programs actually enforce such requirements. States also may now petition the federal government for lower ages, and New Jersey is considering age 2 as we write. A Governors' Conference report has proposed the age-3 "divider," and one current administration proposal suggests 6 months. A pending bill sets age 3 as the cut-off but allows states to go down to 1 if child care is assured. A new rationale is required, against which states may exercise their options.

First, we note that in some sense the young mothers who do not avoid the AFDC trap may find it more difficult to break out. David Ellwood has reported that young women who are placed on the AFDC recipient rolls with children under age 3 are most likely to become fixed in that status and to receive aid for a long time.

Some 40 percent in the group remain recipients for more than 10 years, even though the "average" AFDC case opens and closes within two years. Bane and Ellwood have been able to show that of those mothers who left the welfare rolls because of adequate earnings, two-thirds were mothers with preschool children.[21] Moreover, although those with more children were less likely to give up welfare for work, among those leaving for work, "the age of the youngest child seemed to have little *independent* effect on durations or on the method of exit." Thus, "Women with young children are a bit less likely to become wives, but if anything they are slightly more likely to have earnings exits."[22]

Are children ever too young to have their mothers leave for work? When should the work requirement begin? We have in our earlier research explored and elaborated current maternity/parental leave and related policies in the United States and elsewhere in the world.[23] Society has a stake in guaranteeing a mother time to recover physically from the childbirth experience; in the United States the norms are six to eight weeks, and longer for Caesarians and birth complications. Society has a stake, also, in ensuring fathers and mothers opportunities as parents to participate through their personal presence (perhaps taking turns) in the early development of their child. Parents and children need time to start their lives together, and society is apparently the gainer when such opportunity is available, in the sense that the early parent-child relationship contributes significantly to socialization.

What is needed is a job-protected and paid "maternity/disability" and parental leave with substantial wage replacement—not the unpaid leave proposed to Congress and to some state legislatures at this writing. Whereas at present the United States offers very brief post-childbirth leaves and modest wage replacement (about half an average wage) to about 40 percent of its female labor force, European leaves are much longer, are offered at full or close to full pay, and are available to all working women. In Europe, a 12-week paid leave is minimum, and 5–6 months is usual; 9 months at full pay plus 3 more months at a low replacement is the entitlement in Sweden.[24] Some countries offer an additional 1–2 years of unpaid, job-protected leaves after the paid leave.

All of this would suggest that no work requirement should go into effect any sooner than the typical "maternity/disability" period in the United States—the 6–8 weeks after childbirth (and 2–4 weeks before). However, infant care is the most difficult to obtain, and the most expensive. Single mothers and their children are the most vulnerable, and the likelihood of their child care plan being in place most problematic. A society that should enact, but has not yet enacted, childbirth-related leaves of at least 6 months might nonetheless consider such an interval after childbirth as the minimal starting point for a work training requirement tied to AFDC. Even this is too little, we believe. As parental leave policies improve, we would do well to attempt a one-year period of "adjustment time," and parenting time especially for the beleaguered single mother.

This viewpoint has yet another rationale. While the child care supply has been improving, infant and toddler services are in shortest supply. Many available resources are in the unlicensed, underground family day care. Yet it is the young infant who is the most vulnerable and whose care is least understood and validated. Therefore, we would recommend that work program requirements be deferred, perhaps until the child is at least one year old. We believe that to delay until the child is age 3 may create overwhelming obstacles to the eventual employability of many of the young mothers. A good phase-in policy might require at least part-time work when the child is age 3 but would encourage it once the child is 1. Such a policy also could require school for a teen mother who has not yet completed high school and whose child is 1. The policy could be reevaluated when the infant/toddler child care supply improves—and as the experience is assessed. As noted earlier, this subject remains a field which must draw upon somewhat inconclusive and controversial child development research.

When the child is age 3 (or perhaps even when the child reaches age 1 or 2), the mainstreaming philosophy calls for single mothers to be in the work force or in school/training and their children with relatives or in child-care arrangements. The evidence is that all will be better off for it, because the family income situation will be improved and it will be easier to protect mother and child from social isolation and continued deprivation. Clearly, the public consensus is moving in such a direction.

Income Supplementation, To Complete the "Package"

The core elements in our proposed economic strategy for single-parent families are private transfers in the form of child-support payments by the noncustodial parent—and work. Work, in turn, will be facilitated and buttressed by educational and training opportunity. But will this plan yield enough income? What if it does not? Is there a way to fill the gap without work disincentives?

For middle-class families, fair child-support payments added to the salaries of women with better-than-average education will yield manageable incomes. Nonetheless, many could experience some decline in living standards. At least this is the best estimate one can currently make on the basis of federal data on alimony, child support, and salaries of women in the workplace.

For working-class families and the poor and "near poor" who now depend on salaries or public assistance income (AFDC, or "welfare"), the likelihood is that despite the child-support payment and work efforts, total income will be marginal. A two-person family, mother and child, in which the mother earns the current minimum wage of $3.35 hour and works full-time, has an annual gross income below the poverty line. The two-child family falls even further below the poverty line. While the data are inadequate, meaning that conclusions in either direction are challengeable, our view, which is based on the facts currently at hand, is that child support payments in such families would be important but also would leave the children deprived. Child support would not convert one-earner families into two-income families.

One basic issue to be confronted is that of the marginal economic position of all one-earner families in what has become a two-earner economy since World War II. Working with 1982 data, Blanche Bernstein estimated that "it takes about 1.3 wage earners per four-person family to achieve the Bureau of Labor Statistics lower-level standard of living ($15,323 in 1981 prices), 1.7 for the moderate level ($24,407), and 2.0 for the higher level ($38,060)."[25]

We have already noted (in Table 5–2) how important the mother's work is in affecting poverty rates, whether in two-parent or one-parent households. However, even when single mothers work, the poverty rate is high.[26] First, current costs leave many low-earner families in poverty if the family has only one salary. Second, the female-headed household is affected as well by the lower wage of female workers, overall. Despite recent improvement, women earn 70 percent of what men earn; poorly educated women hover close to minimum wage in various service jobs. As suggested earlier, part of the long-range improvement depends on equal employment opportunity and greater pay equity for women at work. Improvement would be furthered, as well, by a raise in the minimum wage, which has lagged badly behind inflation.

This does not solve a problem of concern throughout the 20th century: The salary of the working adult is determined by various conditions in the labor market and is not geared to family needs. Two people doing the same work and with the same seniority earn about the same wage. One may be supporting a wife and four children, and the other may have no dependents at all. At times, workers have advocated a basic "family wage," a minimum salary adequate to support a worker, his wife, and two children. In general, employers have resisted, although at times some countries have had variations of the policy (Australia and until recently, The Netherlands).

There are several known "solutions" to the problem of the lack of connection between wages and family needs, and they all involve variations on the idea of supplementing the wage to take account of the added burdens of child rearing. As far back as the 19th century in France, private employers paid voluntary wage supplements to workers with children, thus avoiding general wage increases. Later, there were mandatory "equalization funds" with the same results. Subsequently, there were special allowances for one-earner families. Finally, almost universally after World War II, industrial societies established family allowances, which varied in a number of ways but generally adopted the notion of societal sharing in the costs of child rearing. Most such allowances are universal, and are available regardless of family income. As described in Chapter 3, they consist of regular payments, worth more in some places than in others, usually made monthly, and usually for all children. Some are motivated by the pronatalist goal of encouraging people to have more children (of doubtful impact), others by the desire to equalize family burdens to avoid child poverty, and still others by the desire to compensate for the possible gap between wages and family needs. All feature concern for children and social justice. We, among others, have elaborated their history and impact elsewhere.[27]

There is in all this an important lead for the shaping of an economic policy for single-parent families. If the wage income could be supplemented not only by child-support payments but also by a universal payment to help meet the costs of child rearing, one could with conviction argue the merits of work, even of low-pay work. Many scholars have shown that the low-skill, low-earner mother cannot provide her children with the equivalent of a welfare budget in a good-standard state (including food-stamps, Medicaid, and perhaps access to housing benefits) through what she can earn from work.[28] The disincentives could encourage the setting up of "welfare-supported" single-parent households and discourage work. On the other hand, universal (non-means-tested) child allowances made available to all families with children would supplement low wages very effectively and avoid possible work or marriage disincentives. Given some progress on Medicaid for low earners, plus child support, the family would remain better off economically, even when salaries were low. There would be positive work motivation—something desirable both as a "mainstream-ing" and a normalization instrument, as well as a vehicle toward a better living standard and improved self-respect.

Not immediately relevant but worthy of an "aside" is the fact that an income supplement to help with the costs of child rearing would be of enormous importance as well to two-parent, one-earner families in the working poor category—families not currently eligible for AFDC. That is why we stress that what most single parents need are universal and noncategorical social policy improvements, shared with all other families with children.

Obviously, such a proposal arouses controversy in this country—or has in the past. Some have objected to the possible (but questionable) pronatalist impact. They worry that people (or the "wrong" people) might be encouraged to have more children. Others see here an economically inefficient device, since it would distribute funds to many families who already had adequate income. One could say as much, of course, about the even less efficient personal exemptions in the income tax system. The exemption is not available without adequate income—and it is worth more to high-income than to low-income people.

More important, for those concerned with the inefficiency of a universal child allowance, it could be made taxable or even "recoverable" at tax payment time from high-income families. Indeed, several countries have shown ways to integrate tax exemptions and child allowances by creating child tax credit or child benefit systems that become positive payments for low-income families and tax credits for others.[29]

Here we wish only to stress that the economic strategy which includes work and child support is incomplete. A program of income supplementation for one- and two-parent families with children is also needed. The evidence suggests that family allowances in their several variations can become potent components in the repertoire of anti-poverty and mainstreaming benefits for such families.[30] The choice of a specific program device will depend on the expectations with regard to tax policy in the United States. If, following the 1986 tax law reforms, this is to be a period of resistance to use of tax measures as a way to enact new social policy, it would be wiser to seek child allowances (albeit taxable or recoupable allowances). On the other hand, it could become politically practical to consider some trade-offs between projected, increased personal exemptions in the tax system and some types of tax credits to aid families who rear children.

As the income supplementation debate intensifies, as it must, attention should be paid to the specific proposals and cost estimates offered by Garfinkel and McLanahan, Schorr, and others.[31] They vary in generosity, rationale, and political feasibility and must therefore be judged in context. They are part of the much-needed initiative for putting the issue on the policy agenda. Our own earlier research documents possible variations and potential impacts.

We expect that before long the argument will be made out of societal concern over falling birthrates:[32] Who will pay future social security benefits, serve in the armed forces, build the economy, if birthrates decline further? Will immigration fill the deficits? The weak pronatalist case need not be made—only that it is fair to share the high costs of child rearing with those parents who do choose to have children and to ensure that children are not deprived.

If such viewpoints take hold and reinforce an income supplementation policy, the economic situation of the single-parent family would improve significantly. And so it should.

Transitional Aid—And the Longer Term

What has been outlined is not limited to poor or uneducated single mothers but does include them. Indeed, it focuses particularly on them because they make the larger demands on public resources and thus the larger claim on public policy attention. Insofar as those served by AFDC are concerned, the proposed combinations of work, training, child support, and income supplementation may be seen as what is commonly called *"welfare reform,"* and it will take the following form:

- AFDC will be turned essentially into a program concentrating on education, training, job search, and placement. Its task will be employment entry. (Child support will be handled separately, as already discussed.)
- There will be a parallel "public and community work" program for those unable to find private sector jobs, after the maximum preparation for which they are eligible or in which they have interest.

Three components of this "reform" remain to be specified:

- The terms of the transitional financial aid for those using the program in ways already described.
- The terms of financial aid for those who cannot be expected to become self-supporting.

- The policy response to those who refuse to follow the pre-
  scribed pathways.

The social infrastructure necessary to make this reform meaningful
is specified in the next chapter.

Currently, the establishment of financial eligibility for AFDC
via a means-test begins a period of long-term or short-term entitlements. However, cases are not differentiated. Most cases have brief
"spells" of assistance; some, we have seen, "settle in" for 8 to 10
years, constitute a large component in any current caseload, and
account for a large portion of costs. There is a strong argument for
differentiation at the outset. There are useful precedents in the
British, French, and the Norwegian traditions.

The Norwegians, we have seen, have an income-tested transitional benefit. While the specifics (particularly the long years of
coverage) do not suit the philosophy we have outlined, the concept
does. The more modest means-tested French transition lasts one
year—or up to three years for women with children under age 3.
We propose that for the United States program covering single-
parent families with minor children, those newly divorced or
separated mothers, or out-of-wedlock mothers who are in or have
a right to independent households (not young adolescent mothers
not yet emancipated from their own parents), should be defined as
needing transitional help. Theirs could be an implied or even an
explicit contract: enough economic aid for a sufficiently long period
to cover an individually designed education-training-work experi-
ence-job search program and a transition into a self-supporting job.
The program should and would become attractive.

Aid of this kind (and related child-care service and medical
benefits) must be more generous than AFDC payments currently
are in many states. There is need for clothing, lunch money,
transportation, books, and/or work supplies. Nor can a mother
thus engaged be expected to devote herself full-time to seeking
out free or very low-cost ways to "get by" for herself and her
children. The assistance budget must be adequate.

The obvious reform to accomplish such arrangements is a minimum, income-tested, national benefit—a kind of federalized version of AFDC, but more like Supplemental Security Income—and
at least 25 percent above the poverty line. Such a transitional
program needs a new kind of doorway. The "eligibility" worker
must be a social worker-counselor, qualified to clarify the "contract" and make referrals to specialists who will develop the
education/work strategy with the mother. Such social workers must
be more than the currently popular coordinating-types of "case

managers." There is need for counseling, support, following progress, adjusting plans, and individualization.

Both the mother and the society have a stake in a brief "transition," but educational and training programs could continue for some time. We have not found an empirical basis for specifying an outside limit, but tend to favor a plan in the 6-month to 2-year range, individually designed. Individualized plans might allow teen mothers more time to complete basic schooling, but progress would be monitored. One would not permit anything more than this except on the basis of the recommendation of a "career development review panel," which could urge a longer public investment in a limited number of particularly promising trainees whose performance merits recognition. Loosely administered "discretion" has a way of getting out of hand and becoming inequitable.

The time limit (we favor two years but could see a case for one) would both symbolize the contractual intent (there are those who favor a written "contract" or agreement) and avoid undesirable disincentives that a generous program might create. In any case, the responsible social worker would be expected to monitor progress and initiate removal from the "transitional benfit" to the less generous and thus less attractive "long-term" program of those showing inability to use the opportunity for self-betterment.

At the point of application and also during and after the work program exposure of the transition-benefit recipients, the "eligibility" social worker also will identify those who are *not* expected to take part in the work program. The following are two categories of mothers who would not qualify:

- Emotionally or intellectually limited mothers in a number of categories whose handicaps do not translate into eligibility for Social Security Disability Insurance (DI) or Supplemental Security Income (SSI), but who are deemed able to protect and rear their children.
- Mothers whose children have various types of handicaps, limitations, and problems and whose special needs could be better or perhaps satisfactorily and more economically met by an at-home mother. One could explore including on an optional basis the small number of mothers of three or more children.

Relevant to the program but not to our present focus, also, are grandmothers and other relatives who are rearing young children but are of an age when the training investment can be questioned—and who do not choose that option.

For mothers who should not be expected to take part in the

work program, a "long-term" benefit could be designed that would cover the period until children completed middle school. It would not have to cover work or educational expenses for the mother, but it would have to be at a high enough level (indexed to the poverty line?) to allow decent child rearing—assuming availability as well of Medicaid, housing help, and money to meet special needs of children with various difficulties and limitations. Where at all possible, there would be child-support money. As would all other parents, the recipients of either the long-term or the transitional benefit also would have the child allowance supplementation as soon as it was added to the public policy repertoire.

In short, (1) an attractive transitional benefit would aid those who have "contracted" to be on their own after a defined period of public help to cover a defined program of self-improvement; and (2) a respectable but less generous long-term benefit (reversing the British tradition of a *more* generous long-term benefit) would help those not eligible for the transitional aid—or who make a serious effort in the work program but fail. The latter should be few in number because even if they do not gain enough skills for the private market, mothers could be assigned to earn their benefits in the public program.

Those Who Refuse

There could be another group. We assume that there will be, but that it will be small. Some mothers who are defined as qualified for the work-training program may object to participation; they may not want to make an agreement. Or some who complete training may not find work, and may then refuse to join the public-community work program. What about financial support for them and their children?

Current WIN and CWEP legislation states that those adults who will not cooperate are to be removed from the family's welfare budget but that benefits are to continue for the children. We do not deem this as an answer, since one result could be that the family would end up managing on a drastically cut budget; whatever the "principle," in fact, the children would be punished. The 1987 GAO survey reported very limited use of sanctions because programs in fact could not accommodate many mothers, because the "conciliation" machinery avoided some actions, and because sanctions were difficult to apply. [33]

We believe that well-developed programs of work/training and transitional aid will attract eligibles. Those who cannot and should not be expected to work because of personality and character problems should be channeled to the long-term aid program by the social workers who assess eligibility.

The small residue of work and training failures and "refusers" will need individualized assessment and attention. Some will be found eligible for long-term aid because they are confused, disturbed, or of limited capacity. Some will have grievances about procedures; there should be ways for their problems to be addressed, also. Some others may respond to counseling. In some cases, it may appear that children are not being cared for or fed adequately, and society will have to use the powers in its neglect legislation—to offer help under specified conditions—or in the final instance, to remove and protect the children. In brief, if the parents are found to have severe problems, an assessment should lead either to accepting the fact that they cannot comply with work rules but should be helped anyway, or should convince authorities of the need to protect the children whom such parents place at risk to defy a law with which they disagree.

We stress, again, that this is a discussion about small numbers—if also about important principles. The society will want careful assessments, not punitive bureaucracies. Yet it also will need to be clear as to its policy.

Summary

Studies of the life situations of lone mothers, and surveys of these women and their children in the United States and other industrialized countries, all conclude that income, or more adequate income, is the number one priority for these families. In the United States, as in most countries, government income transfers alone will not maintain these families at a decent standard. To argue that single mothers should be supported at home while most married mothers with similarly aged children are already in the work force is to argue against current realities and to further isolate and segregate single mothers from other women rearing children.

We propose, instead, an income package that includes earnings, child support, and government transfers to supplement other income. In the main, the transfers would be part of a universal system and available, as well, to two-parent families. Earnings would—and should—constitute lone mothers' core income as it does for other families with children. Private income transfers— the payment of child support by the noncustodial parent—would constitute a second, significant part of family income, too, partially guaranteed and advanced, as well as collected, by the government in situations where the absent parent cannot or does not pay enough to support the child(ren). The third component would be income transfers provided by government to supplement family income and earnings when wages are low, to support these women when they are in educational or training programs and preparing for work, or to support them when they or their children have special handicaps that preclude their working.

In the next chapter we turn to some other pressing needs of single-parent families—the remainder of the policy and program "package."

Endnotes

1. Sheila Rothman, *Woman's Proper Place* (New York: Basic Books, 1978); Edwin Shorter, *The Making of the Modern Family* (New York: Basic Books, 1975); Carl N. Degler, *At Odds: Woman and the Family in America from the American Revolution to the Present* (New York: Oxford University Press, 1980).
2. Rothman, *Woman's Proper Place*.
3. Committee on Ways and Means, U.S. House of Representatives, *Children in Poverty* (Washington, D.C.: U.S. Government Printing Office, 1987), 636–45.
4. Ibid., 637.
5. Ibid., 632.
6. Cheryl D. Hayes and Sheila B. Kamerman, eds., *Children of Working Parents: Experiences and Outcomes* (Washington, D.C.: National Academy Press, 1983).
7. Sheila B. Kamerman and Alfred J. Kahn, *The Responsive Workplace: Employers and a Changing Labor Force* (New York: Columbia University Press, 1987).
8. U.S. Bureau of the Census, Child Support and Alimony: 1983 (Supplemental Report) *Current Population Supports,* series P-23, no. 148 (Washington, D.C.: U.S. Government Printing Office, 1986).
9. Irwin Garfinkel, the initiator, and his collaborators have reported extensively on their studies and proposals in Wisconsin. See Irwin Garfinkel and Sara S. McLanahan, *Single Mothers and Their Children* (Washington, D.C.: The Urban Institute, 1986), 151–55, 181–83. For a child support overview, see Committee on Ways and Means, U.S. House of Representatives, *Background Material and Data on Programs Within the Jurisdiction of the Committee, 1987 Edition* (Washington, D.C.: U.S. Government Printing Office, 1987), 452–91. On the potential of child support we quote from an editor's summary:

    Bergman and Roberts conclude that merely improving the enforcement of currently existing child support awards would not have a large effect on welfare expenditure or on the proportion of single mothers in

> *poverty. To eliminate poverty among single mothers by child support payments alone would require payments that probably exceed absent fathers' ability to pay. [Clair Brown and Joseph A. Peckman, eds., Gender in the Workforce (Washington, D.C.: The Brookings Institution, 1987), "Introduction," p. 10]*

Also see Philip K. Robins, "Child Support, Welfare Dependency, and Poverty," *American Economic Review*, vol. 76, no. 4 (September 1986): 768–88. He concludes: "Child support enforcement may represent an effective means for reducing welfare program costs but is unlikely to have a dramatic effect on reducing either poverty or welfare dependency."

10. Joyce Everett, "An Examination of Child Support Enforcement Issues," in *Services to Young Families*, ed. Harriet McAdoo and T. M. Jim Parham (Washington, D.C.: American Public Welfare Association, 1985), 75–112; contains broad bibliography. For U.S. and European developments see Alfred J. Kahn and Sheila B. Kamerman, eds., *Child Support: From Debt Collection to Social Policy* (Newbury Park, Calif.: Sage Publications, 1988).

11. For example, see:
    (a) "Welfare and Work," a special issue of *Public Welfare*, vol. 44, no. 1 (Winter 1986).
    (b) *A New Social Contract*, Report of the Task Force on Poverty and Welfare, Submitted to Governor Mario Cuomo, Albany, December 1986.
    (c) Isabel V. Sawhill, "Anti-Poverty Strategies for the 1980s," *Discussion Paper* (Washington, D.C.: The Urban Institute, December 1986).
    (d) Judith M. Gueron, "Interim Findings from the Demonstration of State Work/Welfare Initiatives" (Paper presented at the meetings of the Association of Public Policy Analysis and Management, 26 October 1985). A brief version appears in *Public Welfare*, Winter 1986 (see above) as "Work for People on Welfare."
    (e) Jack A. Meyer, ed., *Ladders Out of Poverty* (Washington, D.C.: American Horizons Foundation, 1986), especially 85–98, Theresa Flynn, "State Work and Welfare Initiatives."

12. United States General Accounting Office, *Work and Welfare: Current AFDC Work Programs and Implications for Federal Policy* (Washington, D.C.: January, 1987); Gueron, op. cit.

13. Committee on Ways and Means, *Background Material and Data . . .* , 391–400.

14. GAO, *Current AFDC Work Programs . . .* , 4.

15. Gueron, "Work for People on Welfare," 12. Also see Judith M. Gueron, "Reforming Welfare with Work," *Public Welfare* (Fall 1987); Judith M. Gueron, "Reforming Welfare with Work," Paper 2 (New York: The Ford Foundation, 1987).

16. GAO, *Current AFDC Work Programs*, 20.

17. "Work and Welfare," 26. In a report prepared at the request of the Senate Budget Committee, the nonpartisan Congressional Budget Office (CBO) has gone over ground similar to that in the GAO report and also endorsed the notion that these are useful activities but that expected overall results are modest, not spectacular. Indeed, most states have exposed only limited

numbers of welfare recipients to such programs. See *Work-Related Programs for Welfare Recipients* (Washington, D.C.: CBO, 1987).

18. GAO, *Current AFDC Work Program,* Ch. 5.
19. Alfred J. Kahn and Sheila B. Kamerman, *Child Care: Facing the Hard Choices* (Dover, Mass.: Auburn House, 1987).
20. "Work and Welfare," 21.
21. David Ellwood, *Targeting "Would Be" Long-Term Recipients of AFDC* (Washington, D.C.: Mathematica Policy Research Inc., 1986); Mary Jo Bane and David T. Ellwood, "Slipping Into and Out of Poverty: The Dynamics of Spells," *The Journal of Human Resources* 21 (1986): 1–23.
22. Mary Jo Bane and David T. Ellwood, *The Dynamics of Dependence: The Routes to Self-Sufficiency* (Cambridge, Mass.: Urban Systems Research and Engineering, 1983), 44.
23. Sheila B. Kamerman, Alfred J. Kahn, and Paul Kingston, *Maternity Policies and Working Women* (New York: Columbia University Press, 1983).
24. Sheila B. Kamerman, "Maternity, Paternity, and Parenting Policies: How Does the United States Compare?" in *Family and Work,* ed. Sylvia Ann Hewlett et al. (Cambridge, Mass.: Ballinger, 1986), 53–65. Also, Sheila B. Kamerman, "Maternity and Parenting Benefits: An International Overview," in *The Parental Leave Crisis: Toward a National Policy,* ed. Edward Zigler and Merryl Frank (New Haven: Yale University Press, 1988).
25. Blanche Bernstein, "Welfare Dependency," in *The Social Contract Revisited,* ed. D. Lee Bawden (Washington, D.C.: The Urban Institute Press, 1984), 146.
26. U.S. Bureau of the Census, "Characteristics of the Population Below the Poverty Level: 1984," *Current Population Reports,* series P-60, no. 152 (Washington, D.C.: U.S. Government Printing Office, 1986), Table 21.
27. Jonathan Bradshaw and David Piachaud, *Child Support in the European Community* (London: Bedford Square Press, 1980); also, Sheila B. Kamerman and Alfred J. Kahn, "Explaining the Outcomes: Social Policy and Children in the U.S. and Europe," in *The Changing Well-being of Children and the Aged: The United States in Comparative Perspective,* ed. John L. Palmer, Timothy Smeeding, and Barbara B. Torrey (Washington, D.C.: The Urban Institute Press, 1988).
28. Garfinkel and McLanahan, *Single Mothers and Their Children,* 22–23; Bernstein, "Welfare Dependency"; Jack Meyer, "Budget Cuts in the Reagan Administration," in Bawden, *The Social Contract Revisited,* 54.
29. Alfred J. Kahn and Sheila B. Kamerman, *Income Transfers for Families with Children: An Eight Country Study* (Philadelphia: Temple University Press, 1983), 200–14.
30. Ibid.
31. Garfinkel and McLanahan, *Single Mothers and Their Children,* 183–85; Alvin L. Schorr, *Common Decency* (New Haven: Yale University Press, 1986), 87–95.
32. "Birth Rate Hits New Low," *The Wall Street Journal,* 5 May 1987.
33. GAO, *Current AFDC Work Programs,* 62.

Chapter 6

TIME AND HELP: MANAGING WORK, FAMILY, HOME, AND PERSONAL LIFE

Single parenthood on the one hand may mean never having to explain "Why?" to a spouse, although there may be twice as many "Whys?" to respond to from a child. If a marriage was bad, divorced and separated mothers find their single status relieves them of the additional strains of conflict and tension; they are free of husbands who maybe gave no help anyway and, in addition, had their own needs that they expected their wives to meet.

On the other hand, one-parent families, almost by definition, are unlikely to have another adult in the home with whom to share any part of their responsibilities. Married working mothers may often feel overburdened, overextended, and inequitably treated, but some, at least, have husbands who do share in the stresses, strains, and decisions of everyday life and in some of the tasks and responsibilities of child care and rearing, and household chores. Coping with all this can be especially difficult for the single mother. While occasionally, the single mother may have a some-time-cohabitant-friend who may be helpful, or a relative, neighbor, friend, or older child to provide an extra pair of hands, most have no one on whom they can depend regularly, or to whom they can turn in a crisis.

Some years ago, during our study of working mothers with young children, a single mother with an active 2-year old and a full-time job made a lasting impression as she described what her life was like. It sounded overwhelming:

With long blond hair pulled back in a pony tail, wearing blue jeans and a heavy sweatshirt, she looked more like 16 than 26. Her

187

husband left her a year ago, and she has received no support from him except for $20 at Christmas. Her mother, who lives two blocks away, has tried to help her, but since her own husband became ill, she has little time or energy for help, let alone money. Sandy works as the office manager in a law office and makes a good salary, but it's still only one salary and it barely covers necessities. She lives in a one-bedroom apartment, selected because she can walk to work and shopping. She has no car. Her 2-year-old, Caroline, is in a day care center, and the fee is partially subsidized. Because the day care center is not within walking distance, and Sandy has no car, she has arranged with another mother who lives not too far away to pick up her child and bring her home at the end of the day. Sandy gets up at 6:00 a.m. five days a week, in order to get the baby and herself ready by 8:15, when the child is picked up and Sandy leaves for work. If she's going to work late and therefore going to be late getting home, she phones the woman during the day and asks her to bring Caroline to her home, waiting for a call from Sandy to tell when she has arrived. Sandy pays for this "extra" child care by the hour, in addition to paying for gasoline for the car, for the trans-portation to and from the center.

Most evenings, when Sandy comes home she bathes the baby first, gets her in pajamas, and then they play for a while. Then Sandy fixes supper and reads to her daughter. Housework and laundry are done occasionally in the evening, but usually Sandy says she's too exhausted to do much. The only real cleaning is once a week on the weekend. She hates the look of "sloppiness" but says it's hard to manage even straightening up during the week. Marketing is a Saturday task for which she takes the baby with her. If the weather is bad or the baby has a cold, it is a problem. Another problem is that the director of the day care center thinks parents should be "participants" and visit the center for parent meetings several times a year, but this requires a sitter to stay with the baby, and that's not part of Sandy's budget. Sometimes her mother sits. The health clinic has Saturday hours, which has made bringing the baby for a checkup possible, but there are always other problems around schedules. It's hard to arrange for repairs if something like the washing machine breaks. Last week the baby was sick and Sandy couldn't get out even to market. She's just asked a friend to sit for a couple of hours, in return for her doing it with the friend's baby, another time.[1]

It was in this arena of household and child care tasks, chores, and responsibilities that we first began to identify the extra bur-dens of single-parent families. For these families, extra-family supports are particularly important, be they informal supports, natural support systems, or formal supports. The themes repeat in our research, in the popular press, and in books of advice and help.

Obviously, a major difference between one- and two-parent families is economic. Family income is significantly reduced when there is only one wage earner in a family. And, as we saw in Chapter 1, that reduction is even more marked when the sole wage earner is a woman. The problems of jobs, training, occupational segregation, pay equity, and wage supplementation were addressed in the last chapter, as was the other aspect of financial support for mother-only families and their children—child support. We have found, however, that if inadequate income is a central problem for mother-only families, from another perspective so are inadequate time and help. Almost a decade ago, Robert Weiss wrote, and he did not exaggerate, that "To be a single parent is to head a family that is often understaffed."[2]

A considerable amount of case material, along with anecdotal reports, ethnographic studies, and testimony, describe the stress and psychological impacts associated with single parenthood and the "time poverty" of mothers alone, rearing young children. Much of this suggests that being a working single mother often means living under constant pressure, with less time, less energy, and less support than what is needed, both in and outside of the home. A review of the more comprehensive and rigorous national surveys, however, offers little that would make for a systematic national statistical overview of the time and stress problems of these families that would be comparable to the picture we have of their economic situation. In itself, this is a revealing and interesting finding.

The Institute for Social Research of the University of Michigan conducted two major national surveys of mental health adjustment, one carried out in 1957 and the second in 1976.[3] In this careful overview, by far the best, attention is directed to problem distribution and to coping strategies, classified by many demographic variables. Single women are differentiated from married women, and employed women from at-home women. However, no analysis focuses on the presence of children of various ages in one- and two-parent households or on the relationship of such circumstances to stress, adjustment, and mental health problems variously conceived.

We therefore suggest that even as late as the mid-1970s, while the media and the professional literature had much to say about social problems or economic difficulties associated with and resulting from single parenthood, the status "single mother (or parent), raising children" was not yet a major category of interest for

exploring problems of personal adjustment. Indeed, we are aston-
ished at the analyses relating to employed and at-home women
that do not attend to the issue of whether these women were
simultaneously caring for children.

Along similar lines, a major program of research on time use was
carried out in the 1960s and 1970s and supplemented and analyzed
in the 1980s by outstanding American specialists in another unit of
the Institute for Social Research. Like the studies just mentioned,
this one also carried out most of its analysis with attention to almost
every socioeconomic variable of interest, except for the combination of single parenthood and the presence of children (let alone
young children). Gender differences and differences by marital
and employment status were attended to, but not by marital status
and presence of children. In a sophisticated, scholarly volume of
more than 500 pages, only one small section in one chapter (which
we review below) reports on the time-use patterns of single mothers.[4]

Again, we must conclude, that the status "single mother (or
parent), rearing children" has not, until very recently, become a
salient one for systematic data collection about daily living experiences, problems, and needs. Only the problems caused for the
society—whether costs imposed by welfare or the care of troubled
children—have been visible, even in the recent past.

We note, however, that the neglect may be ending. Of considerable interest is recent work by Duane Alwin, Philip Converse,
and Steven Martin, again at the University of Michigan's Institute
for Social Research. Reanalyzing a data set from their 1978 Quality
of Life survey (conducted with Angus Campbell), they explored
the relationship of living arrangements to social integration and,
ultimately, to psychological well-being. While it is frequently
assumed that individuals living alone are more isolated and less
socially involved than those who live with others, the analysis
found that "in general, people who live alone are not more socially
isolated than others of comparable marital status. Instead they are
generally *more* likely than others to be socially integrated outside
the household." However, there was one dramatic exception: "It
turns out that the true social isolates tend to be women who are
single parents (including never-married, separated, and divorced
women) who are living alone except for their children." It was the
single mothers, especially the never-married, although sometimes
separated and divorced women living with young children, who
showed up most poorly on such measures of well-being as "reported psychological distress," "reported satisfaction in various life

domains," "degree of positive feelings about one's present life," and "feelings of effectiveness in dealing with life."[5]

Clearly, in our effort to think ahead about social policy, we need a more complete understanding of what single parenthood means on a daily living basis for those who participate in it. In this we are aided by one major survey of children's time use,[6] some material from the above-mentioned time study, an earlier economic analysis of the issue,[7] and by small studies and surveys of specialized subgroups in special locations.[8] These studies do not provide a national statistical portrait but do sketch in a suggestive and useful way the broad outlines of situations which call for discussion and response.

In this chapter we document the problems and the consequences of not having enough time, help, or energy; at the same time, we point toward some of the proposed remedies which are properly in the public policy and program domain. Obviously, most of this topic is and must be left to the choices people make in their personal lives and to the diverse preferences which they exercise.

Time Poor

Clair Vickery (Brown) pointed out in an influential article published in 1977, that if the minimal level of consumption for the nonpoor requires both money and household services, then the official poverty standard does not correctly measure household needs. "Any income-support program that corrects for money differences but not for time differences across households will discriminate against households with only one adult."[9] In effect, the household's assets and the number of adult hours that are available to earn income in the market or to produce consumption goods and services both in the market and in the home constitute the totality of household and family resources. For a family to be adequately fed on a limited food budget, for example, assumes (1) the time (and ability) to do careful and comparative shopping for food as well as other items; (2) the time to prepare and cook meals; and (3) eating meals at home, not at a restaurant.

Using data from a time use study of husband/wife households and estimating patterns for single parents, Vickery concluded that a single parent with two children, working full time (40 hours a week) at a minimum wage, would be "short" at least 23 hours per week in order to carry out some minimum household and family tasks, in addition to having income below the poverty threshold.

Her conclusion was that in most cases, a family with two or more children must either have the productive efforts of two adults, both in the home and in the work force, to fulfill the family's minimal needs, or more money in order to purchase the services that must be foregone at home if there is only one adult.

Like married couples in husband/wife families with children, single-parent families spend time in paid work, on family and child care, on household chores, on personal care, on socializing with friends and relatives, on recreation and leisure time activities, and on sleep. Masnick and Bane, in their analysis of the situation of American families and their projection of trends, point out that "two sets of decisions basically define how single-parent families cope with the demands on their time: decisions about working by the single parent and decisions about the number of and allocation of household tasks to be performed."[10]

Most single mothers work, and, overwhelmingly, those who work, work full-time. Of some interest, when it comes to single parents with children under 6, the proportion with some work experience during the year is lower than that of married mothers. In contrast, however, among those who do work, the proportion working full-time is substantially higher among single mothers with school-age children than married mothers with children of this age, and slightly higher for single mothers with children under age 6.

This suggests that for the economic rewards of a job to be adequate for single parents, full-time work is necessary. Increasingly, the choice for single mothers is full-time work or no work (e.g., AFDC or welfare). The conflict between the need for time and the need for money becomes quite apparent. The choice seems to be weighted toward money when children are of school age (single mothers of school-age children work mostly full-time). In contrast, the choice is weighted toward time when children are younger (single mothers work less and accept even inadequate financial support in order to remain at home).

Some data from the Michigan Time Use Study confirm this trade-off, which many single mothers face.[11] In general, employed mothers spend considerably less time during the week doing housework than nonemployed mothers (and many whose experience we have tapped directly talk about the deliberate decision to compromise on housework, laundry, and cooking). The Michigan interviewees also report less total time taking care of children, less time eating and sleeping, and less time in personal care activities. Dual-earner families spend less time on household tasks and services than husband/wife families with only one wage earner.

Obviously, at-home mothers can and do perform more household and family tasks. The biggest difference found between single and married mothers is that single mothers spend more time working in the paid labor force; on average, single mothers work 6 hours a day, while married mothers work 3.5 hours. In a study of 1981 time use patterns, 86 percent of the single mothers were employed versus only 62 percent of married mothers. Among all the employed mothers, single mothers worked an average of 8 hours a day, while married mothers worked only 5.

A second difference between single and married mothers, in particular those with younger children, is that the former reduce their work time less but still manage to maintain their child care time. They do this by reducing their personal care time, especially sleep and recreation and leisure time.

Single mothers do, however, spend more time watching TV on weekends than married mothers—2.5 hours versus 1.5. Since the children of single mothers also spend more time watching TV on weekends than the children in two-parent families, and the children in single-parent families are more likely to watch with their mothers, we could conclude that TV watching may be an inexpensive form of family recreation.[12]

The Medrich et al. study of children's time use focused on 11- and 12-year-olds and their mothers, living in a major West Coast city.[13] This study is a particularly rich source of data on single-parent families because more than 40 percent of the sample were single-parent families. Moreover, the majority of mothers—and fathers—in the study worked, including more than half of the sole mothers. Furthermore, the vast majority of the single working mothers (75 percent) worked full-time. These researchers, too, found that the amount of time parents spend with their children is constrained primarily by work time. They found that the older the child the less time parents felt they needed to devote to either physical or nonphysical care; and that nonphysical care is usually ancillary to doing some other activity. To identify and characterize the parents who are "time poor" in their study, the researchers "attempted to develop a measure of time poverty that included: number and ages of children; labor force status of adults in the household; and estimates (taken from other studies) of the amount of time adults spent on housework, leisure, and personal maintenance."[14] They found that such a measure did not tell them any more about time poverty than did the number of parents and their labor force status. In effect, almost as a rule, a single parent, working full-time at a paid job outside the home, was likely to be more time poor than a single nonworking parent, than two working parents in a husband/wife family, and certainly poorer than a two-parent family in which one adult was at home or one or both adults worked less than full-time.

Time poverty was found to be especially severe for lower-income, single-parent families. One result was that single-parent families, generally, both white and black, were less likely to have gone to a variety of recreational places with their children (beaches, museums, libraries, entertainment centers) than two-parent families, either because of time constraints or money constraints, or both. Single working parents, regardless of race, were less likely to be involved in their children's school-related activities. Overall, the researchers concluded that the differences on measures of time use among families of different incomes, race, family structure, and even mother's employment status were not as pronounced as they and others would have expected (p. 130). However, and here directly relevant, the only truly time poor in relation to their children were the low-income working single mothers and to a lesser extent, two full-time working parents in husband/wife families.

In another California study of the time use patterns of one- and two-parent families, carried out in 1977–78 as part of an 11-state study of time use in two-parent, two-child families, researchers found that single mothers who were employed spent the least time in household tasks (1.8 hours per day), while married mothers who were not employed spent the most (6.0 hours).[15] Most of the time differences occurred in meal preparation, dish washing, and house cleaning. Time spent in child care was statistically lower for employed mothers when age of younger child was controlled but lower for employed married mothers than for single mothers. Employed single mothers spent about one-third less time per working day than at-home single mothers (1 hour instead of 1.5 hours), but the overall amount seems remarkably small. Most of the difference related to physical care of the children; time spent in nonphysical care did not differ across family types.

The biggest difference between single and married mothers, and employed and at-home single mothers, with regard to time use had to do with personal time, especially sleep, rest, and personal leisure. The single employed mothers spent the least time on personal care—between one and two hours a day less than all other categories of mothers; and both single and married working mothers spent about half the time on recreation as the at-home mothers. Once again, single mothers have the least time of all. The researchers found that employed single mothers have the least amount of time to spend on household tasks, child care, personal care, and leisure and recreational activities. Single working mothers spend slightly more time in child care than their married sisters but somewhat (not much) less time than at-home mothers. To meet the time demands of their families, single employed mothers sacrifice time in personal care activities. The researchers conclude that coupled with less time for recreational activities, the long-term consequences of this pattern of time allocation and its known relationship to stress warrants serious concern. We have cited the more recent Alwin, Converse, and Martin findings along similar lines.

Social Isolation and Inadequate Help

Surveys of family service agencies indicate that single mothers constitute a disproportionately large group among their clients.[16] Reports from various types of counseling and treatment services suggest a similar pattern.

Child care is often described as the most important problem facing all working mothers, but single mothers especially.[17] Numerous studies report how essential child care is as respite and enrichment, but most of all as an essential service if single mothers with young children are to be expected to take a job. The vast majority of children in publicly subsidized center and family day care programs throughout the country come from mother-only homes (not including those using child care tax credits). Despite this, single mothers at home and at work decry the shortage of affordable, good quality care. If working mothers generally list child care as their single biggest problem, single working mothers are almost obsessed about the issue. A breakdown in their child care arrangements can create an immediate and overwhelming crisis.

A Census Bureau report confirms that for employed women with young children, the time constraints of combining both roles implies that some sort of trade-off occurs between working and caring for the children.[18] In an attempt to assess the nature of such a trade-off, they asked women who were not in the labor force whether they would look for work if child care were available at reasonable cost. Forty-five percent of the nonworking single mothers said they would, while only 22 percent of married women, husband present, said so. Similarly, 21 percent of lone mothers working part-time said they would work full-time if additional satisfactory child care were available at reasonable cost.

Robert Weiss, a well-known expert on the experience of single parenthood, characterizes the problems of single parents' household situation as the result of "understaffing."[19] The traditional view of the family has described the "two-parents plus children alone" nuclear family as disadvantaged because they lack access to extended family members for practical daily help or to dissipate emotion and tension from time to time. But, "if two parents are too few, what about one?" Weiss puts it thus: "As in an understaffed office, much of the time there is no problem. But now and again demands on those within the office exceed their capacities. Then everyone must pitch in as needed, no matter what the person's title and official position. Some tasks must be done hurriedly; others cannot be done at all. At the end of the day the people within the office are likely to be exhausted; they may feel that too much has been asked of them; they may be resentful that they have had to do so much."[20] For Weiss as for others, what is special about these single parents is that they are "going it alone"—that they are parenting alone.

Weiss recognizes and describes the differences among the widowed, the divorced, and the never-married. The numbers, ages, and sexes of the children are important variables. Fathers-alone rearing children are not the same as mothers-alone. Education and economic status, and thus access to amenities and hired services, make a great difference. And, obviously, if one contrasts the well-functioning, well-managed single-parent family with a highly disorganized two-parent family, or one in serious conflict, many of the generalizations do not hold. The end result, we may comment, is that we can describe tendencies without being able to attach precise numbers to them or fully weigh their significance for the society.

Nonetheless, one can and should be aware of both tendencies and variations as the society changes, even if uncertain about the application to some subgroups or representativeness of specific case stories. The main image which emerges is that the typical "working and managing" single mother "just about" gets everything done by great effort and some trade-offs, unless and until there are special problems and demands, as in the instances of a child's illness or accident, a breakdown in the house's plumbing or electrical system, or a personal problem. Then there is little leeway and a desperate need for backup or support. If there are friends or neighbors to be counted on, the specific crisis will pass. If not, the presence of another line of defense in the community, a line of "public support," can be critical.

The issue for community and society is whether, in the recognition of the tight coping regimes in so large a proportion of households, there can be some assurance of *supports, infrastructure, and policies* that will ease the lives of families with children (and, also, for that matter, frail and dependent elderly people). In the case of dual-earner families, the need may be as great as that of the lone mother and her children. Should the policies discussed in the previous chapter be adopted more generally, converting more "at home" welfare mothers into members of the labor force, the numbers dependent on public policies and supports will expand further.

Providing Help

"No Time to Do Tasks? Agencies Can Help." So reads the headline of an article in *The New York Times*.[21] The story is about commercial services and agencies that are performing the household tasks that one or two decades ago women did at home, at no direct financial cost to the family. Described in this article are household-management agencies that take care of such routine tasks as house cleaning, catering for small dinner parties, preparing take-out meals, waiting for repair services at home, shopping for groceries, taking care of business at the motor vehicle bureau, gardening, and so forth. "One-stop-agencies" is the familiar term used to describe many of these or other services which may also offer home care services for the elderly; sick child care; baby sitting; and taking children from school to a friend's house, a dentist appointment, an after-school activity, and then home. Among the names of such agencies are "At Your Command" (in California), "Mothers N' Need" (in Massachusetts), and "The Stepford Wives" (in Connecticut). One agency, "Sitters Unlimited," is described as a child care, elder care, and tutoring franchise operation, launched first in California and now having outlets in about 20 locations around the country, including Washington, D.C., Miami, Chicago, and Honolulu. Behind their development is the dramatic growth in the numbers of married women in the labor force. The consumer group for these new and often expensive commercial service agencies is largely upper-middle income, dual-earner families.

Everything we know about single mothers underscores the needs these women have for similar services; they do not have the time to produce many of the essential home-based services themselves, yet they usually lack the money to purchase them in the market. Caught in the squeeze of not enough money to buy help, not enough time to produce the services, and no way to cope and manage alone all the time, these families have an interest in whether they may expect any sort of societal or community assistance in meeting their needs.

Child Care

Child care services that are near home, reasonably priced, and of decent quality are the single most important support services for single parents and the highest priority on single parents' wish lists. We have been told this in many interviews in all parts of the country. Parents view the child care experience as an important part of a child's education and development and as a source of friendship and companionship for the child. Sometimes, for the parent, the child care service connection also is an opportunity to become informed about what to expect about and from one's child at different ages. Most of all, child care is the service that makes it possible for a single mother to get a job, work, and not constantly worry about her child or children.

Although there are probably more child care services available at present than ever before, much of what exists is either of poor quality or more expensive that most single parents can afford, or not physically accessible. Women working full-time in 1986 at minimum-wage jobs earned less than $7,000, an amount under the poverty threshold for a three-person family, the typical mother-only family. Median family income for all mother-only families with children under age 18 was $9,858 that year; in such families where the mother was employed, median family income was $15,420. None of these families could afford market price child care that in 1986 was averaging more than $2,500 a year in the major cities for full day care for children aged 3–5, and more for younger children. From the perspective of income, low-earner single mothers usually are eligible for subsidized child care. In fact, they use 90 percent of it. However, subsidized care is still not available for most of these families because sufficient funds are not voted. AFDC, or welfare, permits mothers who take a job to deduct only a maximum of $160 per month per child, for a total of $1,920 a year, still well below the market rates in most of the country. (As we have seen, AFDC rules have discouraged work by all but 4.8 percent of all such mothers.) Low-income working mothers who fail to find a place in a subsidized center for their child now must purchase care that is available at below-market rates in most of the country. This is a discouraging prospect, since the "choice" may have to be unlicensed, unregulated, and often "underground" care.

Single mothers often find themselves working nondaytime shifts, in an effort to find a decent, well-paying job.[22] A large proportion of these women (almost half of those working full time, nonday hours) manage to have a relative who provides care. Almost as many, however, 42 percent—far more than for any other category of working mother—depend on nonrelatives. In effect, single mothers with young children "seem to be doubly handicapped: child care is likely to be more costly than for married women because it is more commonly provided by nonrelatives than by relatives; and unmarried women have less family income than married women and thus are less able to afford child-care costs."[23]

Working single mothers, like all working mothers, want good quality care for their children. And most stress the importance of a strong educational component, recognizing the need for their children to be as ready for school when they enter primary school as are the children from families who can afford to pay for private nursery schools.

The 5-year-olds of single mothers, like those in two-parent families, are all attending kindergarten; and where possible, they attend a full-day program. The 3- and 4-year-olds of affluent families, however, also attend preschool programs at least part of the day, whether or not their mothers work, while the children of this age from low-income families are often placed in informal family day care or poor quality center care.

Schools are increasingly entering the child care domain, extending kindergarten to a full school day, and beginning to serve some 4-year olds. To establish a child care system that is open to all children, and does not contribute to the development of a two-tier system—one for the poor and another for the middle and upper class—support for the continued growth in school-based programs would make the most sense. For working parents who want the convenience of child care located near their home, schools are the natural solution. For a universal, accessible, and affordable child care service, a school-based preschool program serving all 3- and 4-year-olds whose parents wish them to participate would be the best solution. Parents wanting their children to go only part of the day could choose that option, while parents wanting and needing their children to be enrolled in a program that covers the full workday could have such an option as well. The school-day program, like school generally, would be free; the extended-day program—and the summer and holiday program for the children of working parents—would charge income-related fees.

For primary school-aged children, aged 6–10, before- and after-school programs should also be available, provided either at the school or at another community facility, with transportation linking

school and the after-school facility. Here too, fees would be income-related and free to children from low-income families.

For 1- and 2-year-olds, a more diversified system would make
sense, including an improved type of family day care for parents
who prefer such small-scale programs for their children, as well as
centers.[24]

Counseling, Support, and Information

Our survey of service for single parents in a major East Coast city
revealed a surprising lack of special services for "adult" single-
parent families, a plethora of programs serving teenage single
parents (Chapter 4), and a very limited concept of the problems of
"adult" single-parent families and the kinds of help needed. In
effect, most agencies serving families with children focus either on
teenagers or on low-income families, assuming that by doing the
latter they will inevitably tap single-parent families. Only one
specialized agency exists, and it is described below. Otherwise,
the prevailing pattern of help offered is through "self-help" or
"support" groups.

Parents Without Partners (PWP) is the largest national organization constituting a kind of self-help and support group for single
parents. PWP is a 27-year-old volunteer, mutual help, nonprofit
organization for single parents—separated, divorced, widowed, or
never-married—who are raising children alone. There are 210,000
members in more than 1,000 local chapters (plus international
affiliates). Educational, family, and social/recreational activities
provide opportunities for participants to gain a perspective on
their own situation through contact with other single-parent families. The membership is 65 percent women, overwhelmingly divorced or separated, and largely middle class. Members' average
age is in the 40s, and typically, they have teenage children.

PWP is also an active advocacy group for single parents. The
organization publishes *The Single Parent* magazine, research reports, educational materials, and fact sheets about single-parent
families. They take public positions on such issues as tax reform,
child support, social security, and housing. The organization has a
library and extensive resource services, including a toll-free tele-
phone line for the general public, professionals, and the media.[25]

The Single Parent Resource Center (SPRC) originated as an
experimental project of the Community Service Society, a large
social service agency in New York City, over 10 years ago. It has
since been spun off as an independent nonprofit agency providing
direct services to single parents, technical assistance to commu-

nity-based programs in the city and elsewhere trying to serve this group, and advocacy on issues affecting single parents at the city, state, and federal levels. The services SPRC provides to single parents are largely information, referral, advice, and case advocacy. Some short-term, problem-focused counseling is provided, but practical, helping services are no longer available through this agency, because of lack of funding.

The director and founder of the agency is convinced of the need for special services for single parents and is personally dedicated and committed to providing help. Her concern is that public and private funding is difficult to come by, as organizations see little reason for establishing a special service for "adult" single-parent families. She reports that while some agencies may see service to single parents as best developed as part of a more broadly focused family service and others want to offer their services in the context of expanding access to child care, the general public and many professionals have another perspective. Often they think of "adult" single parents either as "welfare mothers" with many children and no interest in work, or as "divorced middle class women" in transition to another marriage.

In the experience of this SPRC director, however, SPRC clients/ consumers are largely of two groups, neither of which falls into the conventional stereotypes: (1) *working black women* with one (occasionally, two) children, who had children unintentionally out of wedlock, who decided to keep their babies, and who now find themselves socially isolated with no one else to help them or to talk to them at home, and often physically exhausted; and (2) *divorced and separated women,* both white and black, who feel themselves under constant pressure from ex-husbands, parents, and in-laws, and who are often concerned about losing their children. Recently, there has been an increase in inquiries from men who are searching for information about how to obtain joint custody of their children. In part because of the availability of special-category funding, the agency has also established projects related to homeless single-parent families and women prisoners.

The agency director highlights the following as the major areas in which single parents seek help:

- *Income*. Single parents are largely poor or working poor families.
- *Child care*. If single parents are to work, child care is an essential service; it is important in transitional periods also, when women are in training or seeking work, and important for children in difficult family situations.

- *Support*. Support is needed either from informal networks of family and friends or from semi-formal networks of support groups.
- *Legal services*.
- *Housing*.

Our community exploration reveals that the most consistent service provided specifically for "adult" single parents is some form of "support group." One such group, organized under the auspices of a large community center, was specifically designed to serve parents whose children were in the agency's after-school program, yet only one of the participants fell into that category—a divorced mother with two sons age 6 and 8. The other participants included:

- A European-born woman, now a U.S. citizen, with a 9-year-old boy, whom she had out of wedlock with a Latin American man. Her son lives with her but spends summers with his father.
- A recent divorcee who works as a receptionist in the corporate headquarters of a multinational company and has a 5-year-old daughter.
- A secretary, a former army sergeant, with a 4-year-old daughter whom she had out of wedlock with another army sergeant; they currently have no contact.
- The father of two teenage children, whose wife left him a few years ago.
- A widow with one 10-year-old daughter (her niece) whom she adopted after the death of her husband and her sister.
- A graduate student at the city university, the never-married mother of an 8-year-old boy.

The group included 12 members, two of whom were black, and the rest white. Among the reasons participants said they joined the group were (1) to get help with problems of raising children alone; (2) to find emotional support; (3) to get a better understanding of how other single parents cope; (4) to become a better parent; and (5) to meet other single parents.

The group met six times. One session was devoted to issues related to child rearing and time scheduling, to meet both parents' and children's needs. Child care, baby sitting, choosing schools (including maneuvering to get your child into a "good" public school), and relationships with grandparents and surrogate grandparents were major subjects of attention. Another session was devoted to the "single" aspect of being a single parent: feelings of loneliness, sexual feelings, how to develop a social life, and how to cope if none develops. A third session was devoted to the problems of adolescence and rearing adolescent children alone.

Most members appeared to find the experience a positive one. They ended the series feeling better about themselves as parents and understanding more about the universality of their experiences and feelings. They also, however, concluded with some sense of frustration and righteous indignation about the inadequacy of formal services—child care, housing, health care—of financial support, in particular child support, and about the rigidities of work for those trying to cope with jobs while rearing children alone. (We had similar feedback from a church-based group in the 30–40 age range, assembled especially to identify key issues and needs.)

Even in the two-parent family, the young mother who does not live close to her own mother or mother-in-law or close to extended family members often finds herself in need of information and advice during pregnancy, or when raising young children and not knowing where to turn. How much more can this become an issue for the isolated, pressed, single mother who lacks time and contacts. General and quite specialized forms of parent education and parent information programs have sprung up throughout the country under many types of auspices and have proven to be popular and useful. Some are sensitively and effectively tailored to the particular questions which arise in child rearing in the single-parent context. Obviously, access to such programs will vary with educational background, employment status, ethnic and religious preferences, economic circumstances, attitudes to the family, and many other variables. Therefore, it is no surprise that quite diverse, positively evaluated programs that attract mothers' participation can be found in churches and synagogues; in family service, child welfare, and community development agencies working in poverty areas; in public and private schools; in child care centers or in conjunction with information and referral services in the child care field; and in public and private health settings. While we have assessed many of these initiatives positively in earlier work,[26] we would stress here that there is no case to be made for uniformity, monopoly, or excessive standardization. The subject is raised to indicate that the initiatives are so important that in low-income communities, at least, they are worthy of governmental and private philanthropic support—and given so as to protect diversity. Moreover, there is much to be learned, in a changing society, about content and ways of delivering such educational and informative services. Here, too, public backing is a good idea.

Unlike the income, job, or child care programs, these are not the expensive public provisions required for public policy with regard to single parents or all families. The proposals for advice and counseling are also smaller-ticket items in this perspective.

Housing

Child care and other types of help are clearly critical components of support for single mothers. Another is housing, both as a basic necessity for living and as a component of a social support system.

In the 1980s housing emerged as a problem for many young families, as the supply failed to meet the needs of the baby boom population in its peak child-bearing years, and the costs of housing placed it beyond the reach of many low-income families in some parts of the country. Access to affordable housing is critical. As we mentioned in Chapter 3, many other countries provide income-tested housing allowances to subsidize the costs of adequate housing and permit families to enter a housing market which they could otherwise not afford. In several countries (for example, Sweden), depending on the year, between one-third and one-half the families with children have received such subsidies.

A second aspect of housing, however, has to do with design and amenities, incorporating into housing some of the components of a supportive community. Several researchers familiar with the problems of single parents or with the housing and shelter needs of families with children have suggested an approach to housing that would include services other than shelter.[27] Multiple-dwelling complexes with extensive services have become familiar aspects of urban housing for the "Yuppies" for the 1980s, with health clubs, recreation facilities, valet services, concierges, maids, and so forth. Here, instead, the urgent need would be for small-scale service complexes that would include an on-site child care facility, eating facilities—either a shared kitchen and dining area or a cafeteria-type facility—as well as recreational facilities. Once again, this is a pattern that has been incorporated in housing in other countries, in particular Denmark and Sweden,[28] and in some experimental projects in the United States. Whether such a model should be designed for single-parent families specifically or whether this suggests an approach to housing for some families with children generally needs further exploration. Here we are in a field requiring research and development and not ready for significant, large-scale action. Indeed, the severe shortage of low- and moderate-cost housing for families in general in American cities would make it difficult to do much that is special for the single-parent group.

Employment Policies/Workplace Adaptations[29]

Most single mothers are in the work force, and most work full-time. If married women who have jobs have problems managing work and family life, these problems are far worse for single mothers. The time crunch is overwhelming, and the potential for getting help at home, negligible. Like married women with children, many single mothers with young children cope with their child care problems by "pairing" or sharing care. Married mothers may work different shifts than their husbands; single mothers may share child care with a sister or sister-in-law or have a mother who is willing and able to help. But by and large, they remain dependent on their own resources for child care, primarily using purchased care.

As already discussed, for single working mothers, the most important resource is adequate and affordable child care. Closely related to the need for regular child care services is the need for help when a child is sick.

One southern state government established a near-worksite child care service for its employees after surveying its personnel and concluding that many of them lived relatively close to the main office building and that there were few services available in the nearby communities. Nonetheless, some time after the new program was in operation, and despite an enthusiastic response by those using the center, employee absenteeism, a major concern, did not decline. Subsequent investigation found that the primary problem these worker/parents had concerning child care had not been with the lack of available services, but what to do when a child was ill and the usual service would not or could not provide care.

Husband/wife families often manage between them when a child is ill, by alternating who takes days off, or by having the one with the "less important" job (usually the woman) take time off. Single parents characterize such times as "crisis time." They have no one else to help, and even if fortunate enough to have family or friends who will help out, need time to make arrangements. Most working mothers talk of these times as typically beginning with a middle-of-the-night or early-morning illness and fever that does not permit advance planning. And, depending on the age of the child and the nature and severity of the illness, some parents will not want to leave their child.

Many, but not all, employers permit some time off without loss of pay when an employee is ill. Most, by far, however, will not knowingly permit an employee to use any of his or her personal sick leave to care for an ill child at home. And almost no firm in the United States provides special additional paid sick leave to care for an ill child, although this is becoming an increasingly prevalent statutory policy in several European countries. (In Sweden, for example, workers are entitled to up to 60 days a year to care for an ill child under age 8 who needs to be at home. In West Germany, workers are permitted a minimum of 5 days off with pay to care for an ill child, but 10 days is now more typical, in firms subject to collective bargaining agreements.)

Some employers provide paid "personal days" to their employees, but workers complain that although in theory these days should be able to be used for personal emergencies as well as personal recreation, most employers require advance notice and approval, something that is out of the question for working parents who have to deal with the problem of a suddenly ill child.

Some workers are convinced that they might be able to manage, and to work out an emergency arrangement with a relative or friend, if they had a little time. As one woman told us, "I could get someone to help out and come to my house, or agree to care for my daughter (age 4) if I brought her over, but it takes time to make those arrangements. If she wakes up at 4:00 A.M. throwing up, or at 6:00 with a slightly sore throat, even if she seems just mildly sick by 7:30 when I usually leave, I can't call anyone earlier than that. If I could come in about two hours late, I could manage to make alternative arrangements. The problem is that where I work, if you are not there by 9:00 at the latest, within a half hour of when we are due in, we are counted absent. So if I am going to be one or two hours late, there is no point in coming in. Yet if I could come in, I could make up part of the time I missed by skipping lunch that day; and make up the rest during the week. They would end up with less absenteeism and a lot of women's work records would look better."

Flextime—the ability to begin and end work within a flexible band of time—would alleviate many such problems. Firms that have such a policy permit workers to begin their work one or two hours earlier—or later—than the standard 8:30 or 9:00 A.M. starting time, and to end their normal work day with the same options. Thus, a single mother working full-time can select a work schedule that fits her needs; as important, if she has an emergency, she can call in and say that she will be in later, and either make up the time by staying later that day, or by adjusting her schedule a little on several other days.

A critical time for many working parents is pregnancy, childbirth, and the time immediately following. Most big firms let a woman take off some weeks as "disability" leave, and provide some disability insurance that pays part of her salary. Most medium-sized firms require women to use vacation and sick leaves when they need time off at childbirth; very few offer *paid* disability leaves. And almost no small firms have job-protected disability leave policies (let alone paid leaves) which are offered voluntarily. Some states (California, Hawaii, New Jersey, New York, and Rhode Island) require such protection of all employers, regardless of size. Many union contracts provide for leaves elsewhere (but most firms are not unionized). Some employers permit working parents to take off some additional job-protected but unpaid time following the end of the paid disability leave.

Most single mothers have their children while married, thus a supportive policy is important to the large numbers of married women who work throughout their pregnancies and intend to return after a few months at home. But about one-quarter of all single-mother families are headed by women who have their children while unmarried and who have to work out by themselves how to manage the first few months. And some working mothers face the devastating experience of having a husband leave them during their pregnancy or shortly after childbirth, and they have to cope with the trauma of being left by their husband at the same time they adjust to a new baby. Job-protected, paid leaves for some months after childbirth are essential for all new mothers, be they natural or adoptive, married or single parents.

Here, too, the international standard is far more generous and more responsive to the new work and family realities of the industrialized world.[30] In Canada and Europe, somewhere between four and six months of paid, job-protected leave is available with usually an additional year of unpaid, job-protected parental leave. The Scandinavian countries provide much more. Moreover, a country like Austria provides a special extended paid maternity leave for single mothers, for two years beyond the standard one-year paid maternity leave available to all working mothers.

Fringe benefits are another aspect of jobs that are important for the single mother in the labor force. Health insurance, for example, is an absolute necessity, yet many single mothers, working for small firms, still have no medical insurance coverage, leaving them either making insufficient use of medical care or subject to potentially devastating financial burdens as a consequence.[31]

A major public and media issue for much of the 1980s has been this issue of balancing work and family life. As important as achieving a better balance may be for working wives, this issue is critical for employed single mothers. Without a more supportive work environment, managing job and family becomes an over-whelming burden. By now discussion and research have yielded a rich menu of possibilities, and other industrialized countries have tested a variety of solutions.

Conclusion

Much could be said about the problems and needs of single mothers that goes well beyond the topics appropriate for a public policy agenda. Much could be described about the daily lives of single mothers that inspires admiration and wonder. Much that is discussed by and about single mothers suggests the need to learn more and to do more rigorous research, so as to better understand the choices they make and to become familiar with the useful public opportunities for understanding, support, and advice.

Available descriptive and analytic studies, the research over-views that build upon knowledge and offer advice to individuals (in the manner of Robert Weiss), and the assembled opinion and proposals of self-organized single mothers yield a list of important and diverse topics:

- trading off housework and laundry for time with the children
- packaging enough income to manage
- deciding between part-time and full-time work
- relying on one's relatives and neighbors
- taking care of a house without a man around
- finding personal time in the midst of a work-, child care-, home-management routine
- managing emergencies
- finding occasional respite
- dating and the problems of privacy and one's children's responses
- the sex life of the single-mother
- coping with "his" and one's own parents
- managing visitation
- dealing with problems of child support
- locating supportive resources for oneself and one's children
- interpreting the experience for children of different ages
- understanding the differences between girls and boys
- realizing the hazards of treating one's young children as though they were marital partners when discussing problems or needing help coping with emotional needs
- making long-range plans for where to live; the children's

education; one's social life and possible marriage/remarriage; school, work and career.

This list, incomplete and only suggestive, is meant only to reinforce the point that, in dealing as we have with work, income, time, and support, we have presented a large and complex agenda from the *public's* point of view, but we have by no means attempted to answer most of the central *personal* questions about daily life for single mothers and their children. Social policies, infrastructure, and benefits are essential. They attempt to create context. Without the kind of public responsiveness outlined in this chapter and in Chapter 5, and without the several essential policy differentiations by type of single mother described in Chapter 4 and elsewhere, the society leaves an unconscionable vacuum. Then the more individualized issues of preferences and values, and the more personal aspects of adaptation, relationships, and child rearing, may never even become areas of personal consideration and choice. If context can be somewhat protected, more single mothers may free their time and energies to begin to work in their private and personal ways on a good life for themselves and their children.

Endnotes

1. Sheila B. Kamerman, *Parenting in an Unresponsive Society: Managing Work and Family Life* (New York: Free Press, 1980), 80–81.
2. Robert S. Weiss, *Going It Alone: The Family Life and Social Situation of the Single Parent* (New York: Basic Books, 1979), xi, xii.
3. Gerald Gurin, Joseph Veroff, and Sheila Feld, *Americans View Their Mental Health* (New York: Basic Books, 1960); Joseph Veroff, Elizabeth Douvan, and Richard A. Kulka, *The Inner American* (New York: Basic Books, 1981).
4. F. Thomas Juster and Frank Stafford, eds., *Time, Goods, and Well-being* (Ann Arbor: Institute for Social Research, University of Michigan, 1985).
5. Duane Alwin interview as reported in *ISR Newsletter* (Autumn 1984), 3–4. Also see Duane Alwin, Philip Converse, and Steven Martin, "Living Arrangements and Social Integration," in *Research in the Quality of Life*, ed. Frank M. Andrews (Ann Arbor: Institute for Social Research, University of Michigan, 1986).
6. Elliott Medrich, et al., *The Serious Business of Growing Up: A Study of Children's Lives Outside of School* (Berkeley: University of California Press, 1982).
7. Clair Vickery (Brown), "The Time Poor: A New Look at Poverty," *Journal of Human Resources* 12 (1977): 27–48, and summarized subsequently in "Economics and the Single-Mother Family," *Public Welfare*, vol. 36, no. 1 (1978): 18–21.
8. For example, Margaret M. Sanik and Teresa Maulden, "Single vs Two Parent

Families: A Comparison of Mothers' Time," *Family Relations,* "Special Issue: The Single Parent Family," vol. 35, no. 1 (January 1986): 53–56.

9. Vickery, "The Time Poor," 27.

10. George Masnick and Mary Jo Bane, *The Nation's Families: 1960–1990* (Dover, Mass.: Auburn House, 1980), 107.

11. Jacquelynne Eccles, Kerth O'Brien, and Susan Goff Timmer, "How Children Use Time" in *Time, Goods, and Well-being,* ed. F. Thomas Juster and Frank Stafford (Ann Arbor: Institute for Social Research, University of Michigan, 1985), 363, 371.

12. Ibid., 373.

13. Medrich et al., *The Serious Business of Growing Up.*

14. Ibid., 103.

15. Sanik and Maulden, "Single vs Two Parent Families."

16. Alfred J. Kahn and Sheila B. Kamerman, *Helping America's Families* (Philadelphia: Temple University Press, 1982).

17. Kamerman, *Parenting in an Unresponsive Society.*

18. U.S. Bureau of the Census, Child Care Arrangements of Working Mothers: June 1982, *Current Population Reports,* series P-23, no. 129 (Washington, D.C.: Government Printing Office, 1983). See, especially, pp. 15–16.

19. Weiss, *Going It Alone,* xi, xii, xiii.

20. Ibid.

21. *The New York Times,* 29 January 1987.

22. Harriet B. Presser, "Shift Work Among American Women and Child Care," *Journal of Marriage and the Family* 48 (August 1986). Also see Sheila B. Kamerman and Alfred J. Kahn, *The Responsive Workplace: Employers and a Changing Labor Force* (New York: Columbia University Press, 1987).

23. Presser, "Shift Work Among American Women and Child Care."

24. We have recently elaborated the rationale for this approach in our book, Alfred J. Kahn and Sheila B. Kamerman, *Child Care: Facing the Hard Choices* (Dover, Mass: Auburn House, 1987).

25. For more information on Parents Without Partners (PWP), see Kahn and Kamerman, *Helping America's Families;* Weiss, *Going It Alone;* and the PWP magazine, *The Single Parent.*

26. Kahn and Kamerman, *Child Care: Facing the Hard Choices,* 54, and *Helping American Families,* 151–152. See David Harmon and Orville G. Brim, *Learning to Be Parents* (Beverly Hills, Calif.: Sage Publications, 1980).

27. Jacqueline Leavitt, "The Shelter-Service Crisis," in *The Unsheltered Woman: Women and Housing in the 1980s,* ed. Eugenie Ladner Birch (New Brunswick, N.J.: Rutgers University Press, 1985). See also, Susan Anderson-Khleif, "Housing Needs of Single Parent Mothers," in *Building for Women,* ed. Suzanne Keller (Lexington, Mass.: Lexington Books, 1981); Robert S. Weiss, "Housing for Single Parents," in *Housing Policy for the 1980s,* ed. Roger Montgomery and Dale Rogers Marshall (Lexington, Mass.: Lexington Books, 1980).

28. Alfred J. Kahn and Sheila B. Kamerman, *Not for the Poor Alone* (Philadelphia: Temple University Press, 1975 and New York: Harper & Row, 1977, paper).

29. For an extensive review and analysis of what has happened at the workplace

as more women have entered and remained in the work force and of creative responses, see Kamerman and Kahn, *The Responsive Workplace*.

30. Sheila B. Kamerman, "Maternity and Parenting Benefits: An International Overview," in *The Parental Leave Crisis: Toward a National Policy*, ed. Edward Zigler and Merryl Frank (New Haven: Yale University Press, 1988).

31. Kamerman and Kahn, *The Responsive Workplace*, Ch. 2.

Chapter 7

SOCIAL CHANGE
OR SOCIAL PROBLEM:
DESIGNING A POLICY

In some ways, society regards mother-only families as "problem" families, because they are either experiencing difficulty or are causing trouble for the rest of the society, or both. In other ways, society explicitly or implicitly acknowledges that such families are indicators of social change—gender role changes, the growing economic independence of women, family life-style changes, and so forth. Single mothers may be viewed as a family type or category or status, which may or may not be in trouble.

Some of this confusion and ambivalence is inevitable. Lone-mother families are not a homogeneous group. They include the poor, uneducated, unskilled teenage mother; and the middle-class, professional mother by choice. The category covers, also, the divorced mother with a good support agreement; the divorced family in which the noncustodial parent is constantly behind on small monthly payments; and the deserted unmarried mother who is raising children on AFDC with no support from the absent father.

As much may be said of children in single-parent families. The category covers some who are in families in which the custodial parent, usually the mother, moves rapidly from the "divorced" to a "remarried" status. For the children, a problem may arise out of the need to sustain both new and continuing relationships with natural and step-parents and step-siblings—in what can become multiple complex patterns. Children in other single-parent families, however, may be reared in the isolated, poverty environment of the never-married mother, living at the margins of survival in a

212

low-benefit public assistance jurisdiction, with little stimulation, opportunity, or access to society's offerings. Or, despite economic problems, a single-mother, dependent on assistance, could be raising her children in an environment enriched by a network of friends, relatives, and church programs, while taking advantage of the Head Start system and various other supportive social services.

Nor do these possibilities even begin to suggest the variations occasioned by educational, labor-force participation, ethnic-racial, religious, familial, and geographic differences. Such variations and the very fact of rapid social change will probably sustain continued public uncertainty as to how to regard single-mother families and will continue to feed the debates as to what government, social welfare organizations, and private groups should do. In the light of what has been developed in earlier chapters, we offer an approach to overall policy with regard to single-mother families and suggest some of the implications for specific issues and programs.

Prevent the Development of Single-Parent Families?

People in this and other countries ascribe many social problems and much social pathology to single-parent families and conclude that it is the obligation of public policy to combat the phenomenon. For present purposes, we need not fully unravel the complex tangle of causes and effects which find some single-parent families and their children at the center of the statistics on crime, mental illness, school failure, addictions, and dependency. Clearly, causation goes both ways, and the cycle, once launched, is in some sense self-renewing.

It is essential to recall, however, that these generalizations—which need qualification and specification—refer to a subgroup of single-parent families and children. The majority of such families, certainly the vast majority of those who are separated, divorced, or "nonteenage" mothers by choice (a small group) seem to show no more pathology than do other families. There is some evidence that, for lack of adequate support payments, divorce may create economic problems for custodial mothers and children. It is also probably the case that there is emotional suffering and the residue of trauma attached to divorce as well. Yet none of this is of such a nature or degree as to justify the very intrusive and controlling public policy it would take to block separation or divorce. Indeed, there is no knowledge as to the relative personal and societal price of legal constraints and prohibitions of divorce or separation, as contrasted with the practical or emotional consequences of permitting these measures. Nor do developments in Italy or Ireland in recent decades, including significant growth in single-mother families, suggest that formal constraints on family change really block the family break-up processes.

No serious argument in the mainstream of public policy would "solve" the problems arising from separation and divorce through "preventive" legal controls and restrictions. (It would take police-state measures to do so at this point!) After all, the liberalization of divorce in recent decades followed a long period of pressure for change because of the psychological price paid by adults and children for forced continuation of difficult relationships—or the lack of legal recognition and protection when relationships had to break up no matter what the law or custom said.

None of this would discourage all the many efforts to create family support programs, marriage enrichment movements, positive family environments through community provisions—as well as counseling, mediation, and other programs which might intervene when families are endangered. Such efforts should both be encouraged and studied. Little is known as to efficacy—and with whom, or at what cost.

If, then, the response to the single-parent family is not to be found in vigorous legal or social "prevention" of divorce or separation by prohibition, what of the mother by choice? Here we refer to the relatively sophisticated and educated women, mostly in their 30s, who want children and see no prospect of marriage as they confront the "biological clock." Their means vary: adoption, artificial insemination, deliberate pregnancy through intercourse with willing or casual and unknowing partners with whom they do not wish to share parenting. The several moral issues, as well as the psychological and interpersonal elements of such practices, are currently being debated on a wide front, as all these phenomena— as well as the related surrogate mothering by contract—are made more visible, and the issues they generate are posed more clearly. Without fully exhausting the topic, we offer a perspective.

This pluralistic society has functioned best over its two hundred years as it has kept church-state-family properly separated. The state has avoided institutionalizing one among many religions, or favoring religion over nonbelief. Our federal government has left the laws of marriage-separation-divorce-adoption-guardianship-foster care and the rest to state government; and states have shown various philosophies. Such pluralism has made it possible to respect cultural, religious, and ethnic differences, as well as personal preference. Major value issues have not needed to be "settled" and confrontations thus are avoided. A diverse people has, despite this, created a unified polity, a national culture, a productive economy.

Increasingly over the past decade, there have been those who have responded to changes in the family by reaffirming traditions and seeking to utilize government, even national government, to legislate and enforce their preferences. Early in the second Reagan term, a White House report on family trends—without garnering wide support or even serious discussion—argued that "It simply is not true that what we do is our business only" (p. 4). While "many family problems are not amenable to policy solutions the public sector can nonetheless influence patterns of culture. . . . Although government cannot mandate cultural change, public officials can, as opinion leaders, influence its direction" (p. 7). The Reagan White House has led the anti-abortion, anti-family planning and sex education, pro-school prayer, and pro-traditional family lobby, occasionally seeking to go beyond influence to administration and to depriving legal programs of legitimate funds. Yet, while the influence of government is hardly to be denied, or the President's legitimate role as a shaper of opinion not be disputed, our cultural traditions and protection of rights call for a continued pluralism and the avoidance of legislative or administrative action which constrains choices. Family law continues as a state domain, and the country would do well to head the advice of the White House report that government's starting point should be "do no harm," assuming the "reasonableness of parental action, and the authority of the home should be respected except in cases of substantial risk of harm" (p. 6).[1]

In full recognition that out-of-wedlock parenthood by choice, cohabitation, separation, and divorce violate many people's sense of what is right, threaten tradition, and may even impose economic costs on the society and some psychological costs on adults and children, one can argue that each has pluses and benefits. A case can be made that the cost-benefit equation is uncertain, and the ultimate assessment rests deep in the value system of the observer.

If this is the case, we can conclude that it is not for government to "prevent" adult single-parent families through coercion, compulsion, or restriction. It can and should do much, we have shown, through family budgets and social infrastructure, to make the more traditional and conventional family life attractive, viable, and enriching. It is essential, too, that public policy not create perverse incentives, such as assistance for mother-only families but a refusal to aid two-adult families in need; job opportunities or child care services for one group—those on welfare, for example—but not for another—the working poor, for example; and so forth. Obviously, such policies seldom develop deliberately, but they are often the by-product of policy making by impulse and reflex.

Our community life will pay too high a price if government legislates and administers citizens' codes of morality. Our society would be threatened by any imposition of legislative brakes on primary group changes growing out of larger economic, technological, scientific, and political shifts in the society around us.

To all this we add two caveats: It is important to prevent teenage out-of-wedlock parenting, and it is urgent to protect children against neglect and abuse.

Preventing Adolescent Parenting and Protecting Children

We have argued against limited, categorical policy focus on single-mother families because of the heterogeneity of these families and their needs. There is, however, one type of single-mother family that does warrant very special attention, and that is the adolescent, unwed mother. We would argue, further, that at present, the one type of single-parenthood to be actively "prevented" is teenage, out-of-wedlock parenthood.

The stories of the "children who have children," the school dropouts, poverty, poor education, lack of skills for the labor market are well known and have been reviewed earlier (Chapter 4). The group has been in the spotlight in the 1980s. The young women and their children have poor lives and dismal prospects. Those who grow up in such families often can do little except repeat the pattern. From society's point of view, prevention is justified both by social and economic costs and the picture of wasted or unhappy humans. It is difficult to make a case for "benign neglect."

Until there are more notable successes, however, it will not be easy to specify a targeted prevention program for unmarried mothers under age 18. The following are among the more promising initiatives being supported, studied, and (we feel most important) being combined in more holistic strategies and should be pointed to both potential fathers and potential mothers:

- Better and easier access to sex education and contraceptive supplies through a diversity of delivery systems until the greater efficacy of some is better established (health clinics, school medical services, private doctors, family planning programs, pharmacies, community social agencies).

- School drop-out prevention efforts.
- Part-time and full-time job opportunities, growing out of a diversity of training, placement, and apprenticeship strategies, including cooperative education programs—and not so operated as to encourage dropping out of school.
- "Mentoring" programs based in community agencies and substituting positive role models from one's community and social groups for the "missing" parents and relatives in one's lives.
- Strongly led and well-supplied peer-support groups, oriented to raising self-esteem, expanding future options, remaking one's life, community change. This would include church, ethnic, racial, activity-oriented options (schools, theater, sports, music, politics, charity, etc.)
- Media campaigns using TV, radio, billboards, and posters to change community perceptions of teenage sex and irresponsible parenting. Young men as well as young women would be targeted here, as in all the other programs listed.

Choosing Among the Policy Options

These "categorical" prevention efforts apart, what of those who do need financial and other aid? How may we sum up our perspectives on the specific policy options posed at the beginning (and which we can now characterize more precisely)?

1. *Extending AFDC to all poor two-parent families.* A means-tested cash benefit available to low-income families, and thus also to single mothers of children under a specified age, that would make it possible for them to remain at home, and societal acceptance of an at-home role for these women (*an anti-poverty strategy*).
2. *Improving AFDC on the 1960 model.* An income-tested benefit only for single mothers that would permit most to remain at home until their youngest child was well along in primary school (*a categorical single-mother strategy*).
3. *Borrowing from several European countries.* A cash benefit supporting child rearing with special additional aid for a parent (married or single) with very young children (under 3) at home (*a universal family and young child strategy*).
4. *Joining family concerns to labor market opportunities.* Making work feasible, supporting child rearing, and supplementing family income when earnings are low. The expectation is that where there is economic need, and adults are employa-

ble, they will work; neither being a mother of young children, nor being a single mother precludes this approach *(a
universal work and family support strategy)*.

Labor force participation rates (LFPR) of single mothers are
clearly a function of cash benefits, available jobs, wage levels,
tradition, and culture. In countries where the first or second option
is in place, single mothers do take advantage of the policy and stay
at home—either because they have a special financial benefit
available to them that is designed to make this possible, or because
they can claim an income-tested benefit and the difference between the net income available to them when they work and the
cash benefit makes work not worthwhile financially. In countries
where such a policy is in place, married women have higher labor
force participation rates than single mothers. Some of the advantages and disadvantages of the policies have been suggested in
Chapter 3. It is difficult to imagine their being reinvented today.
Indeed, these policies were established in earlier years, before
married women had high LFPR, and when the objective was to
help single mothers achieve a life-style similar to that of married
women. This was the AFDC goal in the United States. In some
countries, high unemployment rates provide implicit support for
such policies today, when other objectives for women might lead
to change.

In the United States, when and where AFDC benefits (plus
Medicaid) have made it possible for some mothers to stay at home,
they have done so, albeit without full social approval or even full
acceptance. We have seen the current AFDC limitations. Efforts
at making this a more viable alternative for these families have all
failed, and a uniform, adequate, national minimum benefit has
never been legislated. By now, with a growing trend for married
women to be in the labor force, an expanding labor force (and a
possible future labor shortage), and with continued ambivalence
regarding low-income single mothers generally, the likelihood of
establishing a more generous and less stigmatizing policy to support single mothers at home through either anti-poverty or categorical single-mother programs alone seems negligible. The growing discussion of "workfare" already indicates a shift from the prior
paradigm.

The first two policy options no longer fit the ideology or meet
the new reality that already includes high LFPR of married mothers with very young children.

The countries that have chosen the several versions of Option 3
are variously motivated by explicit or implicit pronatalism, a desire

to support adequate parenting when children are very young (until age 1? or age 2? or age 3?), eagerness to buttress the more traditional family, or the need to encourage low-skill women to remain out of the labor force when their labor is not needed (since quality child care can be more expensive than at-home maternal care). The evidence for each of these policies is in some eyes mixed, lacking, or negative—but the case for each can be made effectively in some contexts. The United States will not act out of pronatalist goals at this time; nor will it deliberately seek to lure women from jobs. On the other hand, the option of more traditional family patterns should not be blocked, and parents ready to make a larger investment in parenting should be met halfway with public participation as well.

The real problem with Option 3, we have seen, can be its specifics: what kind of support for parents of young children, for how long, under what circumstances? If the program is so designed as to attract young women, not men, if it does not encourage labor force attachment before childbirth, and if it offers at-home support for long periods of time in a world in which most parents have one or two children, it will leave most young mothers in difficult straits as their children enter school and then, after 6 or 10 years, they will face a labor market without preparation and skills. Yet elements of Option 3 are valid, particularly the universal support for child rearing and for parenting. Indeed, this stress on universalism is an important component of Option 4 as well, and is a perspective we are convinced must undergird any policy designed to aid single-parent families in the United States.

Universalism as a Policy Perspective

Doing Better by Mother-Only Families by Doing Better by All Working Families

A primary lesson from all the data, research, and reports of experiences that we have examined is that of universalism—not limiting most public programs to the means-tested poor. It proves very difficult to do special things for very poor mother-only families without creating or seeming to create perverse incentives or inequities. It these mothers are supported at home, at a reasonably decent standard of living, market wages are unlikely to achieve the same standard. In the United States, the result has been more meager support in order to minimize both public expenditure and a work disincentive. Yet, when coupled with the "fringe benefits" attached to welfare, but not always to work (Medicaid or health insurance, for example, plus food stamps), it is still difficult for wages to match AFDC, unless these women work full-time; and that, as we saw in the last chapter, creates an enormous burden on single-parent families when children are infants and toddlers.

If one believes, therefore, that in an era when most mothers of young children work, it is both isolating for the families involved and probably unfair to taxpayers for the society to assume that single mothers will not work, one seeks for an alternative philosophy. One such alternative would focus on integrating single-mother families into the mainstream of the society rather than segregating these families and supporting them on a less than adequate standard. This assumes that a separate, protected status for single mothers is stigmatizing, demeaning—and full of economic deprivation. Indeed, that has been our history. The alternative is to design a policy that is directed at all families with children; lone mothers would benefit along with all parents. What does this mean?

We have suggested, first, opening up educational, training, job-search support, and all possible employment opportunity. For some single mothers this will require public investment, stipends, and other supports—as we have seen. For other single mothers, in particular those with very young children, it may mean assuring decently paying part-time work with fringe benefits (two-thirds, or three-quarters time, for example), in order to allow time for child and home responsibilities. For all women, it requires pay equity and affirmative action in the labor market.

Work for mothers of young children is not possible, as already stressed, without adequate, accessible, and (depending on the policy adopted) free or affordable child care arrangements of good quality.

To protect those who, as married mothers, stay home to rear children—or as married or cohabitant partners work only part-time and at jobs which demand little and pay little—the social security system also will need to take better account of the interests of homemakers. With all the financial problems involved, some variation of the "earnings sharing" approach to benefit equity seems most promising. Payroll deductions during marriage and cohabitation should be pooled as long as the relationship holds—so that the mother, too, builds up independent social security entitlements. To the extent that cohabitant partners are included, children in such families who may become beneficiaries or dependents, while minors, will be better off. (The resulting benefit program under earnings sharing gives benefits to individual adults—not to "dependents.")[2]

Important for all women, indeed for all families with children, is the evolution of a pattern of social responsibility at the workplace which we call "family responsiveness." Demographic variations in the labor force call for variability, individualization, and flexibility in fringe benefits, work times, workplace, constrained by the requirements of productivity and profitability yet shown to be possible and even helpful to employers if carefully conceived and adopted to the circumstances of industry, place, and work force. Mandates by government and international agreements increasingly support such policy in Europe. Some degree of federal or state mandating or system of incentives will be required in the United States, too, or else only the largest and most prosperous firms will inaugurate such policies and benefits. Such mandating has long existed (unemployment insurance, occupational safety, state temporary disability laws) and is expanding.

The premise becomes that just as a workplace is to be made physically safe and its workweek length regulated to protect health and well-being, so should workplace benefits, personnel policies, and some services be expected, the better to mesh workplace routines and requirements with the demands of the family life of those who rear children. This is in the interests of the broader society, as well, in a world in which society needs constant citizen and labor force replacements but individual people no longer need to rear children in order to be protected and supported in old age, and most couples have ever-fewer children, as two parents work; at the same time alternative social and financial supports often are lacking in the community at large.

Family responsiveness at the workplace, we have seen (1) requires a good system of maternity/parenting benefits, which ensures a mother reasonable income replacement (at no less than the unemployment insurance level) while she recovers from the physical experience of childbirth (6–8–10–12 weeks?); (2) allows one of the parents, or the parents sharing in sequence, to remain at home for a longer unpaid period to develop the early parent-child bonds and relationships on which future child development and parenting will thrive; (3) protects job and fringe benefits during the parental leave; (4) allows some days for either parent to remain at home to care for an ill child or respond to an emergency. If the latter right is built into a more flexible concept which integrates personal leave time and vacation time, it could go far toward creating the work flexibility essential while children are very young. Furthermore, the combination of time off after childbirth (increasingly called maternity-disability leave, because of the relevant legislation) and the supplementary parenting leave would make it less necessary for very young infants to be in child care, except by specific parental preference.

All of these measures, we note, refer to working-parent families, not especially to single-parent families. Yet in their totality they would do *much* to make the economic situations and the living routines of mothers and children alone far more satisfactory. This is our theme. If in addition some of the general social support services described in the previous chapter were available to families generally—parenting information and support groups, housing and related amenities, and so forth—many of the other needs which we have identified would be met.

Doing Better by Children in Mother-Only Families by Doing Better by all Children and Their Families

To compare AFDC in the United States or the Income Support (previously Supplementary Benefits) program in England with the family allowance system in France is to see dramatically how important a universal system to equalize family burdens can be. Whether out of social solidarity, concern about child poverty, or pronatalist proclivities, the French offer significant financial help to families who rear children. The help is economically significant and—since much of it covers all families and is mostly not for the poor alone—is largely unstigmatized. It is especially generous while the children are under 3 years of age. A variety of analyses reveal that one by-product of such family allowance policy is that children in single-parent families do not suffer the large poverty gap we have seen in the United States. A few modest measures, effective for a relatively brief period, fill the gap and minimize perverse effects.

We need not repeat the story of AFDC in the United States as a poverty trap and a single-parent family trap. Our response in the earlier chapters has been to make the case for an income supplementation strategy that is universal—available to two-parent and one-parent families and not employing stigmatizing means-tests. Central to the strategy would be a system of family allowances—to equalize burdens for those who rear children and be corrective of the failure of the wage system to take account of the earner's family obligations. There are several ways to devise such an allowance: It could be either a tax credit or a taxable direct grant, and it should be implemented in a fashion consistent with current tax policy developments; it is an essential element. Also critical, again for *all* families with children, is a housing allowance policy granting an income-tested (but not stigmatizing means-tested) benefit to fill the gap between modest income and the housing costs in today's real estate markets.

Finally, there is the issue of medical care coverage. Some combination of national health insurance, employee fringe benefits, and publicly guaranteed health services is essential if families of moderate means are not to deprive themselves of preventive care and necessary treatment because of the financial burdens involved. U.S. medical care policy is currently moving on several fronts: mandating, for a period, the continuation of employee benefits following employee death or discharge (but requiring premium payments); permitting or requiring states to offer services to poor children or to low-income pregnant women, even if they are economically above the state's welfare eligibility levels; trying to ensure better medical coverage at lower cost by encouraging or permitting private fringe benefit systems and government Medicaid and Medicare programs to buy full coverage for people in comprehensive programs which provide preventive as well as therapeutic care of a broad kind (PPOs, HMOs, SHMOs, etc.).

Supplementary income, housing allowances, insured medical care, whether out of a universal plan or one that may be income-tested or taxed (but not means-tested and stigmatized), will provide a somewhat firmer foundation under all families—not just mother-only families. Depending on how all this is done, it may not even be enough to avoid poverty but it will decrease the gap significantly and bring it within reach of additional targeted measures (see below). Most important, *it will support the idea of work, even if the ensuing salary does not meet all needs. Universal grants and income-tested programs pitched well into the income distribution permit unskilled people to work at low-pay jobs and to do so with dignity and no financial disincentives.* The government financial supplements may be accepted with self-respect—burdens are being equalized for those who rear children; housing market and medical inflation problems are being dealt with through government supplements and program controls.

Here we see how well-developed pro-family supports with regard to income supplements and health care can provide all children—and thus also children in single-parent families—with the necessities for daily living. We also have noted that pursuing these universalist courses can avoid segregation by welfare status, whether in living arrangements or associations (perhaps, also, but not as clear, in child care arrangements and medical care). The inclusiveness and mainstreaming could impact on child development.

Nor is this a new idea. For well over a century, universal free, public elementary education has been a major integrating and equalizing force in our society. For a shorter period, and less successfully, we have followed a similar course for secondary education, and we have led the world since World War II in public post-secondary opportunities. To cope with racial discrimination we have even used the courts and their power to implement integrated education since *Brown* vs. *Board of Education* in 1954.

The logic of public education is also the logic of all universalism. There is no better response to the needs of the vast majority of children in single-parent families than to follow a similar strategy for health-housing-medical care. Here we do not, of course, refer to complete support or program operation by government but rather to supplementation strategies on a universal entitlement basis (one possibility: child allowances), by nonstigmatized income tests pitched relatively high in the income distribution (housing allowances), or—finally—perhaps even governmental mandating of employer action and sharing of the costs thereof through tax incentives (medical care).

Doing Better by Mother-Only Families by Doing Better by All Women

As we have seen, single-parent families headed by women are much worse off financially than such families headed by men, even when the women are in the labor force, working full-time all year. At best, mother-only families under such circumstances have incomes that still equal only about 75 percent of the incomes of father-only families. Clearly, attention must be paid to reducing sex discrimination at the workplace and to stressing affirmative action. In addition, women have to be encouraged to move into less traditional and less feminized occupations, and more attention has to be paid to pay equity.

In some ways the mother-only problem is a gender-equity problem as well as a child and family problem. It will show improvement as women's status improves in the labor market, in social-benefits, and in political influence.

Doing Better by Minority Mother-Only Families by Doing Better by Children, by All Mother-Only Families, and by All Families

Given the disproportionately high rate of single parenthood among blacks, one obvious question is whether improving the situation of single mothers generally, even poor single mothers, will be a sufficient response to the specific problems of black families. Indeed, we have argued elsewhere that one reason that the United States has not developed as generous policies in support of children as several other major industrialized countries is that the United States has yet fully to overcome the obstacle of racial prejudice. During the post-World War II years, when other countries were expanding their child and family policies, U.S. efforts were still focused on assuring blacks and unwed mothers of all races equal access to the existing but quite limited social protections of the AFDC program.

Only when the United States is prepared to support minority children as well as white children through a more generous, universal child policy will we be ready for the next stage. We believe that this time may be near. Similarly, policies that make it easier to reconcile work and family life for all employees, not just for the favored few who work for an especially progressive company, would also make a significant difference for working black single, and married, parents.

At the same time we accept the position argued forcefully by Wilson and others that in order to encourage marriage and stable unions among blacks, more must be done to strengthen black males as providers and partners in the family. Clearly, both black males and females, whether or not they are single parents, need access to education, training, and jobs if they are to be buttressed as independent and responsible adults and parents.

A Benefit/Service Package for Single Mothers and Their Children

Building on the principles of universalism, we turn now to the fourth option, the work and family support strategy. This policy option endorses family buttressing for parenting and also the encouragement and protection of labor force attachment. It is a major departure from traditional "welfare" approaches. For the single mother, then, as we have seen, it is the anchor point in a policy which also guards elements as well of the anti-poverty and "categorical" approaches essential to some members of this diverse group.

Expecting work, making it possible, and supporting those who do work, would constitute a policy focus that is compatible with this country's ideology and culture. Income supplementation and transitional and long-term aid would follow the pattern described earlier.

The remainder of the policy package would be premised on doing well by children. Thus, to summarize, the other components of the benefit/service package would include:

- *Support for parents at the time of pregnancy and childbirth*. Such a benefit can be linked to work and limited to those who qualify based on prior work history, with a benefit linked to wages. The policy could limit the leave and the benefit to a maximum of one year, for a paid, job-protected parental leave. Such a policy would increase the incentives for young women to establish a work history and would facilitate an early attachment to the labor market.
- *Health insurance or health service coverage for all in the labor force, and their dependents*. This coverage should be provided by mandated employer provision or by a federal or state plan that employers would be required to buy into for any employee who is not already covered. The plan should provide continuity of coverage between jobs and while unemployed. Medicaid could cover those in the transitional and long-term aid programs.
- *Income or wage supplements, to link earned income to family size and needs*. There should be universal child benefits for all, through the tax system and refundable for those with incomes below the tax threshold, and income-tested child benefits to fill the gap between wages and family income needs.
- *Housing allowances*. These should be income-tested, and therefore, they would be especially helpful to single-parent families; but again, the allowances should be based on need, not family structure, to avoid the experience in some places with perverse incentives.
- *Guaranteed minimum child support*. Such support should substitute, if necessary, for the missing financial contribution of the absent parent, based on rigorous collection and enforcement of parental support obligations (to include mothers' obligations as well) and automatic wage withholding of support. This would incorporate a policy that stresses paternity determination, educating youngsters from junior high school that "making a baby means supporting that baby until age 18," and mandating child support awards in all cases.
- *Workplace policies that make it possible for working parents to manage family life and work with less stress than now*. Details have been offered. One aspect is here emphasized. In countries that provide low-level, means-tested or income-

tested benefits for single mothers, those who choose these benefits are the ones unable to work full-time. Only full-time wages are worth more than low-level benefits. However, full-time work is impossible for most of these women when they have young children; time and energy demands related to parenting and home responsibilities make full-time work at least as impossible for single mothers as for married mothers, unless they are likely to earn enough to pay for services that would substitute for their own work at home. Since this is unlikely for the majority of single mothers, they are trapped. Part-time work is not economically worthwhile when the trade-off is between low-level wages and no fringe benefits and low welfare grants plus medical and food stamp help. Full-time work may not be feasible because of the constraints on the time and energy available for parenting, a major problem for women with preschool aged children. Therefore, in developing a policy premised on work for single mothers, the focus should be on making part-time work an acceptable *option* (25 hours per week?) by making wage supplements available. Moreover, both for those who work part-time as well as those who work full-time, a variety of work-related policies must be in place: flextime, sick leaves for employees and for care of ill children, and personal days available for emergencies.

Beyond this, for the very few who have severe personal limitations, cannot work, but can provide a family environment for their children, there should be a limited program on a much more adequate and improved basis than the current AFDC—and, thus, a federalized program—offering cash assistance integrated with social services. The program by its nature will have supportive-therapeutic components as well as providing necessary resources. Its targets will be families in need of constant community attention and ongoing backing.

Whose Policy?

Who shall bring about this new, broader, more hopeful outlook for single mother families? The obvious, if somewhat trite, answer is: all of us. We need a new public discussion based on new under-standing—and supportive of new actions.

Those who know the composition of the single-mother popula-tion and its diversity need to tell the story in the media, at meetings, in research publications. Those who favor new, universal, mainstreaming policies need to be heard at professional meetings, in organizational assemblies, and at legislative hearings. An adequate base of public support will be needed to sustain the essential state and federal expenditures legislation and provisions on which a new philosophy and action program will rest. These will include income maintenance, social security, taxes, housing, child care, social services, employment, and training.

In the short run, legislators, members of the executive branches in Washington and state capitals, and taxpayers will recoil at probable costs. Consideration, however, will show that investment in people and work is less costly than programs which sustain dependency, however inadequately. Society has begun to see that its economic future and national well-being require new commitment to rearing responsible, competent, creative citizens. The moment is also strategic because demographic trends predict possible labor force shortages. We cannot afford to "waste" any citizens.

The very listing of arenas reminds us how broad are the implications of an effort to depart from a history that goes back to poor law and is so deeply engrained as the practices and attitudes described.

Nor is it as easy as deciding what to do and, then, doing it. There is need for pilot work, demonstrations, testing alternatives— a fruitful field of endeavor for the foundations. There is urgent need for alternatives and competitive models: an arena, as well, for the private sector.

Nonetheless, there has already been investment, testing and evaluation and the broad outlines of an approach can be specified. Indeed, we have specified it on the basis of the work of many scholars, advocates, and program pioneers over the past decade. There is no excuse for not acting—on a larger scale, in a basic and decisive sense, and now.

Endnotes

1. Working Group in the Family, "The Family: Preserving America's Future" (Washington D.C.: The White House, November 13, 1986), processed.
2. Richard V. Burkhauser and Karen Holden, *A Challenge to Social Security* (New York: Academic Press, 1982), chapter 4.

INDEX

Abbott, Grace, 48
Abolitionism, 44
Abortion
  and AFDC benefits, 120
  legalization of, 4
  opposition to, 118
  and teenage pregnancy, 114
Abstinence, case for voluntary, 126
"Adjustment time," for new mothers,
    175
Adolescent mothers, children of, 24.
    See also Parents; Teenagers
Adoption
  alternative of, 45
  and teenage pregnancy, 115, 118
Advanced maintenance benefits
  in Finland, 94
  in Norway, 81
Affirmative action
  in labor market, 220
  need for, 159
Ageism, 143
Aid to Dependent Children (ADC),
    50, 51–52, 54
Aid to Families with Dependent Chil-
    dren (AFDC), 5, 27, 30, 54, 104
  caseload of, 111
  characteristics of, 105
  and child support, 19, 62–63, 160–
    161
  chronic use of, 112, 113
  costs of, 116
  debates concerning, 55
  early dependence on, 173–174
  extension of, 217

and father status, 56–57
financial eligibility for, 180
vs. full-time work, 192
goal of, 218
increase in, 58, 60
limitations of, 155
long-term, 166
as poverty trap, 222
public negativism about, 152
and race/ethnicity, 58
"recidivists" to, 112
role for single parents in, 105–106
targeting of mothers in, 169
and transitional aid, 179
and work, 55–62
Aid to Families with Dependent Chil-
    dren (AFDC) benefits
  abortion rates and, 120
  causes of need for, 110–111
  clients receiving, 22
Aid to Families with Dependent Chil-
    dren (AFDC) programs
  British basis of, 74
  minorities in, 63
  work discouraged by, 198
Alienation, 108
Alimony, 139, 151, 159
Alliance for Displaced Homemakers,
    141. *See also* Displaced home-
    makers
Alms giving, 42
Almshouses, 42, 44
  alternative to, 45
  nineteenth-century, 40–41
American Vocational Association, 144

229

Government transfers, in income
  package, 183
"Grant diversion," 165
Great Society, 60

Handicapped, poor law and, 39
Hart, Hastings H., 45
Head Start system, 213
Health, of pregnant teenagers, 120
Health insurance, 226
  and divorce, 138
  for single mothers, 207
  reform, 144
Healy, Dr. William, 50
Hispanics
  living arrangement of children
    among, 11, 13, 14
  single-mother families, 10–11
HMOs, 223
Homeless, poor law and, 39
Homemakers. *See* Displaced home-
    makers
Homemaking, attitudes toward, 142
Home study, 46
Household management agencies, 197
Household tasks, time spent on, 194–
    195
Housewives, 143
Housing
  help needed for, 202
  need for, 204
Housing allowances, 82, 226
  in Finland, 94
  in France, 87
  in Sweden, 98–99
Hungary, family policy in, 88–90
Hypertension, of lone Norwegian
    mothers, 83

Illegitimacy, 50
Income
  of mother-only families, 15–18
  as priority, 183
  of single Norwegian mothers, 83–84
  of single parents, 201
  Swedish gender differences in, 99

and time-poor status, 191–195
  of two- vs. single-parent families,
    29, 100, 189
Income packages, proposal for, 183
Income supplementation, 158, 175–
    179, 225, 226
Income support programs
  in Britain, 76
  and time-poor status, 191
Indenture
  alternative to, 45–46
  history of, 39, 40
Individual participation plan (IPP),
    122
"Indoor relief," 38
Industrialized countries
  mother-only families in, 71–74
  social trends in, 70
Infertility, increased, 128–129
Inflation, and welfare grants, 107
Institute for Social Research, of Univ.
    of Michigan, 189, 190
Insurance, government child support,
    162. *See also* Health insurance
Ireland, social change in, 214
Italy, social change in, 214

Jobs Training Partnership Act (JTPA),
    61, 142, 164, 165, 169
Johnson administration, 60, 61

Labor force
  married women in, 197
  new female participation patterns
    in, 173
  single mothers in, 20–21
Labor force participation rates
  female, 70
  for married women with children,
    20
  of mothers, 153, 154
  for Norwegian women, 78, 84
  of single mothers, 218
  of single mothers in France, 88
  in Sweden, 95–96
Labor market
  affirmative action in, 220